BACK THEN

NOVELS

Professor Romeo

The Address Book

The School Book

Growing Up Rich

The First to Know

Prudence, Indeed

The New York Ride

Short Pleasures

NONFICTION

The Language of Names (with Justin Kaplan)

What If? Writing Exercises for Fiction Writers (with Pamela Painter)

Walt Whitman: A Life

Mark Twain and His World

Lincoln Steffens: A Biography

Mr. Clemens and Mark Twain: A Biography

The Language of Names (with Anne Bernays)

Bartlett's Familiar Quotations (general editor)

wm WILLIAM MORROW *An Imprint of* HarperCollins*Publishers*

BACK THEN

Two Lives in 1950s New York

ANNE BERNAYS AND JUSTIN KAPLAN

Grateful acknowledgment is made for permission to reprint "mr u will not be missed." Copyright 1944, © 1972, 1991 by the Trustees for the E. E. Cummings Trust, from *Complete Poems: 1904–1962* by E. E. Cummings, edited by George J. Firmage. Used by permission of the Liveright Publishing Corporation.

A portion of chapter 12 appeared in slightly different form in *Fame* magazine.

HarperCollins books may be purchased for educational, business, or sales promotional use. For information please write: Special Markets Department, HarperCollins Publishers Inc., 10 East 53rd Street, New York, NY 10022.

FIRST EDITION

Designed by Gretchen Achilles

Printed on acid-free paper

Library of Congress Cataloging-in-Publication Data
Bernays, Anne.
    Back then : two lives in 1950s New York / Anne Bernays and Justin Kaplan.
    p. cm.
    ISBN 0-06-019855-9
    1. Bernays, Anne—Homes and haunts—New York (State)—New York. 2. Kaplan, Justin—Homes and haunts—New York (State)—New York. 3. New York (N.Y.)—Social life and customs—20th century. 4. New York (N.Y.)—Intellectual life—20th century. 5. Novelists, American—20th century—Biography. 6. Biographers—United States—Biography. I. Kaplan, Justin. II. Title.
PS3552.E728 Z463 2002
813'.54—dc21
[B]   2001059031

02 03 04 05 06 WBC/RRD 10 9 8 7 6 5 4 3 2 1

This book is for our grandchildren—

David

Benjamin

Tobias

Alexander

Samuel

Rachel

—and our friend George Cronemiller

ACKNOWLEDGMENTS

We thank Larry Tye, Doris B. Held, Sterling Lord, Shelly Perron, Jennifer Pooley, and Claire Wachtel, our inspiring and merciless editor.

INTRODUCTION

We were lucky. We met, began our careers and adult lives, and opened our eyes to the world of possibilities in New York, in the 1950s, when the pent-up energies of the Depression years and World War II were at flood tide. You could see this in the rush of crowds, in big fish-finned cars on the streets and in showrooms, in store windows crammed with things that had been scarce for years—high-fashion shoes, kitchen and laundry appliances, generously cut dresses and suits, Scotch whiskey, prime cuts of beef, caviar, imported cheeses, sugar-saturated cakes—and now in the first affordable, invariably temperamental television sets. (To own one, too large to move or disguise, was something of a guilty secret, a cultural sellout according to our sniffier friends.) We discovered the luxury of the inessential—two-tone refrigerators, electric can openers, the conversation pit.

Postwar meant abundance, rapid change, physical and social mobility, a farewell to the lingering effects of the years 1941 to 1945: austerity, scarcities, postponements for "the duration." It also meant urban sprawl, intimations of conflict with a new enemy, the Soviet Union, fallout shelters marked by black and yellow signs, organic anxiety. "Iron Curtain," "cold war," "neutron bomb," and "loyalty oath" entered our vocabulary (along with "junk mail" and "Bermuda shorts"). *Prewar,* meanwhile, had begun to imply a backward glancing recognition of what had been lost: in buildings and material objects—solidity, amplitude, workmanship, humane scale; in mind-set—stability, restraint, generosity, a feeling of community and social connectedness fostered by the presence of a common enemy. The moral certainty driving "the good war" that had just been fought and won gave way not only to guilt over Hiroshima and Nagasaki but also to dread that the Bomb might be used again, this time against us. During this period of nominal peace we built fallout shelters, conducted a "police action" in Korea to contain communism, found Julius and Ethel Rosenberg guilty of espionage and sent them to the electric chair. Meanwhile Edward Steichen's monumental photography show (and the book derived from it), *The Family of Man*, depicting the daily lives of people all over the world, gave hundreds of thousands of Americans an almost sacramental experience of universal oneness. Tranquilizers, developed in France as a treatment for violent psychotics, became the medication of choice for what W. H. Auden named the Age of Anxiety.

Journalists had labeled us—men and women born between

1925 and 1935—"the silent generation," because we didn't make a lot of noise, accepted things as they were, however skewed, were too busy having fun and (in our case) learning what New York had to offer. We had a few insurgent heroes: James Dean, Elvis Presley, Fidel Castro. Some intrepid unmarried couples lived together, but most middle-class young people remained under their parents' roof until the wedding night. Girls drank and smoked in public without hesitation, not realizing their mothers would have been shamed for doing the same. Margaret Sanger's birth-control clinics still refused to fit unmarried women with diaphragms, but there were doctors who would. In the movies, according to an industry moral code adopted in 1934, married couples retired chastely to twin beds. When they embraced they kept one foot on the floor. In real life sex—straight and otherwise—was all around us, just beneath the surface, germinating.

A city that Henry James remembered from his boyhood as a dusky little village was now on its way to being the cultural and economic capital of the twentieth century. Like the famed Paris bookstore Shakespeare and Company, Frances Steloff's Gotham Book Mart at 41 West Forty-seventh Street—its hanging cast-iron sign read WISE MEN FISH HERE—was headquarters for an American literary avant-garde alert to both European modernism and native materials. For us, one of the defining images of the era to come is a 1948 group photograph of writers compressed in varying degrees of discomfort in the bookstore's back room: Auden perches on a ladder and towers over Marianne Moore, Delmore Schwartz crouches in the foreground, Gore Vidal and Tennessee Williams huddle in the rear, the Sitwells—Edith and Osbert—are enthroned like royalty. A postwar generation of bold and original writers came into their

3

own: Truman Capote, Tennessee Williams, Elizabeth Bishop, Gore Vidal, Norman Mailer, William Styron, Bernard Malamud, Ralph Ellison, Carson McCullers, J. D. Salinger, Robert Lowell, Saul Bellow, Allen Ginsberg, Jack Kerouac. Under an imported genius, the choreographer George Balanchine, American ballet produced a classic repertory along with goddesses of Mozartian radiance and grace like the dancer Tanaquil LeClerq. A distinctively New York school of painting was already a force and influence nationally and abroad. The Museum of Modern Art championed the New and dictated taste in painting, sculpture, and design. Sometimes it took its proselytizing mission too seriously, canonized coffeepots, can openers, and martini shakers, and exhibited automobiles on oil-stained white marble slabs as "pieces of hollow rolling sculpture." Rodgers and Hammerstein's *Oklahoma!* (1943) inaugurated a decade and a half of exuberant musical comedies like *My Fair Lady* (1956). There was nothing tentative or sparing about the "big" movies of the 1950s—*Sunset Boulevard* (1950) and *The African Queen* (1951), at the beginning of the decade, *Giant* (1956) and *The Bridge on the River Kwai* (1957) near midpoint.

Still relatively restrained in style, and with as yet only a subdominant glitter, chic, and Babylonian arrogance, New York was hospitable to the young. Subway tokens were ten cents. Newcomers in entry-level jobs, like us in their twenties, could find affordable places to live in the Village, Chelsea, along Third Avenue in the shadow and clatter of the El, on the Upper West Side, and, before it became the East Village, on the Lower East Side. There, in 1950 and 1951 one of us (J. K.) lived in a five-room walk-up in a dumbbell tenement on Pitt Street, with the bathtub in the kitchen, and paid twenty-nine dollars a month for it. At night rats scratched and squeaked inside the walls.

Most of us smoked cigarettes, drank blended whiskey, gin (especially in martinis), and jug wine. Vodka was something Russian and Polish we had only heard about. Occasionally we went to eat at pricey smorgasbord places—Stockholm, the Three Crowns—and piled our plates at assembly-line tables loaded with pickled and smoked fish, iced shrimp, cold cuts, meatballs, and unfamiliar cheeses. The city abounded in sociable cafeterias, aromatic delicatessens, hot dog carts, drugstore and Woolworth counters serving up grilled cheese sandwiches, tuna on white, cherry Cokes, and milk shakes. The standard, minimally worded restaurant menu offered a choice of tomato juice or shrimp cocktail, daily specials like half a spring chicken and Salisbury steak, and apple pie either à la mode or topped by a wedge of orange cheese. Automats dispensed coffee and milk from nickel-plated spouts in the shape of a lion's head, and sandwiches, baked beans, and pies from little glass cells; we favored Nedick's for hot dogs and a pulpy, vaguely orange-flavored drink; Chock full o' Nuts, begun as a nut shop near Macy's, had become a chain of lunch counters, efficiency engineered down to barely tolerable spaces between stools and calibrated dollops of mustard in tiny paper cups.

The owner of Chock full o' Nuts, a white man named William Black, advertised in the tabloids for "light colored counter help," an example of nth-degree job discrimination. The separation of whites and blacks was an embedded fact of American life, "civil rights" an unfamiliar phrase, Harlem another world. In 1956 the city's nearly eight million population was 83 percent white, only 11 percent black. Except downtown in the Village and in other artistic and intellectual enclaves, white people and black people did not mingle. We were accustomed to seeing only white faces as patrons in theaters, restaurants, hotels, and sports arenas. It was only in 1947, when Jackie Robinson, wearing a Brooklyn Dodger uniform, trotted out to second base at Ebbets Field, that the color line in major league baseball was finally breached.

We—the authors of this book—were born and brought up in New York, on opposite sides of Manhattan Island separated by the Everyman's land of Central Park. As much as your address, your telephone exchange was a caste mark: classy names like Butterfield, Regent, and Rhinelander for the Upper East Side, plainer ones for the Upper West Side—Riverside, Monument, Academy. The West Side was exuberant in the architecture and names of its monumental apartment houses—Eldorado, San Remo, Beresford, Majestic, Dakota, Ansonia, Henrik Hudson, Century, Hotel des Artistes, White House. The East Side tended to stick to numbers and to stretches of uninflected and somber blocks of residential masonry. What the Upper East Side lacked in street life along the cheerless canyons of Park Avenue it made up for in elegance, discretion, and exclusiveness. Madison Avenue was New York's Rue de Rivoli or Faubourg Saint-Honoré; upper Broadway, a marketplace promenade in Warsaw or Vilna, an upscale Hester Street with plate-glass display windows instead of pushcarts.

Old New York society, the subject of Edith Wharton's novels, had lost almost all of its clout and coherence during the leveling years of two world wars and disappeared into its clubs, mansions, and Newport cottages. What took over was café society—the Stork Club, the debutante Brenda Frazier on the cover of *Life* magazine, movie stars, the celebrities Walter Winchell and Leonard Lyons featured in their columns. Celebrity began to self-generate—you were known for being known. Style, glitz, and status symbols—handbags from Gucci or Vuitton, a shirt with the Lacoste alligator, shoes from Ferragamo, neckties from Countess Mara—began their gradual and irreversible ascendancy over substance. Still, we could see that life in New York was far more fluid

A.B., late 1950s.

than ever before, and that if you were white and had talent and energy you could start your climb.

During the 1950s we saw the city as if finding something unmatchable anywhere in the world. We took visitors from the South and Midwest to the Fulton Fish market, the meat, cheese, and flower districts, Eighth Street, the Bowery, the South Bronx's Hunts Point Market; Tottenville and the deserted outer beaches of Staten Island; Brooklyn Heights with its dazzling view of Manhattan and mingled odors of waterfront rot and roasting coffee beans; Times Square, advertising itself as "Crossroads of the World," offering, in addition to first-run theaters like the Paramount and Roxy, cheap hotels, and Hubert's Flea Circus and Museum of Freaks.

Together—our first experiment in collaboration—we wrote an

article (for *Barnard Alumnae Magazine*) about walks in New York. The piece's breathless tone conveyed our excitement as well as too much immersion in fashion magazine prose. Virgil-like, we guided our readers to Wall Street, silent and ghost-ridden on Sundays; the Baghdad of the Lower East Side with its compaction of bridal shops, tombstone makers, underwear peddlers, and Katz's delicatessen (order "corned beef on club"); the "pastoral quiet" of the Sheep Meadow in Central Park. "For the West Bronx Walk," we wrote, "take the 8th Avenue subway marked 'Grand Concourse' but follow your whim to wander west toward Hunter College, south along Creston and Morris Avenues. Here you are in suburbia: the tiny lawn, the well-tended hedge, the detached but neighborly villa. A little below Kingsbridge Road the city signs begin to thicken: delicatessens, bakeries, dressmakers, caterers. As you quicken toward Fordham Road, you're on your way to a supreme glory: Alexander's department store. There you will find more people per square foot finding better bargains per stretchable dollar than anywhere else on earth. It's likely that, overburdened with your own buys, you may have to call it a day."

These wonders were new to us, natives who were beginning to respond to the city like recent settlers. But we were proud of skills that set us apart from these newcomers. We knew how to fold and read the broadsheet *New York Times* or *Herald Tribune* while standing in a crowded subway car; we found our bearings immediately, on automatic pilot, when we came up the station steps. We knew how to cross streets—against the lights, cutting corners, in midblock, on the run, facing down drivers, waiting behind El pillars—always counting on the rabbit reflexes, peripheral acuity, and acquired immunity to danger that those who survived had possessed for years. We stood "on line" for buses and the movies, not "in line," and said "Sixth Avenue," never "Avenue of the Americas." We weren't solicited by tour agents stationed along Fifth

J.K., 1950.

Avenue or horse carriage drivers by the Plaza. Maybe it was the way we walked—purposefully, hard-faced, looking straight ahead, and avoiding eye contact with strangers. If we carried cameras we hid them, so as not to be taken for out-of-towners. We could thread our way through crowds like the Artful Dodger.

We were both children of privilege. We had gone to progressive schools in the city, then on to high schools grounded in a classical approach to education—a lot of memorizing and Shakespeare, an exhaustive application to history, literature, and the sciences. Both of us went away to college, majored in English, and, back in New York, found jobs in book publishing—a business (or profession) many young people with similar backgrounds and similar

9

educational equipment hoped to enter. At night we headed downtown and to the Village to enter what, in the 1920s, would have been called "bohemia." It was now inhabited by a new generation, turned on to grass and psychedelics, that called itself "hip" and "beat" and introduced "beatnik" into common speech. Both of us went into psychoanalysis.

Here, then, are some personal, occasionally parallel or overlapping, narratives of life in a particular time and place: New York City between the mid- and late 1940s, when we came of age, and 1959, when, parents of two, we moved to Cambridge, Massachusetts, and followed new careers: novelist and biographer. In writing *Back Then* we wanted to let people and events speak for themselves, within the framework of the period, and without benefit (or distortion) of hindsight, regret, and reconsideration. You won't, we hope, find us introducing a point of view that has been allowed to ripen and change in the intervening years. We've changed the names of a few of the people in our story.

Our habits, manners, language, attitudes in the 1950s were so different from what they are now that in some respects we could almost as well be writing about the era of Theodore Roosevelt and the Gibson Girl. The events of September 11, 2001, widened the chasm between back then and right now. Still, we've tried to convey some of the density and texture of private, social, and working life in the 1950s as the two of us, not altogether untypically, experienced it.

PART I

CHAPTER 1

Where we lived in Manhattan had a lot to do with how my father, the person who made the hefty decisions in our family, chose to be perceived by the world beyond his front door. And this, in turn, had a lot to do with his profound and nervous reluctance to be identified as a Jew. His reluctance was the chain on which many of the beads of daily life chez Bernays were strung. Being Jewish was something we almost never talked about, just as we avoided the contagion of cancer, poor people, and sex. Naturally then, cancer, poor people, and sex took a tenacious hold on my imagination, hung there like a cat halfway up a tree. Oma Hattie, my mother's mother, was one notch less inhibited than my parents about the subject of Jewishness; whenever she wanted to indicate that someone was Jewish she said, sotto voce, "*M-O-T*"—Member of the Tribe. It made my father wince whenever she said it. If I read his thoughts correctly, they were saying, "Why do I have to hear this? What does it have to do with me?" Oma Hattie was just as circumspect about malignancy—she wouldn't say the whole word but whispered its initial: "My friend Bessie was just operated on for *C*, poor thing." People with *C* almost invariably died of it.

Each era earns its particular codes and proscriptions, some more demanding and painful than others, depending on the temperament of the times and the moral force of what has preceded it. As I grew up the language I spoke was heavily encoded, a condition due in part to my hothouse upbringing and in part to the period itself. Because my parents were born before the turn of the century (my father in 1891 and my mother in 1892), many of their regulations hung in suspension around us like the smell of something nasty. Not once did I hear my father or my mother say anything more freighted than *damn* and *hell*—and then only when, like Rhett Butler, they found themselves pushed to the limit.

I found it a constant challenge to decipher what someone really meant when they used this coded language, and since I wanted to believe what I heard, I wasn't all that adept at instant understanding. It took me a long time, for example, to understand that "Will you go out to dinner with me?" more often meant "I want to fuck you" than it did "Let's share a meal." When I accepted a dinner invitation I didn't think I owed the man who had extended it any favors; often, he did. "Good friend" or "Great and good friend," a staple of *Time* magazine euphemism, meant lover or mistress. A "long illness" might have been lengthy but it was also specific: it meant cancer. "Died suddenly" meant a suicide and "he was a confirmed bachelor," homosexuality. "New Yorker" was the equivalent of Jew. When a woman said, "I have to go wash my hands," you knew she was headed for "the little girls' room," another euphemism. As for a girl's periods, they were known by many names: "the curse," "the monthlies," "falling off the roof," and, inexplicably, "grandma's come to visit." Your periods put you in a condition about which boys and men pretended to know nothing. The term "social disease" was code for syphilis or gonorrhea; they were both potential killers and, before antibiotics, often were. On the other hand, it didn't strike us as inconsistent that words like *retarded, crippled, foreigner, spinster,* and *old lady* were never disguised but were allowed to emerge starkly, like naked children at a picnic.

Our pervasive language code fortified the pretense that ours was a polite and well-regulated society—at least at its upper reaches. And along with this, "good manners" were passed more or less intact from one generation to the next, fortified by books of etiquette that changed very little from decade to decade. You knew how to behave in front of and talk to intimate, casual friend, and stranger alike.

When one of my boyfriends, a former sailor, inserted "abso-fucking-lutely" into an otherwise bland conversation, I was dazzled. "What did you say?" He repeated it. "Navy talk," he said.

As a result of these taboos, the shock value of smutty language was as loud as an air raid siren. You could calculate the seriousness of a girl's determination to be "her own man" as much by the words she spoke as by how many guys she had slept with and which substances—and in what quantities—she poured, inhaled, or injected into the temple of her body.

If you can say any word any time you feel like it, it loses its bang; if you save it for the exact right moment it's going to do its job and rip through your adversary like a dumdum bullet. You tucked your list of precious forbidden words and phrases into your deepest pocket, fingering them as you might someone else's gold coins. And, like Russians under communism, like Aesop, we tended to tell our stories in altered form, hiding the truth in assorted disguises. Self-censorship is supposed to be dehumanizing, and perhaps, ultimately it is. But it forces you to be inventive and sly. You got away with something, you slid the true text past the censors as you sneaked absinthe past Customs; you slipped out the window when they thought you were in bed, sleeping; you had sex when they thought you were at a wedding shower.

My father was a gilded creature, shimmering with a vanity that had as much to do with his forebears as it did his considerable brawn in the world of commerce and celebrity. He was Sigmund Freud's double nephew: a brother and sister, Sigmund Freud and Anna Freud, had married, respectively, a sister and brother, Martha Bernays and Eli Bernays, in Vienna in the late nineteenth century. This kind of pairing was not uncommon then, especially among Western European Jews who, xenophobic and cautious anyway, were reluctant to marry outside their tight social circles. It happened, as well, at about the same time, on my mother's side of the family, when two brothers married two sisters. My father's parents were Eli Bernays and Anna Freud (after whom I was named). Almost every time I saw her in her Upper West Side apartment, surrounded by the smallest and dearest of what must have been a substantial collection of glassware, silver, and other gemlike household items, Anna would tell me, "Siggy was such a clever man." My mother confided to me that even in old age Anna was still harboring a grudge against her brother because their father had sent her out to earn her living as a nursemaid even as he paid Sigmund's way through medical school.

16

My father was so proud of his blood connection to Sigmund

Freud that he made sure everyone he met was aware of it by the end of the first encounter. A waggish New York newspaper columnist, who felt my father had exploited this connection—managing to insert "my uncle" into any conversation—called him a "professional nephew" in print. This probably didn't bother my father at all, because, in one sense, that's what he was. Working with his brother-in-law, Leon Fleischman, a founder of the publishing house of Boni and Liveright, my father had been responsible for the first translation and publication of a Freud book in the New World.

When I was a child the name Freud was only a sound, although my father gave that sound an ardent inflection like that used by the devout when speaking of the Divinity. I knew Freud was important; what he had done to deserve this didn't register with me until I was in my teens, when word of his unusual preoccupations had seeped down to the general populace. Whenever I was asked about my own connection to the fabulous mind doctor whom I never met, I got defensive: "It doesn't have anything to do with me." Although of course it did and my great uncle knew it: to mark my birth Freud sent me, via my parents, a postcard headed "Prof. Dr. Freud," upon which he had handwritten, "Welcome as a new output of life on the day great grandmother [his mother] was buried." He signed it "Great Uncle Sigm."

After leaving Austria in 1891, my father's father became an importer. The family—my father, four older sisters, and their parents—lived very comfortably in a brownstone in a neighborhood that eventually became Harlem. There was always money enough. My mother's father was a lawyer, taciturn and unsmiling—a disciplinarian with no shade of gray in his thinking. Both sides of my family were solid in a way that doesn't arouse much interest from the outside, their conflicts and dramas—if there were any— remained safely inside their skulls.

Edward Bernays was different: inspirational, energized, provocative, bold. He revered his uncle and, believing that traits and talents show up in succeeding generations of the same family, felt that he had inherited a good deal of Freud's flair and ingenuity. He deemed himself the father of public relations, although there was a question as to whether he or a man named Ivy Lee had actually provided the sperm. In any case, after a stint as a Broadway press agent, he coined the phrase "Counsel on Public Relations," and set up a counseling office in the mid-1920s, with my mother as unequal partner, and a staff of more than a dozen. He used his brain the way a superior athlete uses muscle plus timing. He dreamed up improbable things. For instance, with the American Tobacco Company as client, he persuaded "nice" women to start smoking in public during a period when a woman with a cigarette in her mouth or fingers was viewed as a lowlife. He accomplished this by asking several debutantes to walk down Fifth Avenue smoking what he called "torches of freedom."

Throughout the Depression, when most Americans struggled to feed their kids, when hundreds of thousands went jobless, and despair was the most common emotion, my father continued to make piles of money. His P.R. services, like those of bankruptcy lawyers, were considered by many businessmen and institutions to be not a luxury but a necessity. I was used to being rich in a way only someone who has never been poor is used to it. I almost never thought about money.

Under several layers of bourgeois camouflage, my mother was a "bohemian." Among her friends had been the literary moths—Franklin P. Adams, George S. Kaufman, Marc Connelly—who drank and traded witticisms at the Algonquin Round Table. She had been a *Herald Tribune* reporter when most women her age already had a couple of children, and fancied herself a nascent novelist. But for reasons she kept to herself, she encouraged her husband to make the kind of decisions that are often arrived at by both the man and the woman whose lives will be most affected by them. He loved being the boss; she, apparently, was willing to be bossed. Given the choice, she might very well have chosen the West Side; its informality and energy, its fierce sense of neighborhood, suited her temperament. But my father would rather have lived on the Bowery alongside the bums than among Jews and assorted Old Worlders on the Upper West Side. If you put a drop of ink into a pail of water, it will dilute in a few seconds. This was my father's Jewishness—he trusted that it would disappear in the watery East Side. To be fair to him, he was a thoroughly secular man who very early decided to rely on his own imagination, intelligence, and skill to get him to where he wanted to go. The idea of applying to a divinity was, for him, as unthinkable as sacrificing a live chicken every time he needed to change his luck. Having also decided that Jewishness was a matter of religion rather than heritage, he rationalized his impulse to "pass" in the largely Christian world that was Manhattan's Upper East Side and resisted the Jewish label by saying, "I don't believe in God. I have no religion." He expected the same of his children, although he did tell me when I was very little that I was "nothing" and that when I grew up I could choose any religion I wanted. I think he viewed the idea of religion in the same way he chose a street to live on or a pair of shoes—easy to change when the spirit hits you.

For a few years before the war we lived in the Sherry-Netherland Hotel in an apartment that occupied the entire twenty-seventh floor. My sister, Doris, and I shared a bedroom. We had a cook and

Anna Freud Bernays, New York,
late 1940s.

Letter from Freud to A.B., 1930.

a kitchen, but my mother often ordered our dinner from the hotel kitchen; it would arrive under a silver-plated dome wheeled in by a waiter who came up on the back elevator. Although we usually had meat for dinner, whenever my mother went out for the evening she would order a vegetable plate for Doris and me, thinking, no doubt, that this sort of food was healthier for children. We had boiled and naked cauliflower, carrots, mashed potatoes, string beans, and asparagus arranged prettily on a round platter. I looked in vain for the meat.

The hotel doorman was suited up like a Russian general, with golden epaulets and something that looked like a coiled minia-ture fire hose pinned to the front of his uniform. Since this was the favorite New York hotel of visiting movie stars, there was always a crowd clutching autograph albums and waiting under the canopy to pounce on Rita Hayworth or Tyrone Power or Spencer Tracy. One Saturday morning, in the grip of mischief, my sister and I decided we were goodie-goodies and better do something about it. Excited, howling with rapture, and starting out on our floor, we scrambled down twenty-seven flights of back stairs, overturning a large laundry cart on every floor, spilling out used sheets and towels. We were inexperienced vandals, and when we reached the ground floor, instead of retreating back upstairs via the elevator, Doris locked herself in the lobby's men's room while I gave myself up and confessed. The manager, obvi-ously torn between rage and servility, assured our mother, now on the scene, that it was just a childish prank and not to worry. He banged on the door of the men's room, pleading with Doris to come out.

The Central Park duck pond, which froze in winter, lay directly below our living room window. It had a bucolic, ad hoc shape and a graceful, arched stone bridge like something in a fairy tale; I waited for trolls. When we had outgrown our governess, my mother hired a series of Barnard College girls to look after us when we came home from school and before she returned from the office. I fell in love with a couple of them—especially Phyllis, who looked like Hedy Lamarr. I played in Central Park at least three times a week for years, until I was old enough not to need supervision. The park was our front yard.

There was a pony pitch where, for twenty-five cents, you were hoisted aboard the animal and led several times around an oval of soil, while the poor old beast beneath you creaked and rocked like a boat. I considered a pony ride perfect bliss, but it was a pleasure withheld from me—not because we couldn't afford it but because it was deemed bad for me to have what I wanted simply because I wanted it. There was a birdhouse, and llamas, and a tiglon, the only offspring of a tiger and lion in the whole world. Cages were spartan—a concrete floor, a tree stump, and bars. The animals sat there glumly or walked back and forth, over and over again, side-stepping their poop, in a fever of boredom. The polar bears had a cave and a waterfall, the sea lions a small lake with a concrete structure in its center, where the seals sunned themselves and occasionally squawked like donkeys. Zoos were no more than jails for animals, but no one ever said this. All you had to do was look into their eyes.

Living on the Upper East Side meant making a contract with an orderly and predictable style. Mr. Bernays rang for the elevator every morning at eight o'clock to be taken down to the ground floor where he wished the doorman an impersonal good morning and entered his chauffeur-driven Cadillac, which whisked him downtown to the Graybar Building next to Grand Central Terminal and some years later, to Rockefeller Center, where he rented office space in the Time-Life Building. His wife and business part-

Sunday evening party chez Bernays. A.B. sitting on floor *(right)* next to sister, Doris, 1947.

ner—"Miss Fleischman"—repeated this maneuver exactly an hour and a half later, having done the day's grocery shopping over the phone and taken a long, scented bath.

Around 1939 we moved to 817 Fifth Avenue, on the corner of Sixty-third Street, one of the few luxury buildings whose management was willing to rent to Jews. Our apartment had separate bedrooms for me and Doris, a kitchen and a pantry with shelves enough to hold plates and assorted tableware for fifty people, and a dining room my mother had custom-painted by an artist who specialized in interior murals to look like a tropical rain forest full of brightly colored birds and exotic flora. Milk made me gag; I told my mother about it, but she insisted that I drink a glass of it each day. Every morning I emptied my milk glass behind the radiator in the dining room. The spilled milk had been cleaned away by the next morning when I repeated again this small gesture of defiance, the maid, silent as always, apparently unwilling to snitch on me.

The living room, furnished with good contemporary pieces—and equally good antiques—was at least twenty-five feet long. Sometimes we rode in the elevator with a beautiful woman with blue-black hair and severely chic hats with a full-face veil. She was often accompanied by her daughter, a girl about my age, who looked at me with disdain. We never spoke, but I stuck my tongue out at her behind her back. My mother said the woman was Gloria Swanson, a silent movie star put out to pasture.

Except for the dining room our apartment was as neutral as a model room on Bloomingdale's furniture floor. There was no way to tell what sort of people lived there except that they had oodles of money and liked original artwork. My parents, guided by my father, who knew precisely what he liked and rarely questioned his own taste, had bought several paintings while on their honeymoon in Europe: two by Raoul Dufy, one of them an oil of a French harbor. There was a Jules Pascin that embarrassed me: two girls sitting on an armchair. You could see the underpants of the older girl; I always looked away from it. On the piano stood a two-foot woman made of polished wood, all curves. This was the work of the sculptor Elie Nadelman, who, when an impoverished immigrant artist, had asked for the hand of one of my father's sisters, Judith, and was turned away on the grounds that his poverty and prospects made him an unsuitable suitor.

No one left shoes or socks, apple cores, magazines, or cigarette butts around; if they did, the maid was instructed to pick up and do the necessary with these gritty reminders of daily life. If she failed to do this there was no second chance. Likewise, Sixty-third Street was always swept clear of detritus—no scraps of paper flew up and around, no garbage cans overflowed with grapefruit rinds and dog food cans. No old chairs were left in the gutter, empty boxes, or dead cigar butts. Outdoors was just like indoors. It was an area rather than a neighborhood, just one gray, severe apartment building after another, most of them erected in the 1910s and 1920s; and home to thousands of people who dressed up to go outside, rarely spoke to strangers, and threw away or mended things as soon as they showed signs of wear. Every apartment building in the area had a freight elevator used by boys delivering food from local shops, drugs from Larrimore's, and spirits of various kinds from Sherry Wine and Spirits. All the gears in this machine worked smoothly and silently, oiled with money. You rarely heard of a robbery or other violent crime. We felt as secure as a safe in the vault in the bank at the corner of Madison and Sixty-fourth Street.

Early one morning, still in my pajamas, I went, as usual, into my parents' bedroom and saw my mother sitting up in bed, crying into a linen handkerchief. I had seen her cry only once before, when I was very young and had wandered out to the porch of a rented summer house and found her alone, sobbing quietly. Now, crying with more vigor and blowing her nose, she paid no attention to me. I'd never seen her distraught, and it sent prickles along the skin of my arms and legs. My father told me that Germany had just invaded the Sudetenland and there was probably going to be a war. My mother said it was the end of the world. My father had steely blue eyes that refused to transmit messages—except those that said "off limits." Eight years old, I wasn't sure what a war involved, but it didn't sound promising. I looked at my mother's face, streaked with tears, and began to worry; to ask her about it seemed out of the question—she had retreated somewhere she did not want me to enter.

And still, we lived an Edith Wharton kind of life, though somewhat scaled down from the plush way of life her characters enjoyed—we never had footmen. My father, an eccentric shopper, bought the mummy of an Egyptian princess at an auction; it lay inside its glass case, a thick X-ray film, lying over its chest like a shield, and disclosing the shadow of a pistachio-size scarab under the bandages. I enjoyed having it there in my living room and viewed it not as a corpse so much as a royal personage. But my mother hated it, would not look at it, and badgered my father until he had it removed and installed in his office, where it lay for years atop a table in his conference room.

My East Side smelled like money. Money to buy things, beautiful clothes, antiques. Money to eat at expensive restaurants and eat berries out of season. To have repairs made as soon as something was torn, broken, or leaking. To hire people to pick up after you, to cook meals and wash up after them. That's how we spent our money, and still there was more. But money was not the whole story, as there were plenty of high-priced places to live on the far side of Central Park, like the Dakota and the Apthorp.

From the time I was about ten, it was obvious to me that the Bernays family had more money by far than most people in the United States. This gap increased my determination to look like everyone else my age; the impulse to blend was an imperative stronger than the one instructing you to "be yourself." I had but a dim notion of who "myself" was, and besides, I hated it when people looked at me, certain they could see something embarrassing that I couldn't. Was my slip showing, were my stocking seams meandering? Was a dog turd stuck to my shoe? My hope was to be a generic young lady, smartly turned out but never, never eye-catching.

However irrational a notion, it seems to be true that people who don't have much money find the lives and disorders of the rich more piquant than their own. The fact of being rich makes a person automatically interesting even if they have a boring personality. I was ashamed of being rich, of living in a hotel and of being driven to the City and Country School, where we went until 1939, by Jack, the Bernays' uniformed chauffeur. My sister and I

Jack, the Bernays' driver, late 1940s.

made Jack stop the car several blocks from the school building, where, mortified by the possibility of being recognized for what we were—extremely rich kids, far more so than the other rich kids who attended this private school—we would get out and walk the rest of the way. Jack motored members of the Bernays family around the city in a Cadillac for many years until the war and gas rationing made a private car impossible—unless you wanted to trade on the black market, something my parents refused to do. Jack was released from his job. I never knew his last name.

My parents had no reluctance or even mixed feelings about having money. They never apologized, denied, or even tried to disguise their riches. Whenever my mother needed something made of leather—handbag, wallet, passport case—she headed for 27

Mark Cross on Fifth Avenue. A dress? Bergdorf Goodman, where the saleslady knew her name and size. A tie for my father? Countess Mara's shop on Park Avenue, where every tie had impressed on it a medieval tiara. Shoes? Ferragamo. She bought fish at a place on Madison she called "Tiffany-by-the-sea" but was actually Wynn and Treanor. A jewel or two? Cartier, a store both more posh and more personal than Tiffany, where you were apt to bump into tourists and arrivistes. And on and on, always top of the line, the most exclusive, cleanest, quietest, perfume-smelling swishy, and above all designed to make the customer feel desirous and desired.

When my sister and I were very young our mother bought our shoes at Indian Walk on Madison Avenue. They X-rayed your feet to make sure shoes and feet were a match. They gave you a paper Indian chief's headdress or a balloon when you left the store

Before heading to a party young girls inserted themselves into party dresses with stiff buckram to make the skirt stick out like a tutu. Before the war, these were light-colored silk or Egyptian cotton with puffed sleeves and a wide belt. During the war you were in danger of growing out of your clothes and not being able to buy replacements as pretty. In any case, a girl's delicate party dress underscored the prevailing assumption that we were expected to behave like angels-in-training. "Sugar and spice and all things nice—that's what little girls are made of"—we heard this with nauseating regularity.

Little boys wore short wool pants, gray or dark blue, a cutoff version of men's trousers. When they reached a certain age—around ten—they graduated to long pants. This passage was so significant—the sartorial equivalent of rites of puberty or a bar mitzvah—that the phrase "he's still in short pants" indicated a stage of emotional growth rather than mere age. Some boys wore woolen knickerbockers, called knickers, a kind of trouser that ended just below the knee in a tight cuff and were also known as "plus fours."

From the time a girl's breasts materialized out of tissue that had looked remarkably unpromising for twelve or thirteen years, her waistline took on a superimportance. You belted yourself as tightly as you could without actual pain; I considered the so-called hourglass figure of the 1890s a silly revival. It was especially hard on fat girls, who looked like sausages. If the 1930s were cool and understated, with women's dresses beltless and sinewy, often cut on the bias and enclosing their wearers in their own aloof concerns, the 1940s and 1950s required women to flaunt it—breast, waist, hip, leg—as if men needed that extra visual jolt. In most postwar closets there hung a medley of clothes to meet a medley of social requirements, for each of which there were rules, explicit and otherwise. If you didn't abide, you were stared at. My mother added rules of her own: Always wear a slip under a skirt. Never wear black and brown next to each other, or, for that matter, blue and green or red and orange. Why? "They clash." Never leave the house without at least one pair of white gloves.

I owned a lot of sweaters and a couple of sweater sets, a short-sleeved pullover to be worn under a cardigan of the same shade. If you were fortunate enough to own one, you added a subtle string of cultured pearls to your ensemble. Some of my sweaters were cashmere, a kind of supple wool that made me perspire and itch; I never wore them. I knew nothing about Jewish holidays; they were as invisible as our many cousins in Austria and Germany who did not survive the war. Thoroughly assimilated, we marked Christmas with a tree and presents; my mother gave me a cashmere sweater every Christmas for years.

During the day a young lady wore a woolen skirt and tailored blouse and either a cardigan sweater or a jacket cut like a man's. Sensible shoes: low-heeled pumps or polished penny loafers. If you were going to meet someone at an office or restaurant you wore a dark-colored wool or silk dress. And tan stockings held up either by a garter belt that cut into your hips' flesh or a panty girdle, depending on whether you thought you were thin or fat. Before the war, women wore silk stockings of a gossamer thinness. During the war silk disappeared into parachute factories; stockings were made of thick, orange rayon. Brassieres were cone shaped and made you stick out in front. If a man could unhook a bra without fumbling you figured he was promiscuous.

For going out or entertaining after dusk you had a separate wardrobe comprised of "party dresses" and "party shoes." You transferred your stuff from a daytime handbag into a smaller, fancier evening bag. Dresses hit you just below the knee until the "New Look" in 1948, when they abruptly dipped to midcalf, rendering your old dresses and skirts obsolete. Party dresses were generally made of silk or taffeta that shimmered and made a swishing sound. Shoes had high heels, and often were open somewhere, to show off naked toes or heels. (On our honeymoon in 1954, I bought a custom-made pair of blue suede pumps in Rome with four-inch heels; they squeezed my toes so hard tears came to my eyes and I wore them only once.) Even when you were invited to a friend's house for an informal dinner—"it's going to be just us"— you changed from your daytime clothes into a nighttime outfit. You put on more casual clothes—slacks and sneakers or Top-Siders—for strenuous outdoor activity. Only beatniks and hipsters, artists and writers, jazz musicians, actors and hard-core Village inhabitants defied the Uptown dress code and wore whatever they felt comfortable in. I knew a couple of Ivy League men who considered themselves cool enough to be seen almost anywhere in a torn oxford shirt, a pair of chinos, and blue sneakers, the more beat-up the better.

A man who worked in an office was supposed to show up every morning with a clean shirt—white, blue, or pale yellow—a tie and a jacket. After work, at home, he might remove the tie and jacket. A hat, usually a "fedora," made of felt with a snap brim, was so standard that if you saw a man without one, you wondered what was the matter with him—was he trying to tell you that he was a rebel? Convention had a firm grip on most of us—at least on the surface.

For any woman a hat was considered as essential an element of her city costume as a pair of shoes, although of course it wasn't, it merely said of its wearer, "Here is a lady." After the war my mother, who thought she was ugly but wasn't, had her hats custom-made by Mr. John, whose atelier was on East Fifty-seventh Street. Mr. John (I didn't know whether this was his last

A.B. (*right*) and Mary Myers,
Brearley graduation day, 1948.

name or his first) looked like Napoleon Bonaparte and made the most of the resemblance, brushing his hair down low over his forehead and to one side. The creative procedure involved in making one of his hats was long and painstaking and largely a matter of theater, starting with an initial visit to develop a concept and consult on design and fabric. A week or so later, Mother returned to his workroom to try it on—her first "fitting." Mr. John pinched and tweaked, tilted one way then the other, consulted again with his customer, took it off gingerly, and instructed her to return in two weeks when the confection would be ready. To me, all her Mr. John hats were nearly identical, a small pancake of buckram with some decorative item sewn onto it, a flower or ribbon with a veil like a black spiderweb to be drawn down over the chin, where it fit snugly against the nose. Mr. John's hats were wildly expensive.

My mother asked him to design and make my wedding veil, and dutifully, I went for at least two fittings before he was satisfied. It was a lace mantilla with delicate lace leaves sewn into it. I heard later from a mutual friend that Mr. John was terribly hurt at not being invited to the wedding. This would have distressed but surprised my mother. Because Mr. John had sold her something, she viewed him as "in trade," and no matter how much you liked them or how gratifying they were to be with, you did not invite such people to weddings or to any other social occasion. The postwar period was fluid enough for old ways—my mother's—to persist even as new ones—Mr. John's—were standing in line to displace them. The resulting collision produced plenty of hurt feelings. No change without conflict.

While my sister and I were away at Camp Kuwiyan by the shore of a crystal lake in New Hampshire's White Mountains—this was early in the war; I was about eleven years old—my father bought a double house on Sixty-third Street between Lexington and Third Avenues. He had all our stuff moved from our apartment on Fifth Avenue to the house without telling us. I never had a chance to say good-bye to my room or the doorman.

The house at 163–165 was faux Gothic, with lots of gray stone and ancient wood panels imported from England on the dining room walls. The downstairs hall—which had six doors, not including the front door, giving onto six different spaces—was large enough to hold a chamber music ensemble and a small audience. The house had three storeys and, up a short flight of stairs, a row of maids' rooms and storage closets. Over one end of the thirty-foot living room hung a balcony you reached via a narrow staircase. One wall of this room was made up of mullioned windows. In the downstairs library was a soft couch where I and my boyfriends repaired to kiss, hug, and, occasionally, pet. No one ever bothered us there.

Five houses closer to Lexington lived Gypsy Rose Lee, the world's classiest stripper, along with her third husband, a theatrical-looking, mustachioed Mexican painter not much over five feet tall. Across the street was the house of Chester Bowles, a former advertising power and diplomat who had worked for President Roosevelt. At the corner was the Barbizon, a hotel for women with swimming pool, library, and daily maid service. A girl could book a room there—for as long as she wanted and/or could afford—only by presenting references that attested to the fact that she was unlikely to pull anything that would embarrass the management. Men were not allowed above the first floor and had to meet their girls in designated "beau rooms." There must have been plenty of sneaking around the rules. Because of its reputation, this was one of the few places in the city that mothers and fathers in Massachusetts, Connecticut, Virginia, felt safe about parking their virgin daughters while they waited for eligible young men to come along and marry them. The rooms were only slightly more deluxe than a convent cell.

Before Bloomingdale's underwent a major face-lift and subsequent personality change in the middle 1950s, it was the somewhat fusty department store you patronized not for dresses, coats or shoes, and assorted items esteemed for their style but for sturdy essentials: bed linen, pajamas, a teakettle, a doormat, and "notions." *Notions* was a catchall word for small household essentials like needles and thread, dress shields (to keep perspiration from staining your clothes), darning eggs, measuring tape, buttons. My mother also sent the maids to Bloomingdale's Domestics department to buy their uniforms—black dress, white apron, and a cap like those worn by nurses. Perfectly right: maids were employed to nurse the hearth.

Even as a small child I was aware that each East Side avenue had its own personality. Fifth Avenue was for seeing and being seen on. *Stately* is the word Edith Wharton used to characterize the huge stone palaces built by millionaires Henry Clay Frick, Felix Warburg, and their ilk. In those days before the income tax, there were quite a few of them along Fifth Avenue, as clean swept as a desert after a sandstorm. Between them were apartment houses occupied by people who made more money in a week than some Manhattan families did in a year. If you were far enough above street level you could look out over Central Park—the grandest work of urban artifice in the New World—and try to pretend you were in the country. The park was relatively safe, even at night. Weekly dances with live music, an orchestra, were held in warm weather during the war. It was here I danced to "If I Loved You" with a sailor named Johnny. I was sure I did. Later, Johnny wrote me letters from the South Pacific, telling me about the atom bomb tests at Bikini Atoll that he witnessed from the deck of his ship.

Double-decker buses, some open on top, were the chief means of public transportation on Fifth Avenue. The fare was ten cents, one thin dime (twice as much as the fare on other bus lines). You inserted your dime in a slot in a money-collecting device that whirred and dinged and was roughly the size and shape of a hand grenade; this was proffered to you by a conductor in a smart uniform. Fifth Avenue was a two-way street and never very crowded. The first time my parents took me to the Easter Parade on Fifth Avenue I asked them where the marching band was. The stretch between Fourteenth and Thirty-fourth Streets was known as Ladies' Mile, presumably because men did not shop. Clustered here was an assortment of stores for every taste and bank account, ranging from pricey Altman's to bargain Klein's on the Square.

Madison Avenue, from Forty-second Street to Seventy-second, had no competition when it came to chic and glitter. It was just one adorable shop after another: Georg Jensen, stocked with Danish silver for arm, neck, and table; Crouch and Fitzgerald for the most fashionable suitcases, handbags, and wallets; Liberty Music, where you could take a record out of its album, step into a carpeted booth, close the door behind you, and play it on a turntable before deciding whether or not you wanted to buy. Outdoorsy men and women patronized Abercrombie and Fitch on Madison Avenue and Forty-fourth Street, a block above Brooks Brothers. Scattered over this area were a great many jewelry stores and boutiques for men and women with both a hankering for high fashion and the money to indulge it. Random House occupied the erstwhile Fahnestock Mansion, at Fiftieth Street, in the same complex with New York's Archdiocesan headquarters, where Monsignor Fulton J. Sheen, the world's first television priest, held court.

There was a Chock full o' Nuts on Madison and a couple of Hamburger Heavens, where you sat in a kind of high chair, pulled a small tray table around in front of you, and were served the world's juiciest hamburger on a bun, with sweet pickle slices on the side.

Above Ninety-sixth a great invisible wall had been erected; below it lived the rich white upper-middle class, above it, each in their own ethnic cluster, Negroes, a sprinkling of Puerto Ricans, Eastern Europeans, and other first-generation Americans. The people beyond the wall served those on the other side: waiters, maids, dishwashers, porters, orderlies, messengers, taxi drivers. Although it was a segregated city it was relatively stable, no doubt because only a brave few realized that they could do something other than wield mops and shovel coal. In 1952, five years after Jackie Robinson destroyed major league baseball's color barrier, Ralph Ellison published *Invisible Man*. Bernie Wolfe, a novelist and also Billy Rose's ghostwriter, took me to an evening book party for Ellison in a cramped bookstore on Eighth Street, where I met Robert Penn Warren, southern as all get-out.

Park Avenue was as unexciting as a park bench. Lined on both sides, with luxury apartment houses of similar architectural restraint, these buildings were sturdy and unimaginative, more fortress than palace. One of the few exceptions was the Hotel Marguery, a modestly ornamental structure that occupied an entire block between Forty-fifth and Forty-sixth Streets with a dusky courtyard in the middle. This is where Adlai Stevenson, running for president, rented space for his New York headquarters in 1952 and 1956. I was devoted to Stevenson. I stuffed envelopes and ran errands throughout both campaigns, with a sick, pessimistic feeling about the whole enterprise; Stevenson was too thoughtful to be president.

Apartments in the city were not for sale; everything was on a rental basis. Park Avenue from Ninety-sixth, where the subway tracks emerged, down to Grand Central Terminal at Forty-second Street was a stretch of real estate impossible to warm up to, even during the spring, when the city planted tulips in the long brown tongue running down the middle of the avenue. Impossible to warm up to unless you bought into its self-perpetuating myth, namely, that here was the only place for the rich and powerful to live.

I didn't know anyone who lived on Lexington. Most of the apartments there were above small stores, shoes repairers, sandwich shops, antiques stores, modest restaurants. It was a sort of unbuttoned version of Madison, more crowded, less pretentious, less expensive, the first avenue, going east, that gave off a sense that life didn't happen only after you closed the front door behind

A.B. (*left*) and sister, Doris, at Yale Law School prom, 1947.

you. When we lived at 163 East Sixty-third, we left the house every weekday morning at quarter past eight and walked two blocks up Lexington Avenue to wait for the Brearley bus, passing unassuming shops we had never entered. Our favorite was an antique carpet place with the words R. *Uabozo*, as if it should be followed by a question mark, painted on the front window. I thought it was a joke while Doris thought it was the man's real name: Mr. Rudolf (perhaps) Uabozo. A few blocks down from our grand house and three steps below street level was a plain restaurant my mother occasionally took me to for lunch on a Saturday. The hostess was a middle-aged woman who looked like one of my English teachers. The three or four waiters were beautiful young Korean men whom I couldn't take my eyes off. The menu was simple, running to things like mashed potatoes, tapioca pudding, meat loaf, tomato and rice soup. It occurred to me that, since it was the kind of place that catered to genteel widows on a pension rather than to "career women" like my mother, she found here the kind of food she had eaten as a child and that nourished her in ways you couldn't measure.

Almost every Saturday during our junior and senior years, I met my two classmates Katherine "Donnie" Agar and Mary "Moo-face" Myers either at Liggett's or Rexall's drugstore, where we ate tuna fish or melted cheese sandwiches at the counter and drank calorific frappes. Then we went to one of two movie houses, Loew's Seventy-second Street or RKO Eighty-sixth Street, depending on what was playing. There we saw two movies, a "double feature," plus a newsreel and maybe a "short," stumbling out after almost four hours into a wintry dusk. We favored movies with simmering passion, malevolent delusions, and domestic disorder, done to a turn by stars like Barbara Stanwyck, Joan Crawford, Joseph Cotten, James Mason, Fred MacMurray. One Saturday we watched, horrified, as Richard Widmark pushed Mrs.

Urmy, our Brearley School dramatics teacher, down a tenement staircase as she sat in a wheelchair. Her stage name was Mildred Dunnock; the movie was *Kiss of Death*.

Looming over Third Avenue was the East Side's elevated railway—the El—blocking out great patches of sunlight and creating embroidered shadows on the pavement below. Every time a train rumbled past, the walls of our house vibrated as if we were in the middle of an earthquake. If I was on the phone I would have to stop talking until the train had gone by. I loved riding on the El, mainly because you could look in through the windows of the houses flanking Third Avenue and see people going about their domestic business. They must have hated the trains' noise and shaking. It was something you don't get used to. To me, the El was a novelty, like a nonthreatening ride at an amusement park. The El was demolished in 1955.

East of Third Avenue were ethnic clusters, mostly European. I rarely ventured east of Third. What for? I didn't know anyone who lived there, and my curiosity had not yet extended beyond my own neighborhood and those adjacent to it. Had my mother somehow discouraged me from tasting other foods, smelling other smells, and sticking my toes in foreign waters? She had warned me away from Yorkville, an area in the eighties, from Lexington to Second Avenue—"Nazis live there"—that was all. Queens, Brooklyn, the Bronx, Staten Island, Harlem, the Lower East Side—my horizon did not stretch that far. I knew Westchester County, Coney Island, and Long Beach on Long Island, and South Orange, New Jersey, where my cousin lived, but I had never set foot in Park Slope or Brownsville or even the Botanical Gardens. I knew Cannery Row and Yoknapatawpha County better than I knew 125th Street and Amsterdam Avenue. It wasn't that I felt menaced by places whose only reality was their name, it was that they didn't make even the tiniest blip on my radar.

I was born and lived on the placid East Side, played there, shopped, walked, and went to school there—in a building virtually lapped by the East River. The only times I went to the Other Side was to visit the Museum of Natural History and its planetarium and to get my weekly allergy shot from Dr. Peshkin, whose office was on West End Avenue. I associated the West Side so completely with Jews that I thought the natural history museum was "Jewish." That both my grandmothers lived in apartment hotels on the West Side I saw as a kind of natural progression from old-fashioned ethnicity to the newest of the new, the world my father yearned for, where distinctions like Jew and Christian would be deemed as socially irrelevant as shoe size.

Barnard College, with its scruffy campus on Morningside Heights (where one day on my way to a nine o'clock class a man whipped open his raincoat and showed me his equipment), was an entire book compared with Wellesley—from which I transferred after sophomore year—which was a chapter only.

An institution with a serious endowment, Wellesley was steered, when I arrived in 1948, by Mildred McAfee Horton, head of the wartime WAVES, the women's arm of the U.S. Navy. Although accepted by Radcliffe, where my sister was about to become a sophomore, I chose Wellesley mainly because my Brearley teachers, having taught my sister the year before, and apparently not able to tell us apart, insisted on calling me Doris. Besides, two admirable girls from Doris's class had gone to Wellesley and reported back that it was good. Something like that. So are life decisions made. My father was disappointed: Wellesley was just girls; Radcliffe, at least in his mind, was Harvard.

The Wellesley campus hub, surrounded by a sea of green grass, consisted of vast stone buildings, faux Gothic in style, somewhat like Yale. Wellesley College, about forty-five minutes from Boston by car, longer by bus, was elegant and dead-ish; rarely would you see anyone strolling its many meandering paths or sitting on its kempt lawns. There was an eighteen-hole golf course across the road from the main campus and a lake, named Waban, where in springtime the Wellesley crew oared its way to national prominence. Every year during graduation weekend, the entire senior class tucked up their academic gowns and rolled hoops down the hill from the main tower, named for the female Midas, Hetty Green. The winner of this hoop race would be, according to legend, first in the class to be married.

I worked hard at Wellesley, often falling asleep at my desk, and came up, for all the studying, with only the vaguest sense of accomplishment; most of the work seemed like busywork. I had learned how to write competently enough at Brearley and there I was, in freshman English, diagramming sentences. Mrs. Holmes, our young—and slightly distracted—teacher, demonstrated for us on the blackboard, turning a sentence into a kind of pictograph, with boxes above and below a middle line, and this, she explained, was supposed to help you recognize the assorted parts of speech. For what reason were we being asked to do this? If I knew that the subordinate clause went below the middle line, would that help me write a more fluid or arresting sentence? I doubted it. A substitute teacher came into the classroom one morning looking very sad and announced that Mrs. Holmes's husband had died over the weekend. How could that be? She was so young. A couple of weeks later Mrs. Holmes returned, looking very sad but went briskly on with the business at hand: diagramming more sentences. I daydreamed, watching through the window as the leaves of autumn turned from green to yellow to pink and orange—for a city girl, an alien sight.

I sat high up in an amphitheater listening to a balding professor of psychology gallop through the history of this relatively new academic discipline while two hundred or so freshmen and a sprinkling of sophomores took notes and tried to keep up with him. The teacher, a virulent baseball fan, talked more about the "Sox" and "the Series" than he did about Sigmund Freud. The professor was openly skeptical of any mind science that could not be verified by some instrument other than the mind itself and favored those experimenters who fiddled around with graphs and microscopes. I learned, in his class, to memorize quickly and think shallowly.

When I wasn't mooning about my boyfriend, Bert, back in New York, I was aware my brain was capable of doing new things. Inside my head were unpopped kernels; each time one of these new things heated sufficiently, a kernel would pop. But it wasn't until I took a couple of classes offered by the English department that I discovered I liked reading plays, novels, and poems far more than textbooks; by the end of my sophomore year I had decided to major in English.

Wellesley College was a ghetto designed to protect young ladies from the evils of city and/or modern life. Plentiful were the rules: no men—including brother and father—were allowed above the first floor of the dormitories. The nearest movie house was in the next town over, Wellesley Hills. The nearest bar was Ken's Roadhouse, far away, within reach only by car. There was no staying out overnight unless your parents sent a letter to the administration with specific dates and addresses: "My daughter Jane will be staying with the Merriweather Cabots at 102 Beacon Street the night of April twelfth; she will return to the campus the following day." You were allotted three late nights (until eleven-thirty) per month. But since the Wellesley campus was so far from Boston, and the last bus left there at ten-thirty, the only condition under which it seemed sensible to use them was if your boyfriend had a car. Most didn't. Drinking was verboten. During my sophomore year, when seven girls were discovered in a dorm room sharing one can of beer, all seven were suspended for two weeks. Sex? It was never mentioned by the authorities, even as occasional rumors of abortion riffled through the student population the way chicken pox did every spring.

Generally trusting me not to get into serious trouble, my parents had never laid down parietal rules. So I would have found Wellesley's multiple proscriptions laughable, if they hadn't reflected a basic mistrust of its students. Deans in charge acted as if, were we to be given a drop or two of freedom, we would immediately become unwed mothers, drug addicts, or prostitutes. The mistrust was misguided: the girls I lived and went to classes with were, for the most part, strictly brought up and determined not to offend anyone, especially those in authority. One night, when eight of us walked out of the dining hall because we were being served creamed canned asparagus on toast for dinner the third time that month, we were severely scolded by a dean, made to feel shame, and ordered never to do anything remotely like that again. We figured that if we did try it again we would, like the beer drinkers, be suspended.

After a summer traveling in Europe, I was certain that returning to Wellesley for my junior year would be like going back not so much in time as in age; I would become a little girl again. I was a ripe nineteen, swelling with focused desire and indistinct ambition. I had no fear of the psychic dark or unknown, wanted to meet as many men as I possibly could, although not sure I would ever meet anyone I wanted to eat breakfast with for the rest of my life; I was fickle as a rabbit. Mildred McIntosh, who had been headmistress at Brearley while I was there, was the new dean of Barnard College—I wrote to her in August and asked if Barnard could possibly take me as a commuting student starting in September. I received a prompt "of course."

43

Once enrolled, I elected almost nothing but courses offered by the English department, bowing to requirements in science by taking geology, which I found unexpectedly fascinating: "New York is built upon Manhattan schist." My parents acted as if I were not a daughter, but a houseguest, almost never questioning me about my extracurricular activities or imposing a curfew. I had the feeling, although she never said it outright, that my mother—whom I never called anything but "Mother"—would make life extremely difficult for me if I spent the entire night away from home, and I was willing to go along with this restriction, my part of the bargain for her attaching me to a very long leash. If she or my father (who was too busy to focus on my comings and goings) suspected I was trying out assorted partners and styles, that I spent most of my time in the Village hanging out with men identified in the press as hipsters, she kept her misgivings to herself, the two of us—again tacitly—recognizing that had she made a fuss and started a list of rules for me to follow, I would have disregarded them in the same way that I disregarded my father's middle-class attitudes toward money, class, and social status—all of which I found definitely not to my taste.

Rapture! I gamboled through Barnard, a garden of scholastic flowers, brilliant teachers—most of them female—courses that turned you inside out. You were permitted to take a course in your major across the street at Columbia if a similar course was not offered at Barnard. At Columbia, in an enormous amphitheater, Mark Van Doren delivered a series of lectures on the Hero, one of the first theme-driven courses. Marjorie Hope Nicholson, a large woman who wore long, voluminous, eggplant-colored dresses and looked like the Duchess in *Alice in Wonderland*, lectured for a semester on eighteenth-century criticism. I ate this up like a starving gourmand. Senior year, infected by Nicholson, I wrote an honors thesis on eighteenth-century satire, a project that grew out of an honors seminar given by Eleanor Rosenberg, a soft-spoken middle-aged woman with no particularly striking trait other than her mind.

At Barnard I found friends of a libertarian spirit almost entirely nonexistent in the Wellesley student population. Most of my friends had, like me, transferred from other schools, drawn to New York for the same reason people have gravitated to provocative cities ever since Nineveh rose from the desert. I met Linda Schapiro in a class on William Blake. Linda had a powerful personality, mostly expressed by strong features, impeccable posture, and an air of certainty. One whiff of it and my mother, always concerned that I was too fragile to stand up for myself, warned me to avoid Linda, whom she seemed to think wanted to possess me, not as a lover but as a demon. Linda's boyfriend, Artie Collins, a Columbia student, worked part-time as a soda jerk at Schrafft's on Times Square. Saturday nights Linda and I would go to a movie and then head over to Schrafft's, where we sat at the counter and consumed ice cream sodas made for us by Artie, with extra scoops of ice cream. He wore a paper hat shaped like a boat and an apron tied around his waist. Linda was not only an honors student but she'd also had a short story accepted by *Mademoiselle* during her senior year. After weeks of squabbling with the magazine's fiction editor over whether or not to leave one of Linda's characters with an unshaven armpit, it finally came down to this: remove the hair or we won't publish your story. Mortified at having to cave, Linda removed the hair.

Anna-Maria Vendelos was South American, fullblown and lush like a tropical forest, with Marilyn Monroe curves, dark hair, a full mouth, a fluid south-of-the-border accent. Her boyfriend, Stanley, was a large, messy-looking, lumbering person somewhat her senior neither handsome nor sexy, but he obviously had something that satisfied Anna-Maria. None of her friends knew exactly what Stanley did for a living. He had published a few poems in literary magazines and at one point, down on his luck, sold some of his books to Anna-Maria's friends. I bought a Wallace Stevens first edition from him. Anna-Maria was smitten with Stanley and he, we thought, with her, but not long after we graduated I found out from someone who knew them both that Stanley had been and was still carrying on with Stella Adler, a former actress, known as much for her love of the flesh as for her acting classes.

The star of our small circle—we had not the slightest doubt that we were the hippest girls on campus—was Francine du Plessix, a girl so strikingly beautiful that she had modeled for *Vogue*, wearing a smart suit. Her aristocrat French father had died flying over Spain during its civil war. Her mother was a white Russian, Tatiana, who designed hats for Saks Fifth Avenue. Tatiana's husband, Alexander Lieberman, was art director for Condé Nast publications.

Francine was a transfer from Bryn Mawr, had been born and raised in France, and was both savvy and intellectually gifted. She seemed to me flawless, with the kind of social poise most people don't slip into until they're pushing middle age. Her mother and stepfather gave frequent parties, studded with stars like Salvador Dalí and John Gunther. The older folks stayed mainly in the living room of their house in the east seventies, while Francine and her friends hung out in the library, on whose shelves were clustered a selection of the world's priciest art books, most of them French and Swiss. During one party I watched, open-mouthed, as one of our friends lifted a small book from a shelf and slipped it into his pocket as casually as if it were a shell he'd found on the beach. Aware of being observed during the heist, he shrugged and met my eyes, making me an accomplice. Then he came over to me and explained, "They'll never miss it."

We—Francine, Linda, Anna-Maria, a girl named Vera, and I—decided that we were just short of spectacular, miles smarter than our classmates, more worldly, capable of more fun and more profundity. Armed with a sense of our own superiority, we persuaded our English professor, Barry Ulanov, to tutor us once a week in the late afternoon, on the writing of poetry. We met every week for a year, at the end of which we produced a pamphlet of poems, published at Barnard's expense. Each of us contributed her favorite three poems. The best of the best were by Francine, who showed a genuine flair, while the rest of us had composed competent but uninspired verse. When I showed this little book to my father he said, "People would just as soon sit on a tack as read poetry," having, no doubt, learned his lesson when, as a young press agent, he himself had contributed to a slight book of poems, called *The Broadway Anthology*. During our senior year Francine won the Putnam prize, given annually to the creative writer the English faculty deemed most worthy. You couldn't envy or begrudge Francine her success: she was too generous, lovable.

Lovable: men turned to jelly in her presence. It was a joke among the rest of us. She would meet a man and within a week or two he was her heart's slave. At least three men confided to me that they were insanely in love with her and would do anything to make her love them back. Could I help them? I told them, "Get in line." Once or twice she passed one along to me; I was pale compared to Francine, and they soon lost interest.

Francine invited me to midday Thanksgiving dinner the year we graduated. I arrived at her house in time to see the cook, looking somewhat familiar and wearing an apron over a black cocktail dress, emerge from the ground-floor kitchen, carrying a silver platter on which sat a glistening turkey. "Marlene has prepared our dinner," Francine told me as I took off my coat. The cook was Marlene Dietrich. "This is my friend, *Ahn*," Francine said, introducing us. Dietrich gave me the briefest once-over and then, having failed to acknowledge me in any other discernible way, proceeded upstairs to the dining room with her burden. "Don't mind Marlene," Francine said, "she's a bit rude. But she has a kind heart. Cooking is her passion." I remained unconvinced: Dietrich continued to ignore me throughout the feast. I was upset by her rudeness. Could she, a German and probably anti-Semitic, have known that I was Jewish? But that didn't make sense: her host, Francine's stepfather, was not only Jewish but also had a Jewish nose. In my parents' house the famous were, if anything, oversolicitous to the little girl whose house they had been invited to: movie stars Madeleine Carroll and Edward G. Robinson, publisher Bennett Cerf, and others whose names blossomed regularly in the gossip columns of Walter Winchell and Leonard Lyons (some of them planted there by my father). They made a fuss over the bashful child with long braids and polished shoes, who was thrilled and detached at the same time, feeling, too, that she was just another ornament in her father's house, like one of his pieces of statuary or a painting. The fact that Marlene had acted as if she were royalty and I a filthy street urchin only underscored what I had long suspected, namely that celebrities are long on charm when they want something, short on grace when they don't. The turkey was delicious.

CHAPTER 2

When Annie and I moved from East Nineteenth Street to Riverside Drive in 1957, the Upper West Side had already entered a cycle of decline that lasted for about two decades, during which the city itself nearly went bust. We knew people who claimed as a matter of pride never to have gone to the West Side except to visit their skin doctors and psychoanalysts or—repeating an old quip— to get to Pier 90 on their way to Europe. Riverside Drive was almost as remote as Canarsie from our old apartment. To get there involved a long taxi ride or a combination of subway and cross- town bus. You arrived in what felt like a different city.

Upper Broadway, a gilded ghetto in the years before the end of World War II, had been like a main shopping street in Warsaw, Berlin, or Budapest, its population and collective accent shaped by refugees from Hitler's Europe. On weekends and Jewish holidays family groups in their best, the women in fur coats, promenaded Broadway's golden mile of haberdasheries selling silk ties, "white-on-white" dress shirts, and expensive fedoras, movie houses (about a dozen), bakeries, restaurants, cafeterias, and delicatessens, liquor stores displaying top-of-the-line brands like Johnnie Walker Black Label, Courvoisier, and Hennessey, candy and nut shops, shoe stores enough for a city of centipedes with bunions and fallen arches, and showrooms of vases, lamps, mirrors, overstuffed sofas, and bedroom suites that belonged in a sultan's harem. By 1957 the lights along upper Broadway had begun to darken. Except for the newly arrived Puerto Ricans, the promenaders were less exuber-ant. This was the sad, lonely, and striving avenue of Saul Bellow's *Seize the Day* and Isaac Bashevis Singer's cafeteria encounters. Popular restaurants like Tiptoe Inn and the relatively down-market C & L (known as the Cheap and Lousy) were about to go under. Other local fixtures—Barney Greengrass, Zabar's, Murray's Sturgeon Shop—hoped to wait out the neighborhood's transfor-mation into streets of bodegas, pizza parlors, and Chinese takeout.

The landmark Ansonia, a seventeen-story Beaux Arts apart-ment palace once tenanted by celebrities like Babe Ruth and Lily Pons, Enrico Caruso and Igor Stravinsky, had grown shabby. So had the Endicott, on Columbus Avenue at Eighty-first, where decades earlier guests took tea in the palm court to the music of a string and piano ensemble. The side streets were being taken over by junkies, drunks, and prostitutes. They lounged on the stoops of decaying brownstones—passing citizens walked faster and looked straight ahead. By night the open spaces of grass and wooden benches along Broadway became Needle Park. By day elderly men and women still sunned themselves there, aired their medical complaints and offspring problems, and traded neighborhood gossip. "You know who Phil Spitalny—that All-Girl Orchestra he used to lead—is? Well, his mother-in-law slipped on some cabbage leaves in Waldbaum's and broke her arm."

All the same, despite creeping seediness, the Upper West Side was still a neighborhood, in a way the corresponding area on the other side of Central Park was not. It had kept some of its old character—polyglot street life, joy in food and the senses, legacy of disputation, array of institutions like Columbia and Barnard, Juilliard, City College, and two theological seminaries, and a distinctive population of musicians, psychoanalysts and analysands, students, and refugee intellectuals. I felt as much at home there as I had in the 1930s, when I lived in a ninth-floor apartment at Central Park West and Ninety-sixth Street. This was still the northern boundary of a district of big apartment buildings with canopies, uniformed doormen, bordering privet hedges, and first-floor doctor and dentist offices. Its terminus was the stubby granite steeple of the First Church of Christ, Scientist on the corner, built in 1903, when Mary Baker Eddy's home-brewed religion was growing at such a pace that Mark Twain compared it to Standard Oil. Like Unitarianism, Christian Science offered a moderately comfortable halfway house for Jews willing to go beyond Ethical Culture. They could say (to quote Jonathan Miller's famous comment in the satiric revue *Beyond the Fringe*), "I'm not a Jew. I'm Jew-*ish*. I don't go the whole hog."

To my mind Riverside Drive was still the city's most beautiful promenade and vista, maybe even the hemisphere's. Coming home after work downtown I emerged from the grimy IRT subway station and walked west toward the dazzling open spaces of the Hudson. From our eleventh-floor apartment at Ninetieth Street and the Drive we looked out at a long stretch of the river to the 51

George Washington Bridge five miles to the north. At night you could see the lights of Palisades Amusement Park and its Cyclone roller coaster. Wintry gusts coming off the Hudson were strong enough to blow pedestrians and baby carriages around the corner. It was hard to understand why so many New Yorkers ignored the visual splendors of Riverside Drive and Central Park West, preferring, it could only be for snobbish and conformist reasons, stodgy Fifth Avenue and Park Avenue apartment houses and East River views of Rikers Island, the largest jail facility in the country, and a commercial wasteland in Astoria, marked by giant illuminated signs advertising Crisco and Pearl-Wick Hampers.

The skyline of Central Park West had always delighted me. From the park's moated Belvedere Castle at Seventy-ninth Street—a delicious Victorian-Gothic anachronism overlooking the Turtle Pond and the Great Lawn—I could see a two-mile stretch of apartment houses, punctuated by the gabled Dakota and the immense, turreted bulk of the American Museum of Natural History. Whatever I knew of medieval Europe had come from Sir Walter Scott's *Ivanhoe*, Mark Twain's *A Connecticut Yankee in King Arthur's Court*, Howard Pyle's novels about Robin Hood and the Knights of the Round Table, and my visits across the park to the Metropolitan Museum of Art, mainly the halls of arms and armor. The arrays of bourgeois apartment houses stirred fantasies of castles and fortresses, even though the inhabitants were clearly not lords and ladies, pushed baby carriages instead of riding chargers and palfreys, and sent their cooks out to buy meat, milk, fruit, and vegetables on Columbus Avenue. Still, whether these buildings had authentic grandeur or were merely stage sets and architectural pastiche, it was not too much of a wrench to think, however fleetingly, of Camelot and sometimes Oz.

Dominating the scene were three towered and intricately embellished structures, each a somewhat watered-down example of imitation Renaissance, Baroque, or Art Deco. They had glittering names, each with its own aura of association—San Remo (the Italian Riviera), Beresford (British nobility and military heroes), Eldorado (conquistadors, Sir Walter Raleigh). These three buildings had been put up between 1929 and 1931, a last exhalation of prosperity on the eve of the Great Depression. (For devastated high rollers in the stock market, the motto on the Beresford's heraldic elevator doors was prophetic: *FRONTI NULLA FIDES*— "Don't Trust Appearances.") The Beresford (the largest apartment house of its day), Eldorado, San Remo, and dozens of other buildings—among them the Normandy (Renaissance towers with an Art Moderne base), the Mayflower Hotel, originally festooned with balconies, and the vaguely Mayan-looking Ardsley—were all the work of one architect, Emery Roth. His buildings on the West Side were as iconic, as expressive of the city's style of grandeur, as Henry Hardenbergh's Dakota Apartments and Plaza Hotel. Roth did most of his important work on the West Side, lived there, and died (in 1948) in one of his buildings, the Alden on West Eighty-sixth Street. The double stigma of immigrant (he was born in Hungary) and Jew had for years excluded him from prize residential commissions on the other side of town.

In point of professional and social disabilities Roth's career differed little from the general situation of Jews in New York who, once they were able to afford it, moved to the West Side from shabbier parts of town. They were discouraged from entering professions like architecture, banking, and, through restrictive quotas, even medicine, despite (perhaps because of) the legendary superior skills of Jewish doctors. Desirable East Side apartments were off limits to them. (According to the joke, current in the 1930s, about Pease and Elliman, one of the city's ritzier rental and management agencies, "Elliman waits on the gentiles and Pease on the Jews.") The situation was somewhat different for Jews who were of

"German" rather than "Russian" origin, well connected, thoroughly Americanized, and invariably discreet in harboring the remaining traces of their Jewishness.

Since 1852 the Harmonie Club, now located in a Stanford White building off Fifth Avenue at Sixtieth Street, had restricted its membership to German Jews. The club excluded "orientals," Jews of East European origins (whom Henry Adams caricatured as "reeking of the Ghetto" and "snarling a weird Yiddish"). Creakily bending with the times (and with the rise to world eminence of men like Minsk-born General David Sarnoff, of RCA and NBC) the club relented after World War II, the Nuremberg Laws and Hitler's mass executioners having finally demonstrated that distinctions between one kind of Jew and another counted for nothing: a Jew was a Jew, and "German Jew" an oxymoron. I felt a tiny bit sold out when my brother Howard, a lawyer, became a member of the Harmonie Club. A semitophile like my colleague at Simon and Schuster, Joe Barnes, for all his intellectual acuity and wide experience as a newspaper editor and foreign correspondent, denied the existence of this long-standing caste warfare. How could a people collectively scarred by persecution over the centuries and traditionally liberal in sympathies behave like this—like Nazis? "I just don't believe you," he insisted after Annie and I tried to explain intramural animosities, a degree of which we had to cope with in our engagement and from time to time even in our marriage.

Annie's parents were longtime members of the Harmonie. She says the place was like "a deodorized delicatessen." The club restaurant, otherwise indistinguishable from other select eateries, featured herring with sour cream and put pickles and sauerkraut on the table, a reminder of German-ness: until World War I the club had a portrait of the Kaiser in the lobby. The Harmonie celebrated Christmas with all the fixings, including a tree in the foyer and a children's party with a magician. Pulpit accent, decorum, and liturgy at Temple Emanu-El on Fifth Avenue, five blocks north of the Harmonie, could almost as well have been Episcopalian. Yarmulkes, anything more than a token amount of Hebrew in the service, and the Yiddish word *shul* (instead of *temple*) were as alien there as kreplach and kishkes would have been at the Harmonie.

The Harmonie's East Side and Emery Roth's West Side, the latter typically Orthodox in religion and East European in origins, had different ways, and different degrees, of being Jewish in what had been for half a century and more the largest Jewish city in the world. On both sides of the tribal divide, the Holocaust remained buried in denial, an event to be ashamed of as evidence of Jewish helplessness and long-standing victimhood. And although we were aware of American anti-Semitism before, during, and after the war, we no longer felt marginalized to quite the same extent. Yiddish words like *bagel, chutzpa, kibbitz, maven, schlemiel, momser,* and *zaftig* and even *schmuck* entered the common vocabulary. Jews were conspicuous, even predominant, in music, entertainment, the movies, literature, broadcasting, and book publishing. German Jews owned the *New York Times*, the national paper of record, although they hooded their affiliation, were reluctant to allow page-one bylines, much less editorial command, to reporters with Russian-Jewish names (the excuse being that these names were often too long for the paper's column width). The *Times* covered the liberation of Dachau in 1945 without once using the word *Jew*.

Moving back to the West Side, married now and after years in neutral territories, forced me to examine my own conflicted feelings about being Jewish. I had avoided this for a long time, just as I had avoided thinking about my dead parents. Perhaps psychoanalysis had finally taken hold along with normal maturation and the passage of time.

Tobias Kaplan, my father, had studied to be a rabbi in Vilna, the Jerusalem of Europe. To escape conscription in the Russian Army, he left for America by way of Hamburg in the 1890s. Whenever I asked him to tell me the story of his escape he pulled up his left trouser leg to show me the dent in his kneecap made by the rifle butt of a tsarist guard who had tried to stop him at the border. Even before he arrived in the United States he had decided that a newcomer rabbi in a golden land already overstocked with rabbis might have to live on charity and handouts in order to survive. He had already learned English, partly from reading *The Last of the Mohicans,* and said he used Cooper's novel as a text in tutoring other immigrants. I wonder how useful they found the idioms and speech patterns of Uncas, Magua, and Natty Bumppo. Tobias went into business for himself, made a success of his Dexter Shirt Company, and was shrewd enough in the management of his affairs to emerge from the crash and Depression a moderately rich man. Shortly before he died in February 1939, having outlived my mother by six years, he was planning to retire from the shirt business and spend the rest of his life growing Washington State apples and reading.

He took financial papers like *Barron's* along with the conservative *Reader's Digest* and the Republican *Herald Tribune*—in 1936 he even voted for the G.O.P. candidate Alfred M. Landon, a midwestern fiscal mossback who called F.D.R. a Communist (Landon carried only Maine and Vermont). Tobias subscribed to the regular offerings of the Book-of-the-Month Club and reread the Russian classics. The Dostoevsky titles alone—*Crime and Punishment, The Insulted and the Injured, The House of the Dead*—gave me an irreversibly bleak view of the old country. Despite his rock-ribbed capitalism and his abhorrence of labor unions and Roosevelt's

J.K., Central Park, 1931.

National Recovery Adminstration, he kept his copy of anarchist prophet P. A. Kropotkin's *Memoirs of a Revolutionist* close to hand. He read Samuel Pepys's *Diary* with amusement and James Boswell's *Life of Johnson* with respect. I came to resent Johnson because my father invariably cited him as an authority in regulating my conduct and composing condolence letters. His gift to me on my seventh birthday was an *Aesop for Children* with wonderful pictures by Milo Winter. On my twelfth he gave me a copy of *Bartlett's Familiar Quotations;* I took it with me when I went away to college. For me it was much more than a reference book: an irresistible anthology of the sort of literary passages that Matthew Arnold called "touchstones." *Bartlett,* and any other literary collection, for that matter, infected me with a compulsion to play quotation guessing games with almost anyone I could collar.

For all his faith in business and the Republican Party Tobias remained an observant Orthodox Jew. He put on tefillin and prayed upon arising, obeyed the dietary laws, respected the Sabbath and Holy Days, and attended almost all services at the local shul, Congregation Ohab Zedek (Lovers of Wisdom) on West Ninety-fifth Street. For a year, when we were in mourning for my mother, he often dragged me along to weekday services in the basement, an awful place that smelled of schnapps, bad breath, and moldy prayer books. I suspected he did all of this less out of zeal than habit and resignation. On his deathbed at Mount Sinai Hospital he recited Psalm 22 ("Why hast thou forsaken me?").

Tobias sent me to the Center School on West Eighty-sixth Street, a private progressive school equipped with a swimming pool, gymnasium, woodworking shop, and rooftop playground. The building was one of the first Jewish community centers, part of an emerging movement to socialize and secularize Judaism and release it from the confines of the synagogue. In the early grades we read *Julius Caesar* and *Romeo and Juliet,* built a six-foot-high Mayan temple out of bricks and papier-mâché, mapped the Mexican railroad system, studied French, wrestled with the girls, and—in obedience to the creed of progressive education—never learned descriptive grammar or how to join letters in cursive script instead of block printing them. A home tutor brought me up to speed with weights and measures and the times table. Miss Helen Cushman, the third-grade teacher on the Center School's mostly gentile faculty, lost her left eye to an arrow shot by a student, a sacrifice inadvertently offered to John Dewey's principle of hands-on education: in this case, we were studying the buffalo hunting tactics of the Plains Indians. Wearing an eye patch she came to our apartment once and talked my father into installing a hallway trapeze to improve my coordination.

Weekends, during Sabbath services in Ohab Zedek's airless and overheated Moorish interior, I endured the torments of Gehenna.

They began with boredom, restlessness, and uncontrollable fidgeting and proceeded to a state of acute anguish—I wanted to weep for my imprisoned self, my neck in its collar, my toes in their shoes, and for all the glories of the bright day outside. When sermon time came, the rabbi, an overbearing, golden-voiced, and thoroughly Americanized man named William Margolies, turned into Savonarola. He abused us for allowing our minds to turn to profane things like movies, tennis, and the World Series (which sometimes—God putting us to the test—collided with the Day of Atonement). After four or five years of such pastoral flogging and pummeling Margolies fell like the archangel Lucifer. He had got into difficulties with the law—involving, so the whispering ran, a stolen Buick and embezzled moneys, all of this aggravated, maybe even set in motion, by an affair with a parishioner's wife. Our rabbi traded his pulpit at Ohab Zedek for a cell in Sing Sing. On his release he put himself in the hands of a psychiatrist, transposed letters of his old name into a new one (Gailmore), and resurfaced as a liberal-minded political commentator on a New York radio station. By then the congregation had expunged him from the record, and he was never again seen—or heard—on Ninety-fifth Street.

He had been replaced meanwhile by a newly arrived refugee from Frankfurt am Main, Rabbi Dr. Jacob Hoffman, reputed to be a distinguished biblical and Talmudic scholar. His spluttering English, gargling gutturalisms, steam-engine fricatives, and Moses-like gravity sent me into paroxysms of laughter that mortified and enraged my father. Several times Mr. Turteltaub (turtledove), the shammes, removed me to the lobby.

After the long morning of sermon and liturgy I sang the closing anthem—"Adon Olam" ("He is the eternal Lord")—as if released from the Babylonian captivity. I had a week of freedom ahead of me. At home my father drank his glass of cream sherry and read the Saturday *Herald Tribune* before going in to lunch, invariably a parched chicken salad made from Friday night's soup fowl. Meanwhile I went to my room, closed the door, and in secret conducted a black service of my own devising: switched the lights on and off, handled money (my coin collection), lighted matches, scribbled in my school notebook, drew pictures, laid out cards for solitaire, and tried to think up other ways to violate and desecrate the Orthodox Sabbath. I went away to college in an unforgiving mood—the next time I entered a synagogue after my father's funeral was to attend the funeral of an uncle, and even then I couldn't help giggling.

I was not altogether irreligious, and despite my attempts at desecration, I didn't abhor the Sabbath. In its softer, obser-vances—the lighting of candles at sundown on Friday, the bless-ings over bread and wine—the Sabbath had a sacramental sweetness and purity. But it was hard to ignore the angry old men at Ohab Zedek shushing and glaring at the young. "The scribes and the Pharisees sit in Moses' seat" (I had been reading the New Testament on the sly) and defiled a religion that despite my intol-erance I revered—at least for its fervor and the literary splendors of its Bible. But for me Orthodox Judaism seemed to have no place for joy, spontaneity, celebration, youth; its windows were nailed shut.

As for the women: they were segregated both in daily life and on the synagogue balcony, hidden behind a Jewish purdah (I imag-ined their white thighs). By tradition and inclination they were ignorant of Torah and content to serve as acolytes and handmaid-ens. Both my mother and her sister knew Latin and Greek. Edu-cated in Massachusetts schools at a time when women were fighting for the vote, they were suffragists with a touch of socialist radicalism and outraged memories of the Triangle Shirtwaist fire. But they never questioned what the rabbis told them was their organic inferiority and an uncleanness that had to be washed away once a month in ritual baths. My mother went to the opera, loved Puccini, Caruso, and lilacs, and introduced me to *Gulliver's Travels*. But she had an intransigent mind-set. Nothing in her religion mattered so much as the strictest letter of the domestic observances she learned from her mother: the relentless koshering of chickens and the voodoo purging, with boiling water and red hot stones, of tableware contaminated by accidental contact with food products of an opposite dietary gender.

I lusted after forbidden foods: ball-park hot dogs, supposedly composed of ground-up rodents and slaughterhouse sweepings; glorious, super-American Jell-O, taboo because its gelatin came from the hooves and bones of unkosher animals; pork sausages and bacon. (Despite a few unattractive qualities, including an appetite

J.K. with father, Tobias Kaplan, summer 1938.

for garbage and occasional carnivore ferocity, pigs are delectable creatures, as I recall reading somewhere, "walking butcher shops of hams, chops, roasts, and ribs, with twice as many drumsticks as turkeys.") I lusted after these forbidden delights, partly because I believed millions of Americans couldn't be altogether wrong about such simple (and apparently delicious) sources of gratification, but mainly because they were forbidden. I had my first bacon at a summer camp breakfast cookout at Fort Ticonderoga, New York, a month before I went off to college. I had my first lobster and steamers at the Union Oyster House, Boston, on D day, June 6, 1944. Later that evening, with too much whiskey in me, I broke my wrist and passed out on the sidewalk after a failed attempt to scale the fence of the Harvard Botanical Gardens.

My parents never acknowledged the historical existence of Jesus or the New Testament (the term "New" being in itself an affront to Mosaic law). They dated their letters and checks by the Gregorian calendar, but insisted on B.C.E. and C.E. instead of B.C. and A.D. when it came to locating events in the past. I secretly used the King James Bible as a crib when I was supposedly learning Hebrew. I turned up my nose at Yiddish because it seemed the language of old people who couldn't speak or read English. My parents forbade me to pitch pennies and play punchball with the Irish kids, Catholic and poor, who lived around the corner toward Columbus Avenue—they were "bad boys," "common." Deprived of their company and of education in the streets I was well on my way to sissyhood.

Xenophobic, and at times paranoid, the Jewish mentality that saw the gentile and all his works as the enemy had plenty of justification. Even in the heart of our enclave on West Eighty-sixth Street, as I stood under the canvas canopy of the Jewish Center building, a stranger stopped to shake his fist at me—"Little kike bastard!" We knew about Hitler; the Kristallnacht pogrom, when

Nazi mobs gutted nearly two hundred synagogues while the police looked on; forced expulsions and concentration camps. But our dismay was blunted by resentment of the wave of refugees from Germany and Austria, some arriving with huge crates, parked in the streets, containing entire households of heavy bourgeois furniture. The newcomers made no secret of their assumed superiority to the vulgar, materialistic, self-indulgent American society that had taken them in. Some still believed an awful mistake had been made and that to the end they would remain Germans or Austrians who happened, inconveniently, to be Jewish as well.

A boy growing into adolescence on the West Side could feel a certain airlessness and an urge to escape into the great secular world outside. You had a choice if you thought your distant business was with the written word: to look inward and meditate on the fate of being Jewish, or to look outward, at the risk of being shunned both by the faithful for abandoning the faith and by the others for trespassing on their cultural property. When I reached college and graduate school I wondered what business I had as a Jew engaging with the Christian canon of English literature, much of which was not only alien but openly hostile. T. S. Eliot was the most problematic of all. I worshiped him, and the melancholy cadences of *Four Quartets* penetrated my subliminal being, but it was impossible to reconcile his hold over me (and my generation) with his High Church allegiance, royalist politics, public primness, and, most of all, his pervasive anti-Semitism. "Reasons of religion and race," he said, "combine to make any large number of free-thinking Jews undesirable."

I was baffled by a growing sense of disconnectedness and remoteness in my studies. With the exception of the scholar-critic F. O. Matthiessen, my teachers at Harvard regarded their discipline as 63 hermetic and scorned connections between literature and life. On his advice I took a leave of absence from graduate school and went out to New Mexico. For half a year I cultivated chili peppers, mucked out horse stalls, and pumped gas and diesel in the Glorieta valley, southeast of Santa Fe.

My employers, a retired car dealer and his middle-aged girlfriend, had fled their spouses in Dallas to start a new life, but they missed their old life and talked about it all the time. They had bought a place they hoped to turn into a guest ranch after World War II, but Arrowhead Lodge, as they named it, was still only a truck-stop eatery with half a dozen unheated cabins and a couple of undernourished horses. To re-create her suburban garden back in Dallas Josephine set me to planting jasmine, arbutus, hibiscus, and other shrubs that needed pampering; the soil was so loaded with clay that the holes I dug for them with a pickax, shovel, and buckets of water hardened into their graves almost right away. In line with her taming of this wild land she hired a man from Lubbock, Texas, to set tile in the cabin bathrooms. He arrived in a pickup truck loaded with tiles, cement, tools, and whiskey and was only semiconscious by the end of the workday. Donna, the cook, another of Josephine's desperate wartime hires, was clearly crazy. She would lie on the floor of her cabin after a few nips of Southern Comfort and invite me to watch as she masturbated the large male mongrel she had picked up at the Santa Fe pound. When this exhibition failed to have the intended effect on me, she flew into a rage. One evening she threatened me with a loaded shotgun. The day after, Josephine had her carted off to the state insane asylum.

Josephine's mate, Wayne, needed all of a month to figure out that "Kaplan" was not a Scots name, as he had assumed when he hired me ("able-bodied Harvard student") at the U. S. Employment Service in Santa Fe. (The main business of this office was recruiting workers for a secret military research establishment hidden in the hills at Los Alamos.) "You may be a Jew," Wayne said after we had got the name business cleared up, "but I like you, and I think of you as a white man." We shook hands on this. Presumably we were peers, fellow "Anglos," as distinguished from the "Mexicans" with whom I drank beer in the Glorieta saloon at the end of the day.

Wayne's compliment, such as it was, set me to thinking about the human order in this New Mexico wilderness as it related to my own feelings of belonging. I lived in a cabin on the edge of a vast national forest bounded by the Sangre de Cristo range. Possibly no one had ever walked or ridden over much of this land, not even the Indians. Like many other parts of New Mexico it had remained unexplored for centuries and so "belonged" to no one, meaning, I supposed, that I had as much a right to be there as anyone.

"Every continent," D. H. Lawrence wrote, "has its own great spirit of place." For me the spirit of place in New Mexico was far more life altering than that of Europe when I got there several years later. Among the books I brought with me to New Mexico was Matthiessen's monumental study of "art and expression in the age of Emerson and Whitman," *American Renaissance*. I also brought Alfred Kazin's *On Native Grounds*, a work of discovery and appropriation: a Jewish writer—outsider—son of immigrants, raised and educated in Brooklyn, doing his reading at the New York Public Library on Forty-second Street—laid claims to American literature as his own "native grounds," despite the incongruities.

Henry Adams, anti-Semite and supreme representative of the American social and political patriciate, became the darling of Jewish critics and biographers, perhaps because they fell in love with their tormentor, believing they understood him on a higher, more tolerant plane than he understood himself. They were dazzled by his brilliance, fully as dazzled as Adams himself. The same

65

process of appropriation, maybe even Eucharistic ingestion and incorporation, transformed another *monstre sacre* of American letters, Henry James, whose antipathy to Jews was at least as pronounced as Henry Adams's. Leon Edel, a Jew, wrote a landmark biography that in effect made Henry James his property, and for a while, until it was stolen, Edel wore the novelist's gold signet ring. Even preferring to ignore James's comments on "a Jewry that had burst all bounds" and effected "the Hebrew conquest of New York," I felt sickening dismay the first time I read *The American Scene*, his account of a return visit to his native country in 1904. In one appalling chapter he described the denizens of the Lower East Side—my grandparents, Sir!—as belonging to "the nimbler class of animals in some great zoological garden." They were "human squirrels and monkeys," glass snakes, worms, ants, a "swarm" of insects, and "fish of over-developed proboscis." And yet, as they had done with Henry Adams, Jewish writers like Edel made love to Henry James, enfolded him in their own emerging literary tradition, and emboldened others—like me—to tread on "native grounds."

By the 1950s—at least in New York, Chicago, and on the West Coast—Jewish writers and intellectuals no longer skulked in the alleys of American culture. There was even some danger, given the historical precedents of fifteenth-century Spain and twentieth-century Germany, that Jews as a group may have become too successful and perhaps ought to keep their heads down. They were conspicuous in areas like entertainment, book publishing, "communications," and even the academy, especially in previously off-limits English and history departments. Writers like Philip Roth, Bernard Malamud, Saul Bellow, and Allen Ginsberg challenged the traditional WASP hegemony in American letters. These writers weren't descended from what Emerson had called "the establishment," the pantheon of American letters. Not without opposition they created their own mainstream along with a literary language, this one with a Yiddish and vernacular substrate, that was as formative as the language of Mark Twain, Henry James, and Ernest Hemingway.

One night, over drinks in a Montauk, Long Island, restaurant, Philip Roth entertained Annie and me with an imitation of Prince Sadrudin Ali Khan, publisher and chief patron of the *Paris Review*, speaking at the magazine's annual award ceremony. Roth indicated a dignified hush and then drew out the prince's precise upper-class articulation when he spoke and, in an unintended context of comic incongruity and delicious irony, presented "The Aga Khan award for short fiction, to Phee-leep Roth for 'The Conversion of the Jews'" (one of the stories in *Goodbye, Columbus*).

My pride in belonging to a stubborn, perdurable people had come slowly, along with the recognition that, like the color of my eyes, this was for life, a membership nonelective and nonresignable, and that one had better make the best of it. Jewish collective survival over the millennia, against all odds and all reason, even gave me a faint intimation of impersonal immortality.

CHAPTER 3

As one of two brotherless sisters, I was skittish around boys. For two years I went to City and Country, a progressive school for boys and girls on West Twelfth Street, an institution my father plucked me from after he found out that I hadn't, by the age of eight, learned to read. After that, I went to the Brearley School, a polite and venerable all-girl establishment, then on to two female colleges. Until late in my teens I found men, like raw clams and fast sports cars, something of a novelty, something of a risk.

I was twelve when my periods began, and it was my mother who discovered this before I did. Superstitiously uneasy with her, convinced that she could navigate and chart the chaos of my mind, it dismayed but didn't surprise me that she saw the blood first, as I undressed in front of her, having been sent home from school early with a stomachache. But even before I became a "woman" I existed in a state of heated infatuation with boys. One evening as I sat next to one of these on a piano bench—behind us stood half a dozen formal wedding portraits within silver frames—talking with his eagle-eyed parents, the edges of our shoe soles touched, and I felt a rush of desire so violent it nearly knocked me off my perch. I mentioned my eagerness to cuddle and smooch to no one; it was my secret, kept even from my sister, Doris, who had a way of worming almost anything out of me. Whenever I met a new, good-looking boy (for I had definite standards) at my cousin's house in South Orange or my friend Carol's in Woodmere, Long Island, I couldn't wait to feel his tongue inside my mouth, his member tight against my pubic bone—under layers of clothing— and the melting of the bones in my legs. Most often, I ended up dizzy, loose in the knees, from these baby encounters. I had never seen a live penis.

My passion for movie stars—Ronald Colman, Tyrone Power, Macdonald Carey, Gary Cooper—was not a mere schoolgirl crush on two-dimensional idols but throbbing, stomach-churning, heart-stopping lovesickness. I collected pictures of these and other actors, cutting them from movie magazines and attaching them with thick white library paste to the pages of an album I hid on a shelf in my closet under my ski pants and showed to no one.

Starting when I was eleven, I had so many boyfriends that, lest I forget any, I kept an up-to-date list in a notebook, placing a star-shaped mark alongside the names of those with whom I had shared great kisses. Sex with these youths was passionate but chaste, maybe more passionate precisely because for years, until I was seventeen, "nothing happened." Lust was stalled at a notch or two below orgasm and so my appetite was never appeased. We "necked," we "petted," we jabbed our fully clothed bodies rhythmically against each other, but we never went "all the way"; home runs were out of the question, pregnancy being roughly equivalent to a death sentence.

Constantly on the prowl, juices on the simmer, I was about as steady as a trayful of champagne flutes on a North Atlantic crossing in February. I rated handsome far higher than character, temperament, sense of humor, intelligence, or communications skills. It didn't matter if they preferred Batman comics to the poetry of William Butler Yeats, my boyfriends had to have regular features, sited symmetrically, strong chins and brows, lean bodies, good posture. They also had to be graceful and adept at ordering food from a waiter, paying and tipping a cabdriver, and knowing which shoes to wear when. Raised in a household where being Jewish was a silent reality rather than an imperative, I made little distinction between Jews and gentiles—except that gentiles were more likely than Jews to have the physical style I required.

The following is a sampling of the men I dated, considered, and eventually parted from.

Bert. I was in my senior year at Brearley when we met at a party. He was twenty-five and a devout Jew. A buyer in the management training program at Macy's department store, Bert was a Yalie and a former marine who had been through boot camp at Parris Island as well as some shooting action that he never talked about. Bert lived with his mother and brother in a two-room apartment in the east fifties, a "good" address. The only two windows in this place gave out on a filthy air shaft; it was in constant dusk. Bert's mother, a fragile neurasthenic, slept on a fold-out couch in one room, the two men in twin beds in the other. The kitchen was a hot plate, a tiny refrigerator, and a sink. Although on their uppers, they pretended to be rich; Bert's mother was desperate for him to marry a

"Bert," Wellesley, 1948.

girl with money. His brother, Andrew, also a veteran of the war in Europe, suffered from mild shell shock and was unemployable.

Bert wasn't merely handsome; he had the gloomy good looks of an actor playing a doomed prince, and not necessarily a Jewish prince; he could have passed for the offspring of almost anything but Asian or Nordic lineage. He wore flannels and tweeds, cordovan shoes, black knit ties. His thick shiny hair was so black it was blue, like Prince Valiant's. I was in love with him chiefly because of the way he looked and because his melancholy suggested—mistakenly—both depth and an inquisitive, playful mind. Claiming to be protecting my virginity, he insisted we have oral sex.

Bert wrote catchy song lyrics that he and Andrew sang while a third man, a friend, accompanied them on the guitar and also sang. They were better than "amateur" but never seemed able to find the right door to open, the door leading to the garden of worldly success. I went away to Wellesley and languished there for an entire semester, writing to Bert every day. Letters from him came back in a tiny, exact hand, stuffed with new lyrics. I talked to him several times a week from the pay phone on the ground floor of the off-campus house where I lived with twelve other freshman. My romance with Bert occupied a good deal of talking space in this mandatory family. An ex-marine, an older man, his gorgeous picture on my bureau, sitting on a stone wall somewhere, looking seductively at the photographer. To most of my "sisters," few of whom had gone out with anyone more exciting than the boy next door in Kentucky, Tennessee, California, Texas, Bert was an exotic.

Sometimes Bert made me feel terrible and I couldn't understand why, since we were in love. He told me I was too fat; he called my father a tyrant; he scolded me for the absence of religion in my life; he criticized exuberance and repeatedly told me to stop acting like a baby. His piety was a constant surprise because he was so intent on climbing the social ladder that led to largely Christian territory. How could he be a Jew and be accepted by those who lived there at the same time? Once he took me to Sabbath services in a cramped East Side synagogue off Lexington Avenue, where I sat with the women. The arms of the rabbi's wife were covered with black silky hair, like a man's; I couldn't take my eyes off her arm where she had draped it over the pew in front of me.

Agreeing with most of Bert's estimates of my worth, my family, my appearance, and my failure to act more maturely, I was determined to transform myself into the girl he seemed to think I could be—without ever asking him what about me didn't need fixing. He said we should get engaged and I agreed, liking the sound of it. "I'm engaged to be married." After Bert paid me a weekend visit—in a borrowed car—my housemates—without being asked—told me I was much too cheerful and nice for him; they said he was gloomy and possessive, a grouch. It was pointed out to me that during the two and a half days he was there I hardly said a word. "He's a jerk, you deserve better," they told me. I was sure they didn't know what they were talking about, they hadn't, as I had, bothered to unpeel the top layer and see the wondrous person that lay beneath.

When it came to Bert, my parents made no attempt to hide their distaste. My mother said, "He sulks," "He's a nar-sist." My father said, "He won't look me in the eye. He's shifty-eyed." There were things they could have added aloud but which they transmitted silently, such as Bert was poor and worse: he was a Russian Jew. Having convinced themselves that Bert was the ghost of Henry James's Morris Townsend, with his greedy eyes on the heiress's fortune, they declared a covert war on my romance.

One night after we had been going together long enough for my parents to realize that Bert wasn't simply another of my two-week flings, he phoned me at Wellesley, an expense he saved for emergencies. "Your father is having me investigated. He must be crazy. What does he think I am—a criminal?"

I wanted to tell him he was mistaken but I couldn't; it sounded like authentic Edward Bernays. This was my father, who often picked up the downstairs extension and listened in on my phone conversations. Bert complained that his boss had told him a man had been sniffing around Macy's, asking questions about Bert. A friend in the Yale alumni office reported roughly the same thing. It sounded as if my father might actually believe that Bert was an impostor. In his deliberate and languid way Bert was burning like a tiger whose meal has just been snatched from under his nose.

"That's just my father," I said. "He thinks ravening animals are after me."

"You're making a joke of something terribly serious. . . ."

I told him that my father was relatively harmless, that he might

73

root like a pig after truffles but that he would always stop short of violence. Bert insisted that he had already done violence—"to you, Anne. Don't you see how he's questioning your judgment and your relationship with me? He doesn't trust you to think straight. Anyone with half a brain will tell you he's doing violence to your character—and pulling you down to some awful, mindless level. I don't know why you let him do that to you. . . ."

I started to cry. "I didn't know he was going to do that," I said. "And anyway, I couldn't have stopped him. . . ."

"And I don't know why I keep seeing you under these circumstances. . . ." Not one to take things lightly, Bert sounded like a tired old man.

"Then why do you?" I could hardly get the words past my tears.

"God only knows," he said. "I guess because you have a nice smile."

When I challenged my father his admission was buried under a mountain of excuses: "You don't know anything about Bert." Not true. "I always check up on their background when I meet someone I know nothing about." Also not true. "You said he lives in Midtown in the fifties. I don't see how he can manage that on his salary." That was true enough—if you hadn't seen the size of the apartment he lived in. I was disgusted.

My father's operative found nothing to pin on Bert; in fact, everything he had told me about his history turned out to be true. Yet having failed to get the goods on Bert, my parents persisted to demonstrate their contempt. My mother's face grew blotchy when she talked about him, my father's went pale with malice. They snarled whenever they had to say his name.

They cooked up an alternate strategy to pry us apart; my

mother was its messenger. "Annie dear, Dr. Kubie would like to see you."

"Who's Dr. Kubie? What does he want to see me for?"

"Dr. Lawrence Kubie—he's a psychoanalyst—one of the most respected in the field. He's a member of the Institute. He knew Eddie's uncle."

"But there's nothing wrong with me," I said, "Why would I want to see a headshrinker?" Then it hit me. "I suppose this is about Bert." Reams of undelivered dialogue remained inside my head.

"As a matter of fact—"

"You already talked to this doctor person about me—"

"Maybe I should have asked you before talking to him," she said, her apology somewhat disarming me. But the idea of chatting with Dr. Kubie was about as attractive as having a molar pulled without Novocain. If I paid him a visit I would, in one sense, be admitting I needed help. It wasn't hard to guess what they were up to: the doctor, under orders from my parents, would try to sever me, the swimmer, from Bert, the shark.

Bert didn't want me to have anything to do with Dr. Kubie. He said my parents had overstepped all reasonable bounds. "They had me investigated as if I was a crook or a scam artist," he said. "They despise me. They'll do anything to get you to stop seeing me. You mustn't listen to them."

I reminded Bert I was only eighteen and living at home; it wasn't as if I had adult freedom. "Don't worry," I told him. He frowned terribly, took out his wallet of tobacco, stuffed the bowl of his pipe with it, and then lit up, dragging out the procedure to fill a couple of minutes. "Will you ever grow up, Anne?"

Over Bert's objections, I made an appointment, agreeing to go mainly because I was positive I could resist any attempts to separate me from the man I was in love with. Dr. Kubie's office was in the seventies between Park and Lexington, a choice suite of rooms. He opened the door himself. He was wearing heavy, black-rimmed glasses and a dormant smile—I figured the name of Freud had preceded me like a red carpet. "Come in come in," he said, with more enthusiasm than the situation called for.

We sat down and he began to ask me questions, some of them reasonable, others that struck me as crazy: When had I begun to menstruate? How did I feel about becoming a woman? How did my parents get along? Did I think they were faithful to each other? Had I ever wanted to be a boy? How many boyfriends had I had? Had I had sex with any of them? Had I ever met my great uncle? I tried to answer the way I thought he wanted the answers to go. It was like being onstage in a play, not having thoroughly learned your lines. I was anxious and creative. I told him, for instance, that I'd had sex with a cousin when I was eleven, which was a lie—we had only considered it. I told him that I had run away from home—also a lie; I had considered this too but had been too scared to try it. He didn't take notes but stared at me, as if that would help him bore into my psyche, and sat perfectly still, a heavy presence with the focus of a gold miner on a suggestive hillside.

"Now suppose you tell me about this young man of yours."

I told him Bert worked at Macy's and that my parents didn't like him. "That's why I'm here, isn't it?"

"Why do *you* think you're here?" Was the man hard of hearing?

"Because my parents are scared to death I might marry someone they don't like. They think Bert's bad for me."

"This is not about your mother and father; it's about you. *Is* he bad for you?"

"No."

"Then why do you think they think he is?"

"Because he doesn't have any money and he's a Russian Jew.

He also goes to services every Saturday. We aren't observant at all. My father doesn't believe in religion." I thought this remark halfway witty, but Dr. Kubie didn't pick up on it.

He wanted to know if Bert was Orthodox. "Do you think your parents are snobs? And that's the reason they want him out of your life?"

"Yes. That's part of it. I honestly don't know the rest—why they hate him so much."

"That's a pity," he said. For a moment he looked as if he too had forgotten his lines. Then he asked me if we had ever made love, except he called it "sexual intercourse."

I shook my head. He raised his eyebrows, a cliché of surprise. "How old did you say you were?"

"Eighteen."

"Why haven't you? You say the two of you are in love."

"Only one of my friends has had sex, as far as I know," I said. I realized that this was about as useful as telling him that our dog had recently been run over by a taxi.

"Don't you think it's about time you gave it a try?"

I was so stunned that my thoughts were wiped out. My mouth fell open.

"There's no reason to be afraid," he went on, "there are ways of preventing conception, you know." He said this as his smile stopped being latent and became manifest. Something about it made me want to turn away; it was a lustful smile, and was not so much about his wanting to have sex with me as it was his vision of my coupling with Bert and causing trouble at home, deliberately making mischief, or else why encourage me to break the rules?

"Yes, I definitely think you and your young man should go off together for a weekend say, spend a night or two at a nice inn somewhere in the country. Bucks County is lovely." He paused, waiting for me to say something, and when I didn't he went on. "I

77

mean it. Get away from parental eyes and ears. See how you feel about each other in a different setting. Does he have a car?"

I told him Bert didn't have a car but that he could probably borrow one. Dr. Kubie repeated his proposal. "I think it will be a splendid test. You will think about it, won't you? And after you've gone on this little trip I hope you'll give me a call and let me know how it turned out. You're a big girl, Anne, you have a right to your own life."

It wasn't often that I had a chance to catch up with my parents, who always seemed to be at least a couple of yards ahead of me. When, with sprinting heart and poorly concealed glee, I told my mother that Dr. Kubie had suggested an illicit weekend, she refused to believe me. "No, really," I said. "It's true. He thinks Bert and I ought to go away for a romantic weekend somewhere."

I might have been telling my mother that I had been instructed to dismember the cat and roast it on a spit for dinner. She went to look for my father, who was sitting at his desk, talking on the telephone. Patiently, she waited while I stood just outside the room, where I could hear them.

Betrayed! My father shouted that he was going to get his lawyer to write a letter threatening Dr. Kubie with a malpractice suit. My mother used the word *unconscionable*. My father, still at the top of his voice, said. "And he knew my uncle!" I smiled in the dim hallway, marveling at the extent of the damage I had done.

When I reported back to Bert, he permitted one of his rare smiles to emerge briefly, admitting that he never would have guessed. But in the end, he couldn't get a car and, besides, the places where we would have liked to spend the weekend—Bucks County, somewhere green in Connecticut—were too expensive for him, and he refused to let me pick up the tab. So we visited a Yale friend, who had a house on Long Island, where we were shown to the same guest room. Saturday night we had oral sex, as we had done all along, because, as he told me solemnly soon after we met, he didn't believe in "sex before marriage."

Thereafter, my parents acted as if the Dr. Kubie incident had never happened, and if they spoke to the doctor I never heard a word about what was said on either side; they may have been bellicose but they knew when to cut their losses.

It wasn't until Bert took me to his uncle's jewelry store on Boston's Washington Street to buy an engagement ring that I balked. Standing over the counter looking at the diamonds blinking expensively up at me, I was about to pick the one with the most sparkle when the blood drained from my head, my knees went soft, and the warmth of a swoon started to circulate. "I have to get some air," I said, startling the uncle and eliciting one of Bert's celebrated frowns. We made it to the elevator just in time for me to throw up on his shoes. If I was too stupid, while fully conscious, to acknowledge my own misgivings, my unconscious did it for me. I told Bert I was much too young to marry, hoping, by this fib, to save at least a small piece of face for him. He went berserk; in the end it took me weeks to escape. I think he needed my father-the-tyrant's moneyfamepower more than he needed me.

Ian. I met Ian during Christmas break of my sophomore year at Wellesley. His maternal aunt, Janet Anstruther, was a writer (under the pen name Jan Struther) whose novel about life among the upper classes in wartime England had been made into a three-handkerchief, blockbuster movie of the same title, *Mrs. Miniver*. This fact—along with Janet's acerbic style—impressed my mother, who had made friends with her after they were introduced at a fancy New York gathering. Janet had a nephew, my mother had me; phone numbers were exchanged, Ian called me, we agreed to meet. I was smitten at once; a British accent has a way of disarming

79

the young and naïve. Ian took me to dinner in a dusky Italian place in the Village near his apartment on Horatio Street. A nice touch, the Village apartment, suggesting a free spirit. Ian was as handsome as Bert though the mold he came out of was altogether different. Ian, another of whose aunts—on his father's side—was a niece of Queen Victoria, was obviously the product of careful, aristocratic marriages. He had light hair, a thin, delicate nose, and a perfectly formed, mobile mouth. At the peak of each high cheekbone was a small patch of hair that he never shaved off; "bugger tufts," he called them—all the men in his family apparently wore them as a badge of clannish pride. These tufts struck me as silly, I had to stop myself from saying "You forgot to shave those things," but what did I know about the tribal customs of Scotland? He said he wore kilts back home in the Highlands, along with a tam, and a sporran, a small leather handbag that lay over his abdomen. His cousin was the much married duke of Argyll. An army captain during the war, Ian was private secretary to the British ambassador to the United Nations. This meant dark blue suits, subtly striped shirts of the softest Egyptian cotton, hair brushed to a sheen by the two-handed method favored by upper-class Brits. I felt I either had to dismiss the entire package as de trop or to fall in love with it.

Ian was verbal, playful, slightly bookish, and he loved the United States. He loved New York, even its more dismal neighborhoods and its gritty atmosphere. He loved Massachusetts; in a rented car, we toured New England. He couldn't seem to get over the road sign BEAR LEFT, preferring to read the verb as a noun, and pretty soon he gave me a private name: Bear. A thorough gent, who, surprisingly, did not try to bed me, he gave me the sense that I was no more than a cute American toy for him to play with, and that, for many reasons, he would never yearn for my heart—which I would gladly have torn from my chest and handed to him had he asked for it.

Ian Anstruther in front of Inverary Castle, 1950.

That summer, only five years after the end of the war, I went to Europe with my friend Patsy Fitzsimmons. Her boat tickets back and forth were paid for by my parents. They had been young during a time when rich folk regularly made the trip across the Atlantic on luxurious ocean liners to absorb the art and artifacts of a culture deemed superior to that of raw America. Wherever Patsy and I went we let guys pick us up, drive us around in sporty cars, take us places, buy us things—bathing suits, and four-course meals—and try some innocent kissing. Once an Italian man twice my age nearly raped me while his pal, under orders, had left the car with Patsy and gone deep into some nearby woods to engage in God knows what games. We ended our tour in late August by visiting Ian's ancestral home on a loch in Strachur on the west coast of Scotland. He shared this castle with Dodo, the aunt related to Victoria, and Ian's sister and her two small children, all of them

81

peaches-and-cream beautiful and elegant. Patsy and I went rigid with the cold. Chilly in August in any year, the house, made of stone and uncarpeted, was unheated. The home-front effects of the war, only five years over, persisted like a doubt. There were no napkins—cloth or paper—no red meat, very little soap, stiff toilet paper, half cups of coffee in the morning; meals were tiny, greens from the garden predominating. It wasn't until I stayed with Ian and his family for two weeks that I had any understanding of what the English had put up with since the war started for them in September 1939.

In Scotland, Ian was barely recognizable. Could this remote presence be his evil twin brother? And, if so, what had he done with the Ian I loved? While in New York he was boyish, on his own turf, at Strachur, he was lord of the manor, distantly polite, imperious. It was as if he had been given a fierce purge that had flushed out the young and free spirit, leaving behind a middle-aged reactionary nearly as frosty as the house he lived in. Ian wasn't fun anymore; Patsy couldn't understand what I saw in him, refusing to believe me when I assured her that there were two Ians—one American the other British. Constantly hungry, I suggested one day that we get a snack from the kitchen. "We don't go in there," Ian said. I needed to know why. "It isn't done. That's Cook's place." I asked him if he had ever raided the icebox, and he looked as if I had accused him of stealing from the collection plate. He seemed to enjoy telling me that all the married men he knew slept in their so-called dressing rooms. Pressing him for clarity I discovered to my astonishment that men of his class prefer not to sleep next to their wives.

That was the year I transferred to Barnard. Although I went out with other men, I yearned for Ian. We exchanged letters. He invited me to Strachur again and again I accepted, this time alone—and armed with two thick sweaters and some heavy-duty survival rations. If I had hopes that Ian had somehow dropped the mantle of the laird, the fact that I was wrong—along with the fact that I had gone back—only proved how little room I allowed reality. Ian was the same only more so. He wanted to teach me to sail. For once the day was warm, and so I put on a pair of shorts before we set out on the choppy waters of the loch in a small, swift boat. Within a few minutes, Ian began the lesson, the naming of parts— "sheet," "boom," "jib," and so on. Having neither pencil nor paper, I figured I was supposed to memorize this rapidly issued vocabulary, and also to remember to duck my head whenever we changed directions ("came about"), which seemed to be happening every few minutes. Ian told me to tighten something; I did something else. Without hesitating, he whacked me smartly across my thigh with the end of a rope ("sheet"). "So you'll get it right next time," he said. Where the rope landed lay a pink snake of pain.

We went shooting for small woodland creatures. He handed me a shotgun and showed me how to carry it while walking across the lumpy moor behind the house, which lay below us, starkly splendid in a medieval sort of way. We didn't talk much as we trudged over gorse and brush. "I think I see a rabbit," I said, darting ahead of him on the overgrown path. "Get back here, you damned idiot," he shouted. I froze. "Didn't I tell you never to get in front of someone carrying a loaded gun?" I tried to apologize but nothing came out. He said "damned idiot" again.

The ten sexless days (since he had told me many times how adorable I was, why hadn't he tried to ravish me?) at Ian's house in Scotland that summer were enough to start the process of breaking up and dispersing the particles that formed my attachment to this man who was so loose when abroad, so taut at home. Along about December an envelope addressed in Ian's ornamental hand arrived. I tore it open and found inside an announcement of Ian's upcoming marriage to Miss H. B., daughter of Brigadier and Mrs. So-and-so. There was a note to me from Ian. "She's a lovely girl—I'm sure you'll like her." The dispersal was complete.

By late fall I still couldn't say Ian's name without beginning to tear away the scab that had formed over the wound of his marrying someone else. But neither was I quite ready to take the veil.

What did my friend Patsy have in mind when she decided I should meet her boyfriend Milton's chum, Anatole Broyard? However fond of me she was, it didn't take me more than a minute to realize there might be an element of mischief in her wanting to bring us together; I think she read my parents' correctly: ostensibly liberal, they were emotionally conservative and maybe even as xenophobic as the generation that preceded them. White girls did not date dark-skinned men unless they didn't care if they were ostracized. Patsy told me that Anatole's mother and father were Negroes. "You don't object to that, do you? He doesn't look it, you know. His hair is straighter than yours and his skin is white."

Patsy and I met during the summer of 1945, when I was about to turn fifteen. We were both at a music camp on Cape Cod; all the students except Patsy and me were prodigiously gifted. Patsy explained her being there by saying her mother needed a summer off. As for me, my mother believed—erroneously—that I had the makings of a pianist—or maybe a singer. The camp's directors, apparently persuaded that the ability to perform on an instrument is the natural companion of emotional maturity, left us, when we weren't busy with music, to our own feral devices. The camp issued no rules, and I learned, during those two summer months, as much as I needed to know about the art of kissing, the craft of petting. My parents never suspected the wilder side of the camp they had blithely entrusted me to. It turned out to be a memorable summer in other respects, including, as it did, a fire that threatened to devour the camp, flames leaping and roaring over a nearby tree line and turning the sky orange, the dropping of atomic bombs on Hiroshima and Nagasaki, and Japan's surrender to the Allies.

After that, Patsy and I spent a lot of time together over the next five years, although we went to different schools and graduated from different colleges. Patsy was so smart you had to watch your step with her, always careful not to say anything stupid because she would let you know whenever you did. She was ash blond and brown-eyed, courted risk, and draped herself in an attitude that my parents—who nevertheless liked her—assured me was a cynicism unsuited to someone so young. My parents had paid Patsy's passage to Europe; every so often she punctuated her conversation with a reminder to me about how rich, compared with hers, my family was. This made me uneasy, but I didn't say so, partly because I was afraid of her sharpness and partly because I didn't know what to say. To apologize for being rich is one of the more stupid verbal gestures; it only lands you in even hotter water.

Patsy and her mother (her father had split when Patsy was an infant and her mother had not remarried) rented the top floor of someone else's four-storey house in the Village, a skylit apartment I visited frequently and where we lay on the floor listening over and over to her long-playing record of "Songs of the Auvergne," music that managed to be ethereal and sensuous at the same time and that ignited buried feelings. Patsy and her mother worked uptown, Mrs. Fitzsimmons as a publishing executive and Patsy as a junior copywriter at an advertising agency, a job she loathed. Her heart belonged below Fourteenth Street. Patsy assured me that Anatole and I would get along just fine.

1950 Greenwich Village was still coasting on its reputation as the hub of bohemia, although the word was now almost obsolete,

85

having given way to *beat* or *hip*, and with this, a fixed conviction that almost anything goes. One of my Barnard classmates had posed nude for e. e. cummings in his Washington Mews studio. Drugs emerged into the open. Delmore Schwartz lived there, and Franz Kline, Ad Reinhardt, and Dwight MacDonald. But the area was dangerous only if you were threatened by uncertainty.

On the night we had agreed that I would meet Patsy, Milton, and Anatole, I put on a gray wool skirt and a pink Brooks Brothers button-down shirt (styled for women), told my parents I was going out and ignored my mother's "when will you be back?" I took the East Side IRT subway to Eighth Street, then walked west to Louis' Tavern, a bar three steps below sidewalk level. Dusky, thick with cigarette smoke, and noisy as a subway tunnel, Louis' was stuffed with so many people I had trouble pushing open the front door. Patsy waved at me from a table. "This is Anatole," she said as I came over to them. Was that a smirk on her face?

I held out my hand, which Anatole shook firmly, while greeting me with a remark so muted I couldn't hear what it was. Patsy hadn't prepared me for a man who seemed to have stepped off the stage of a melodrama, an erotic villain who caresses his victims before sucking all their blood, leaving little more than a husk. Anatole, whom I guessed to be in his middle thirties, at least a dozen years older than I, had a round head, great black eyes, strongly lashed, ebony hair cropped so short it looked like a cap, an interesting nose, and a mouth that would have looked perfectly fine on a woman. Patsy stared at us; Milton, a man almost grotesquely ugly, with an enormous, shiny nose and a low hair-line—physically Anatole's opposite—asked me if I would like a beer. "I'll get it," Anatole said, bounding up. He loped away on elastic legs, elbowing his way to the bar.

He came back with the glass of draft beer, which he put on the table without looking at me. Within a few minutes I found myself

A.B. and Anatole Broyard, 1952.

in a state of nervousness, excitement transforming itself into desire. Ignoring Patsy and me, Milton and Anatole carried on a conversation more theoretical than concrete, about a French author I had neither read nor heard of. There was plenty of time to try to size him up—was he showing off or did they do this all the time? Was he deliberately ignoring me in order to make the prize seem more valuable? If so, he shouldn't have bothered. Does a healthy fire need gasoline thrown on it? After a while Patsy suggested we go to the ladies' room.

"What do you think of Anatole?" she said, taking out her comb and running it through her short yellow hair without looking at the cracked mirror above the sink.

"He's sexy."

"You know how some people refer to him—-a giant penis with almost as large a brain."

I asked her how come she wanted me to meet him if he had that kind of reputation. "I thought you'd hit it off," she said. "He does these pieces for *Partisan Review*," she said, naming a journal of ideas and art, a sort of bible of the avant-garde. "Milton says he can write rings around anybody." She told me that Anatole had a job writing copy at an ad agency uptown but didn't like to talk about his work, which he considered beneath his dignity. "I told you he was a Negro, didn't I?"

Anatole was a prize, but I wasn't at all certain what I would do with it if I won it. Like one of those rococo silver cups won for athletic brilliance, did it get passed from one woman to the next on a regular basis?

"He scares me," I said.

"You can handle it," she said. "You've been around." I told her I felt like a child next to Anatole.

Back at the table, Anatole turned to me briefly and said something unflattering but clever about Barnard, something about hens, a remark I swallowed with a smile. He was not a person who carried with him a biographical checklist for a potential girl-friend—"Where did you grow up?" "Where did you go to school?" "Do you have any brothers and sisters?" "What kind of music (movies, books, food) do you like?"—preferring instead to obtain bits and pieces of the life indirectly or with a jerk on the hook. In fact, Anatole wasn't like anyone I had ever known; everything he said challenged the prevailing temper of the culture. Broadway was a sellout; the press and broadcasting and television were the creatures of government; there was only one good publishing house—and that one was in France. This wholesale skepticism appeared to be Anatole's gospel. His attitude not only did not discourage me, but like a shower with antibacterial soap, it also invigorated me. How refreshing to get rid of those germs my parents infected me with, such debatable certainties as: "If you're not sure what to do, call in an expert"; "Don't get matey with the help—they won't understand"; "If you read it in the *New York Times* it must be true"; sister to "If a play lands on Broadway it must be good"; "If you can't see, smell, feel, hear, or taste it, it's not worth a plugged nickel"; "If no one will publish it, it can't be any good"; "Religion is practiced only by dopes."

Anatole turned to me once or twice and alluded to something about me—my great uncle, my father—that he could only have known about via Patsy. It occurred to me that Patsy, a girl whose curiosity had, in the past, been known to swamp her scruples, was waiting, along with Milton, to see what would happen to this Jewish princess out of East Sixty-third Street and the Brearley School, at the hands of the city's preeminent stud. I sensed what was happening to me in the way you know it when someone is about to lose their temper and whatever you do won't make the slightest difference.

Milton and Patsy got up and left for Milton's place on Horatio Street, presumably for a night of dope—something I was too timid to try—and screwing. Anatole asked me if I'd like to go back to his apartment for another beer. Don't go! I could hear this as clearly as if my mother had been standing behind me, shouting, pulling at my arm. Having been pelted with warnings from earliest childhood, I knew what she would tell me: that Anatole was too handsome, men as handsome as he was were toxic to women; he would use me and throw me away like an empty container; he was a Negro—I didn't want a black baby, did I?

My mother as conscience was not powerful enough; Anatole drew me gently out of Louis', around the corner to Christopher Street, up four flights through a dark, narrow, rank-smelling stairwell to his apartment, two rooms with a stamped tin ceiling, a double bed, a refrigerator at least thirty years old, and a wooden kitchen table that seemed too large for the room it was in. Within minutes, Anatole had me naked on this table, flat on my back where, unlike the reticent Ian, he wasted no time in introducing me to the act of sex in a way unlike I had known before; it was as if, like Dorothy, I had emerged from a black-and-white world into one bursting with vibrating colors. The act was accomplished in almost total silence—a slow-moving, well-oiled pantomime whose choreography I seemed to know beforehand. Although my body seemed to know the ropes, I realized that I had about as much common sense as a newly hatched egg. This man was a stranger; I had allowed an exotic stranger to lure me into the forest. As soon as I had put on my proper outfit again, Anatole escorted me down the stairs and out to Sheridan Square. "Have you got enough money for a cab?" I nodded. "I'll find one for you," he said, and loped off to get me a taxi. After stowing me in the backseat, he asked me my address and repeated it to the driver, who sped off, leaving Anatole standing on the sidewalk looking around as if for some late-night action.

The stranger had not only seduced me but had peeled away twenty years of uncertainty. Although touched with guilt (I still thought of myself as a "good" girl whose chastity was high on her list of things to keep) I no longer gave a damn about what my mother might say or how my father might frown. In one electric moment, Anatole had turned me into "me." I believed myself in love with him even as I recognized how hard and cold he was. In the fairy tale, the sleeping beauty is kissed by the prince, whose gift of love brings her back to life. In my case, though no beauty, I had been asleep, and just my luck, the person who brought me to life had not had the same gifts used on himself.

"What's happened to you, Anne?" Two days later this question was lobbed at me by Marian Strang, the modern dance teacher at

Barnard, during a workout in the gymnasium. A member of Martha Graham's original company, Strang was an elegant, muscular woman who drilled her girls like a sergeant in the spasmlike motions invented by her guru. She had an active curiosity, few inhibitions. I suppose I blushed and said, "Nothing." But it must have been visible, some kind of liberation had taken place on Anatole's kitchen table (the first time I had indulged in sex for almost five years) then found its way into my arms and legs, my torso, releasing them and at the same time endowing them with absolute control. "Look at Anne, girls, she's flying!"

The most unsettling thing about Anatole was that you never knew where you stood with him, and I was far too shy to ask. For two years—until my shrink pronounced him a demonic influence and an obstacle to mental health—I saw Anatole once or twice a week, mostly on his terrain. I would eat dinner at home, some-

A.B. (*far right*) in Barnard dance class, 1951.

times with my parents, other times alone, then take the subway to his place, where we engaged in wordless, somewhat sepulchral sex and then go to Louis' to drink beer with his friends. I never knew—and had reason to suspect, from remarks dropped by Patsy or Milton—whether or not he met another girl after he put me in a cab and sent it uptown. Soon after we met, he moved from Christopher Street to a place near Washington Square (not far from the house my parents were living in when I was born), one enormous room in a loft he had underfurnished, stripping his living quarters the way he had stripped his life of anything that did not directly have to do with feeding his sexual hunger or his brain. He had no hobbies, played no games, rarely went to the movies, hated live theater, ballet, and nightclubs. It was books galore. He presented me with a reading list and expected me to comply by going out and buying copies, reading, and preparing myself to talk about them whenever we paused between bouts of wordless sex. His list included *Aubrey's Brief Lives*, the short stories of D. H. Lawrence, *Seven Types of Ambiguity*, by William Empson, and the work of several kinky French writers. Up until then I had believed I had been decently educated.

Anatole accepted nothing at face value, made fun of most objects, people, and institutions I had been trained to venerate, such as the *New York Times;* the Nobel and Pulitzer prizes; the Upper East Side; the work of Rodgers and Hammerstein; best-seller lists; fancy clothes—everything, in fact, admired by most of the city's population. According to Anatole democracy was an unachievable ideal; so it would be better for everyone if smart men were installed in high positions than to have the sorts of elections—catering to emotion and narrow interests—that the United States indulged in. That this was just a notch or two below fascism didn't bother me: Anatole was smart about everything else so how could he be wrong about this?

We rarely broke our dating routine—sex, then meeting up with Milton or another pal, and sitting around talking until midnight—but one night Anatole took me to Delmore Schwartz's place nearby in the Village, where I learned how to shoot craps, with Dwight MacDonald and Anatole as my coaches.

He sent me to a doctor—I suspected from the familiar way he talked about her that I wasn't his first referral—to be fitted with a diaphragm. Embarrassed by the procedure, I forced myself to remain cool while between my spread legs the woman rummaged around my insides. While there, she said, "I suppose you know that it's unwise to have sexual intercourse before you marry." I interpreted *unwise* to mean *immoral*. I wondered if Anatole knew that along with the diaphragm there came, at no extra charge, instructions on the proper way to behave as a single female. When I reported what the doctor had said, Anatole brushed it off. "She's okay. She just feels she has to take a parental interest. Come over here!"

I made a tactical mistake when I gave my mother the issue of *Partisan Review* in which Anatole had published a piece as intellectually subversive as the Museum of Modern Art's fur teacup, Stravinsky's *The Rite of Spring*, or the Armory Show had been forty years earlier, shaking up the bourgeoisie and forcing people to look at things in a new way. It said, in effect, that members of so-called respectable society were the true vulgarians because they lived in a constricted world, never questioned or fought against the tyranny of the status quo. He said this via the most graceful and startling prose. I thought my mother would be won over by Anatole's brilliance and range, but after reading his essay she said, "I don't want you to see this person anymore. He's a nihilist." When I told her Anatole had Negro parents, she went nuts. "Do you want to have a black baby?"

I wanted to shock my mother. But I also wanted to be shaken up myself—everything my parents had done until I went off to college had been designed to shield me from the slightest whiff of danger. They had so thoroughly childproofed my world that I had begun to think I lived inside a bubble through which nothing, no germs—real or metaphorical—could penetrate.

The penetrator—Anatole—was an extreme, way off the scale of normal human behavior. He never paid me a compliment or indicated that he enjoyed my company. We had been invited to a party uptown by one of my few friends he hadn't said anything dismissive about. "I'd like to go," I told him. "Well I wouldn't," he said. "I'd have to put on a suit and tie, and anyway they'll just sit around being clever." I told him that in that case I would go by myself, which seemed to surprise him. I showed up at the East Side apartment, where I found a roomful of young people sitting around being clever. Less than an hour after I arrived, the doorbell rang, the hostess went to answer, and who stood on the threshold, in a suit and tie? Anatole. This was the closest he ever came to admitting that I was in any way important to him.

"What have you got on under that dress?" Anatole said one night as I took my coat off in a loft where a large and noisy party was in progress.

"A panty girdle."

"It's terrible. Take it off. You should never wear anything like that." I went into the bathroom and peeled it off. "I was only trying to look thinner," I said. "You like thin women." I'd rolled up the girdle and stuck it in my purse.

"You're okay without one of those things," he said. And this was the closest he ever came to admitting he found me less than repulsive to look at.

One of his former friends, Chandler Brossard, wrote a novel with a pretentious title: *Who Walk in Darkness*. Anatole was reading it in manuscript, dropping each page on the floor as he finished with it, when I showed up at his place for one of our curious dates. "Chandler's publisher sent it to me to read. They're afraid I might sue." Why would he sue? "This book is largely about me. He implies that I'm a Negro trying to pass as white."

"Well, aren't you?" This was the first and only time we had ever come close to this porcupine.

"It's not about what I am," he said ambiguously, veering off. "I just don't want him to turn me into some fictional character."

I asked him what he was going to do, and he said he was going to threaten the publisher with a lawsuit. "I won't let them publish this garbage." In the end, Brossard, faced with this lawsuit, changed the main character's unspeakable secret to that of being born to unmarried parents. This was an era when social stigmas were disappearing from the scene as fast as virgins, and the novel as it was published had none of the impact that the original version would have had. Who cared if the hero was born out of wedlock?

During my senior year the news office at Barnard named me campus correspondent for the *New York Times*. Since I had absolutely no experience as a reporter, hadn't been on the *Barnard Bulletin*, and didn't even know what a lead was, I could only imagine how the hardworking staffers of the *Bulletin* felt about my getting this plum job. I was just a blithe kid, and although I assumed, justifiably, that my being given this job had a lot to do with my mother, Barnard, class of 1913 (and also related to the Sulzberger family), I wasn't fazed by my connections or my ignorance, and was too arrogant to be scared. At least twice a week in the afternoon I took the Broadway subway from 116th Street to Forty-second Street, walked cooly past a phalanx of *Times* delivery truck drivers who whistled, cheered, and yelled smutty things at me, visited Mr.

Garth, the managing editor, who told me how many words he wanted, sat down at my desk in the city room and typed out my little story on three pieces of paper connected at the top. Sometimes, if it was late, a copy boy would be waiting by the desk, plucking the paper out of the machine as I came to the end of a page. No time for revision. During that year the *Times* published at least one Barnard story a week, not because spectacular things were happening on campus but because Iphigene Ochs Sulzberger, wife of the publisher and president of the Times corporation, was a Barnard graduate—the maternal autocrat. And so I profited by two daughterly connections. Anatole made fun of me and my stringer's job, giving me no credit for my snappy leads—"Cries of 'nike,' Greek for Victory, were heard yesterday for the fiftieth time as the annual Greek Games was held at Barnard College"—or my thoughtful stories, but dismissed the whole enterprise, once again, as a doleful instrument of its middle-brow management and readers.

My friend Mary said, "You make Anatole sound like a vampire."

"I'm besotted. I can't help it."

"Then why don't you marry him?"

"He hasn't asked me," I said.

For months after I stopped seeing Anatole, having been told by my shrink that he'd be forced to discontinue the treatment if I didn't, I walked around like an addict who's gone cold turkey. He was, in fact, very like a drug, and my trancelike state only underscored my need for shoring up from the outside. For this I focused on men, looking for someone like Anatole.

I met Bernie Wolfe at a party in the Village. He was sixteen years older than me and looked even older, his skin thick and wrinkled.

Bernie earned his living as ghostwriter for Billy Rose, a former songwriter, nightclub owner, and theater producer. Rose had maneuvered himself among so many Broadway-connected enterprises that he was identified as a *showman*, a word used to characterize someone who can't quite make up his mind which of his assorted skills he wants to use at any one moment. Among other things, Rose had staged a swimming extravaganza at the 1939–1940 World's Fair known as the Aquacade—a couple of dozen gorgeous girls in swimsuits performing water ballet to music. Rose, born William Samuel Rosenberg, was so popular and ubiquitous that a nationally syndicated column called "Pitching Horseshoes" appeared regularly under his byline. It was written by Bernie. In "Horseshoes," Bernie, disguised as Rose, spread showbiz opinions and dispensed news of the theater and its people.

Bernie's best-known novel was *Really the Blues*, a fat, sassy book about jazz trumpeter Mezz Mezzrow. Published by Random House, it hadn't sold very well, but people who knew the subject assured me it was the best book about jazz ever written. Bernie told me stories: how he had been one of Leon Trotsky's bodyguards in Mexico, where Trotsky lived as an exile after his life was threatened by Stalin. Whenever Trotsky went to the movies, his several bodyguards went with him; instead of looking at the screen they continually scanned the audience for potential assassins, one of whom eventually managed to break into Trotsky's house and kill him with an ice axe. Bernie was short and not fat but squat, as if pushed in from both ends. He looked a little like the movie star Edward G. Robinson and, like Robinson, smoked cigars; he always smelled like sweetened smoke. I wasn't in love with him, and he seemed to love me with a sort of avuncular warmth, aware that I wouldn't sleep with him and having the tact and kindness not to scare me off by insisting we have sex. I was still getting over Anatole.

Bernie lived in the murky two-room basement apartment of a brownstone on Tenth Street a few steps east of Sixth Avenue. He was a Village regular, knew everyone, and was one of the few people I've ever known about whom I never heard a nasty, snide, or envious remark. He kept an office-size typewriter on his desk, and next to the typewriter he maintained a neat pile of assorted candy bars, five or six of them—Milky Ways, Baby Ruths, Hershey bars. He told me he ate them as he wrote, converting sucrose into words. The Billy Rose columns helped pay his rent and his mother's, who lived in Brooklyn and came by occasionally to clean his apartment. She was there one afternoon when I arrived; she was wearing a kerchief that covered her hair completely and had trouble speaking English. I thought she was the cleaning lady until Bernie introduced us. Bernie chafed at having to do the Rose columns; he wanted to write nothing but fiction. I spent a few months seeing Bernie several evenings a week, coming back late at night to the house on Sixty-third Street, where I still lived with my parents. He was so affable and reasonable that sometimes I wished he would chew me out for being a tease, an epithet I had heard a couple of times before and that made me feel as if I had no heart. But he never did; he always asked me what I wanted to do, where we should eat, did I want to go to a certain party—Anatole might be there. Anatole was there one night, and, when he saw who I was with, told me that Bernie was one of the best people he knew.

Bernie was a buffer between my recent past and the rest of my life. We broke up when he realized that I wasn't in love with him and probably never would be.

CHAPTER 4

Before coming to a party, I'd circle the block several times, stop by the front door, light another cigarette, and set off on another round of postponing the inevitable. Disgust with timidity eventually took over. I'd straighten my necktie once again, head for the elevator, enter a room full of strangers, and, I expected, pass through them unnoticed, like a specter. Parties had been different back in Cambridge. They tended to be placid and predictable, populated by academics, junior and senior, who gabbled in departmental gossip, literary tags, and vacation plans. If not baby talk it was at least parochial. But now, at the age of twenty-one, I was in adult territory, a corner of a world I had known about only from reading and hearsay.

At a cocktail party in the East Fifty-sixth Street apartment of Louis Posner, a lawyer and collector of Dickens first editions, I met Somerset Maugham, the prince of cats among popular story-tellers of the postwar era. Highbrows like Edmund Wilson called Maugham's work "a tissue of clichés" informed by "bogus motiva-tions"—"I've settled that fellow's hash," Wilson boasted. But I was awed nevertheless, mainly because Maugham had written a wickedly funny novel about literary biography, *Cakes and Ale*, as well as *Ashenden*, a thriller in the line of E. Phillips Oppenheim and John Buchan. Maugham had based *Ashenden* on his service in British intelligence in World War I, but it was hard to believe that this "Old Party" (as he liked to call himself), bridge partner of dowagers, had once carried a revolver, feared for his life, and trafficked with spies.

Guest of honor, the great man was in his seventies, with yellow pouches under lizard eyes and a neck wattled and retractile like a tortoise's. (To fight off impotence and mortality he was rumored to be submitting his buttocks to massive injections of cells from fetal sheep. The inventor of this sheep-cell therapy, a Swiss, Doctor Paul Niehans, was also treating Pope Pius XII and the duke of Windsor.) Maugham rotated his head slowly, one degree at a time, to peer at me, briefly, but appraisingly enough to make me uneasy. Our host's handsome son, my college friend David, who had invited me to this party, was Maugham's young lover and had been ever since he was a student at Lawrenceville. Although notoriously stingy, Maugham had helped pay David's Harvard tuition in return for sexual services rendered. The woman standing with Maugham announced herself, in the fluttery style of Margaret Dumont, as La Duchesse de Clermont-Tonnerre. She added, considerately—"To make it easy for you Americans"—that her name was pronounced as in "clear mountain air." Apart from a few polite words and

Maugham's stammered "how-do-you-do," these exotics might as well have been stuffed animals, for all the content of my encounter with them. I had a brief colloquy, at another party, with Dame Edith Sitwell, garbed like a Druid priestess in a flowing black dress, on her head a shapeless hat and on her feet shoes from the men's department at Macy's. She said Walt Whitman was a great poet, "wholly unappreciated by you Americans," and then, having delivered this judgment, turned her back on me and attended to her brother, Sir Osbert. Rubbing feathers with such rare birds, although uneventful, was all very well for the thrill and anecdotal value, but for me this was not what parties were about, nor what New York was about either.

The irreducible essence of parties in New York was romantic, erotic. There was always the possibility, heightened by shyness, adrenaline, and anticipation, of adventure, meeting someone who would change my life. New York was about career, but it was also about women, their mystery, their capacity for affection and surprise. Growing up in an all-male family after my mother's death I had missed these tender aspects of the creation, even despite the mitigating affection of our housekeeper Georgia Edwards, a woman from St. Kitts who had been with us since I was an infant. In time I left home to enter the relatively monkish confines of Harvard College. This was before "combined instruction" with Radcliffe, a measure forced on a shorthanded Harvard faculty by the war, brought young men and women together in the same classroom. The first weeks of combined instruction in Longfellow Hall on Appian Way, strictly Radcliffe territory until then, I felt like Adam in the Garden waking from deep sleep. The Radcliffe Eves were clearly undecided whether they should dress up or dress down for the occasion—some were defiantly unkempt and wore what must have been their old bathrobes—and whether the presence of males on the premises was a desirable accommodation or heralded another rape of the Sabine women. For my part, I lacked the courage to talk to any of the girls, but scanned the hall and fell in love every fifteen minutes. On one occasion early in the new era of combined instruction the English department lecturer turned up the sexual heat by spelling out references to orgasm and sexual exhaustion in William Wycherley's Restoration comedy *The Country Wife*.

Even in the freedom and exuberance of the postwar era, language and manners remained relatively demure. In elementary school I had once been isolated in an empty classroom for an entire day as punishment for saying "go to hell." Since then the constraints on "blasphemy" and "obscenity" had loosened only a little. The shock value of "smutty language" was as powerful as an air raid siren. The salt, pepper, and ketchup of G.I. speech, the word *fuck*, supremely adaptable as verb, noun, adjective, adverb, expletive, and "infix" (inserted within another word), hadn't been demobilized. Even three years after V-J Day Norman Mailer's publisher made him adopt a transparent substitute, *fug*, in *The Naked and the Dead*. (This evasion gave the original word an added prominence and supposedly provoked Dorothy Parker to remark, "So you're the man who can't spell *fuck*.") James Jones's *From Here to Eternity*, like Mailer's novel an attempt to show the way soldiers really talked, managed to get away with *fuck* in 1951, but, along with some other indispensable words, it was banned from normal conversation and supposedly worldly magazines like *The New Yorker*. Well-brought-up girls were shocked when they heard it—or pretended to be. An "obscenity," the word remained officially taboo in print until the end of the decade, when D.H. Lawrence's unabridged *Lady Chatterley's Lover* was admitted to the company of permissible books. Before then, we packed our copies of *Lady Chatterley*, John Cleland's *Fanny Hill, or the Mem-*

oirs of a Woman of Pleasure, and Henry Miller's *Tropic of Cancer* in our bags of dirty laundry, a harmless charade for the entertainment of U.S. Customs inspectors. The movies we saw—even *On the Waterfront* and *The Bridge on the River Kwai*—were governed by the inflexible Motion Picture Production Code that banned exclamations like "God," "Jesus Christ," and "hell," and, in westerns, *buzzard*, because it might be taken for *bastard*. The movie (1953) of *From Here to Eternity* featured a scene in which Burt Lancaster and Deborah Kerr appeared to be having sex on the sand while lapped by the Hawaiian surf. But with a few such spectacular exceptions most popular movies were almost as innocent of explicit carnal content as *Little Women*. Movie babies came from central casting.

Sex before marriage remained vaguely illicit for members of my generation. This gave it an extra thrill—the thrill of "sneaky sex." We were cat burglars of pleasure. Even at the end of the decade "facts of life" manuals (for example, *What Girls Want to Know About Boys*, by Arthur Unger and Carmel Berman) were warning young people that "illicit relationships" were "sordid. At home, someone may walk in at any time; at a motel it's necessary to give false names and addresses; and police may be patrolling the local lover's lane," all this in addition to the risk of pregnancy, forced marriage, and venereal disease. But the reality, as we learned from Alfred Kinsey's reports (1948, 1953) on human male and female sexual behavior, was quite different. As a species we behaved like rabbits but knew not much more than rabbits did about sexual physiology. In the 1950s the Freudian ideal of the vaginal orgasm was still the gold standard. The clitoris hadn't yet been publicly "discovered" but merely "detected" (as Oscar Wilde said about America), even though nowhere else, with the exception of Jerusalem's Temple Mount, could be found such a concentration of nerve endings and perturbations in such a small place.

Harvard's parietal rules forbade undergraduates to "have"—the ambiguity was unintentional—women in their rooms after 5 P.M. Before 5 P.M., once you signed in your guest, there was ample opportunity for "having," but also the danger of discovery by a tutor, checking on the sign-in register, who noticed that your door was closed when it was supposed to have been left ajar. In aggravated cases, the punishment for fornication under the Harvard roof could be expulsion from the House. By contrast, drinking yourself stuporous was countenanced as a private matter unless, before passing out, you became a threat to public order. In addition to quelling Yard riots, which went out with the war, one function of Harvard's tiny constabulary, armed only with furled umbrellas, was to rescue intoxicated students from the clutches of the Cambridge police. (One night the Harvard constables, unable to beat a large rat to death with their umbrellas, had to ask the local police to shoot it.)

Sex was easier in New York, although not without the peril of the transgressive when one was discovered. Caroline's parents were watching *Victory at Sea* on the television set in their Park Avenue living room. From our bed in Caroline's room down the hall we could dimly hear the billowing cadences of Richard Rodgers's score as American warships and warplanes sent the Japanese foe to the bottom. Finally noticing our absence, her parents pounded on Caroline's bedroom door. A week later she moved to her own apartment, a walk-up off Second Avenue. Nicki's mother was prepared to be more tolerant than Caroline's. Finding us lying together, quite chastely, with our shoes off (this was a hot summer night), she tickled my feet and told me I had beautiful insteps. The notion that she had begun to fancy me as a potential son-in-law was reason enough to go no further.

As for contraception, dispensing diaphragms or advice to unmarried women was illegal for birth-control clinics. Doctors who performed abortions had to be ferreted out on shabby side streets in Hoboken or Jersey City and paid in cash. Males of my age found that buying condoms, officially vendable only as "prophylactics . . . for the prevention of disease," was both an ordeal, requiring furtive courage, and, in retrospect, once you were out on the street, low comedy. You did not want to be seen or heard asking for condoms at a drugstore counter; you developed a sudden need for cough drops or toothpaste if the salesperson was a woman, or if a woman customer or anyone else, for that matter, stood anywhere nearby. With a show of reluctance, and rather too dramatically for such a modest transaction, the druggist at long last extracted the little flat tin of Trojans, Sheiks, or Ramses (these evocative trade names deserve a history of their own) from a drawer behind the counter and passed it over with a subtextual smirk—"Will these be enough?" The first time I bought condoms I walked a mile or two to a drugstore in Brighton on the other side of the Charles River rather than risk the chance of being seen asking for them at a Harvard Square drugstore.

My brother and I used to watch what we called Hudson River whitefish swimming out of the sewers and floating downstream toward the bay. These pale, dispirited flotillas of used condoms gave an adolescent burdened with homework a piquant notion of how grownups occupied themselves meanwhile—perhaps doing nothing else. If you were walking by the river with a girl you hoped she would not notice a naval parade that could be as embarrassing a sight as the baboons in the Central Park Zoo exhibiting their crimson bottoms. Being responsibly equipped with condoms when the need arose put you in the difficult position of seeming to have assumed too much of your date. You could only say, "Well, you never know," when in a show of maidenly dismay she asked, "Do you always carry those things with you?"

When I met her in the course of one of my job-hunting expeditions, Phyllis worked as a secretary at a publishing house. We arranged to meet after work at a bar on Lexington Avenue, where we had a few drinks and then, as if this was the natural thing to do, went on to my apartment. But after this auspicious start we plateaued, permanently as it seemed, at a debate about moral obligation—she was married and, she said, "perfectly happy" with her husband—versus the pleasure and spontaneity principle. That she was married was not of much consequence to me so long as what she might choose to do she did out of free choice. This was New York, after all, I said, not York, Pennsylvania, which was where she came from. Firing off this ammunition seemed to be having no effect, and we had arrived at an apparent stalemate, when, abruptly, she said, "Okay, I'm ready." Afterward, she asked me to mix us a pitcher of martinis.

During that year, 1953, Phyllis came to my apartment Thursday evenings, when the department stores were open late—shopping was her cover story. Tuesday late afternoons belonged to Edna Lewis, who ran an art school and whom I had met at a dancing party in the Village. She helped me furnish my little apartment on East Thirty-seventh Street in the comme il faut style of the day: unforgiving sling chairs and chairs of molded plywood and plastic, a cushionless Danish Modern sofa covered with itchy wool, a glass and wrought iron coffee table with lethal corners, teakwood nesting tables, nubbly brown rug, café curtains, a Pyrex coffeemaker that looked like a piece of laboratory equipment, brightly colored bowls and plates, and sundry kitchen items from the Museum of Modern Art design collection. Irregular evenings belonged to Laura, once a steady girlfriend, who had taken to showing up unexpectedly, after getting sozzled at cocktail parties;

to Naomi, who wasn't sure she wanted to stay married to her husband, whom she had learned was homosexual, and was willing to consider marrying me so long as I changed my last name to something ethnically neutral; and to Janet, who was, quite simply, generous and enthusiastic—she had never had an orgasm, she told me, but there was always hope. I was also dating cool beauties like Mary-Louise Louchheim, a student in Martha Graham's dance company, and the literary scholar Aileen Ward, both of whom I adored but kept a shy distance from: it was satisfaction enough that these glorious creatures even consented to go out with me to dinners, concerts, and parties. Noticing Aileen as we got off the subway on our way to the Bronx Zoo the trainman drew his fingertips toward his mouth and simulated a kiss, an Italian gesture meaning, Perfect!

There were sometimes weeks of sexual famine during which I did desultory reading, went to the movies, visited friends and my brother. Then came periods of plenty, even glut. Like a character in a French bedroom farce, I scurried back to my apartment after work to straighten the living room, make the bed, empty ashtrays, and remove lipstick from glassware. I was too entranced by sex to give much thought to anything else, especially work. Given a moment to reflect and catch my breath, I recalled the Wife of Bath's word for the loose pleasures of her youth: "Jollity."

Lucy Thomas, with whom I had an open relationship on and off for about five years, came from Nebraska. She pronounced *cookie* as if it had three *o*s and *rinse* with the *s* sounded like *z*. She explored the givens of life in New York with a boldness and enthusiasm I envied. Most of us stayed put for a while once we had found a place to live, but Lucy was restless and inventive and experimented with offbeat apartments, rented or borrowed. When we first met in the late 1940s she was living off Columbus Avenue just below 110th Street, near the southern border of Harlem. Soon after, she moved on: to a place above a fish restaurant in the west fifties; then, one off MacDougal Street in the Village, around the corner from Minetta Tavern, that was reached more conveniently by the fire escape than by the front door. She was briefly tempted by an apartment on the first floor of a converted funeral parlor in Chelsea—the embalming slab, still fastened to the floor by pipes, drains, and heavy feet, would have served nicely as a kitchen table easy to crumb, sponge, and, as needed, flush. Her place in one of the tenement blocks in the seventies between First and Second Avenues began as two apartments that she made into one: with a sledgehammer and crowbar she took down the nonbearing wall that separated them; a neighbor from the floor below helped her frame a doorway. The new combined apartment had two toilets with overhead tanks side by side.

Lucy had been a doctoral candidate in philosophy at Brown and also studied painting with the Provincetown artist Xavier Gonzales—she told me about the freshwater ponds in the Truro and Wellfleet woods. She had the gumption to buy a used British car, a Morris Minor, and then face down the seller when it turned out to need major repairs. Even after the thing was fixed the windshield wipers died whenever it rained—she drove, and I kept lookout from a side window. For a couple of summers we shared a shack east of the Cherry Grove fringe of settlement on Fire Island. It didn't have electricity or running water, and to reach it from the ferry dock we trudged along the ocean beach carrying food, gin, and a block of ice. We occupied the one bedroom while our visitors, most often *Time* researchers and writers, slept on the parlor floor or aloft in an abandoned Coast Guard tower nearby.

At night we walked back to town for beers at the Cherry Grove Hotel, meeting place of gays and straights in an overwhelmingly tolerant community. Wystan Auden was supposed to have said that even the cats at Cherry Grove were queer. In a silent dialogue that epitomized the anything-goes spirit of the place, one bungalow had a sign that declared FOUR OF A KIND and faced another across the boardwalk, this one replying INSIDE STRAIGHT. By the Cherry Grove ferry dock we once watched a water ballet in the form of a flower opening to the sun. The performance by a dozen male swimmers was wildly applauded. It celebrated a mock wedding followed by the departure for the mainland of two young men on their honeymoon.

In contrast to Cherry Grove, New York's gay community, though sizable, was unacknowledged and denied for the most part by the general public uptown and had no overt political and collective identity. The word *queer* was offensive, while in common usage *gay* carried no specific sexual meaning: "Gay Blades" was the name of the popular ice skating rink in Madison Square Garden. But in writing and the arts gays were a formidable presence and, to the extent they had coherence and power as a group, were playfully called the Homintern (by analogy with Comintern, the dread Communist International). The Homintern, as I understood it from the sidelines, had an honorary elder statesman (Auden) in New York and a network of influence, patronage, and membership that extended to San Francisco, Rome, Paris, and sunny places like Marrakech, Ischia, Key West, Provincetown, and Cherry Grove. Among the Manhattan power brokers in the mid-1950s were Lincoln Kirstein, patron of George Balanchine and the New York City Ballet; Kirstein's brother-in-law, the painter Paul Cadmus; Monroe Wheeler of the Museum of Modern Art; Wheeler's companion, the novelist Glenway Wescott, a native of Wisconsin; and Leo Lerman, literary editor of *Mademoiselle*. Truman Capote and Gore Vidal were among the Homintern's younger stars, along with Tennessee Williams. The writer and composer Paul Bowles, a resident of Tangier, was its proconsul; his wife, Jane Bowles, its sibyl.

Morris Golde, a generous and unassuming businessman who knew and was adored by everyone in the arts, had a big house toward the eastern end of Fire Island and a powerboat he drove at terrifying speed across Great South Bay, paying little attention to floating logs and even other boats. The composer Ned Rorem, Morris's former lover, had been replaced by a sweet-natured still-life painter, Alvin Ross. In his garden apartment on West Eleventh Street Morris gave exuberant drinking and dancing parties that mixed gays and straights. They featured huge platters of imported Italian salami and appearances by Leonard Bernstein, Aaron Copland, Marc Blitzstein, the opera and concert singer Jennie Tourel, and similar celebrities. Larry Rivers, John Ashbery, and Frank O'Hara were often there, so was Anatole Broyard, understood by many Village people to be a light-skinned black man who passed as white uptown, where he worked for an advertising agency. He was said to be irresistible to women. At these free-and-easy parties I was reasonably certain of finding an Edna or Janet to go home with. One evening a group of us witnessed a silent comedy scene: the composer and critic Virgil Thomson struggled to liberate his hippopotamus bulk from one of Morris's chairs, a leather and tubular steel sling that challenged even supple occupants to escape gracefully once they were seated. All the while, in his distress and appeals for help, Thomson waved his cane (or "wand," as a taxi driver delivering him to Carnegie Hall was supposed to have called it).

Lucy was a researcher for *Time*, to my mind an enviable and glamorous job. In the magazine's hierarchy the editorial researchers— about fifty of them—were all women, well educated, many of them upper class. Researchers made up the broad base of an editorial pyramid that narrowed toward its apex at the founder, Henry R. Luce. In between were half a dozen and more levels of *Time* editors, about sixty in all, only five of them women; of these five, three held basically administrative and traffic-managing positions. The researchers as a group seemed to accept this caste system as if it were a function of natural law requiring them to be handmaidens to male journalists. Life in the researchers' harem—there was a fair amount of cross-pollination from the writers—was sweetened by generous salaries, frequent performance and seniority raises, paternalistic policies (researchers working after hours were sent home by taxi), free psychotherapy, and, overall, the sense of belonging to a tight-knit elite turning out the world's most successful and powerful newsmagazine. (Lord, how I wanted to be in that number!) Editors and researchers formed an extended family held together by their ability to withstand, even thrive on, intense pressure and short deadlines, a muted opposition to the hard-nosed right-wing policies of their employer, and the assumption, among some of the writers, that they would be doing better things, maybe writing novels, if it weren't for Luce's paycheck. In the early 1950s they could afford to live well—good apartments, good food, entertainment, travel—on the canonical base salary of $10,000 a year and the knowledge of additional money piling up against the future in retirement and profit-sharing programs.

I often heard stories about the magazine's legendary alumni. One was James Agee, novelist, film critic, screenwriter, and author (with Walker Evans) of a classic study of Alabama sharecroppers, *Let Us Now Praise Famous Men*. Agee, who died in 1955, reportedly threw a typewriter out the window toward the end of an office drinking session. In point of notoriety another *Time* editor, Whittaker Chambers, a confessed Soviet courier, was America's (if not his magazine's) Man of the Year for 1948: he had testified before the House Un-American Activities Committee that Alger Hiss, former State Department adviser and president of the Carnegie Endowment for International Peace, had spied for the Soviet Union. One *Time* writer, who knew both men, told me that Hiss and Chambers were equally guilty of lying and spying, but Hiss, who went to federal prison for perjury, was at least prettier. Before he became a national figure I had known the name Whittaker Chambers only in his capacity as translator from the German of *Bambi*, Felix Salten's gentle animal story.

Monday nights I sat with Lucy in a bar on the ground floor of the Time-Life Building while she and others waited for word from above that the magazine had finally closed for the week, leaving Tuesday and Wednesday for the staff to recuperate before taking on the next issue. The *Time* calendar set them apart from most of the city's population, and before I started in-house work in book publishing, I adopted this weekend, which had, among its many advantages, escape from the normal crush of people heading out of the city on Friday. I applied several times for job interviews within the Time-Life-Fortune empire, but the closest I could come to being a member of the family was to live the off-pace weekend with Lucy and her friends on the magazine: Douglas Auchincloss, bearer of one of the fancier names in American society, who for reasons I never understood, was *Time*'s religion editor; an Australian couple, Essie Lee, who worked *Time*'s letters to the editor column, and Alwyn Lee, one of the book reviewers, who told me bawdy and alluring tales about life down under. Lucy and I helped the Lees build a little fieldstone house in the woods at Croton-on-Hudson. Nearby, along Mount Airy Road, lived a community of survivors of the Popular Front, a bygone era of hope and goodwill when the United States and the Soviet Union fought side by side against a common enemy. The children of this community—"red diaper babies"—were now cold war adults.

Lucy was by far the kindest and most intellectually sophisticated of the women I knew up to then. Recognizing that she was too accomplished to remain a researcher and fact checker, her employers at *Time* sent her to France to do a report on the worker-priest movement, the social reform program, anathema to the Vatican, that joined the ideals of primitive Christianity with those of Marxian socialism. I was beginning to get a few freelance writing assignments, and sentence by sentence Lucy tutored me in patience and clarity as I struggled at the typewriter. One of those assignments was to write the introduction to an anthology of anti-woman writings I had been commissioned to put together. Given the nature of the project, Lucy did not seem to mind the incongruity of her tutoring—as a reward for finishing this depressing piece of work she bought me a recording of *Rosenkavalier*. One Christmas, encouraging a direction I myself wasn't fully aware of, she gave me the three-volume Macmillan *Literary History of the United States*. I began a slow return to where I had left off in graduate school—nineteenth-century America and its writers.

For all the tacit openness of our relationship on both sides, she put up with a great deal of faithless and self-serving behavior along with my reluctance, even under pressure, to make any commitment. I kept my apartment, and she kept hers. As a couple we had no future, as much as we genuinely liked each other: whatever spark there had been between us had gone out. One day, crossing Fifty-third Street on the west side of Fifth Avenue, Lucy and I passed Anne Bernays crossing in the other direction. Annie and I barely knew each other then. She wore a little gray suede hat and a rosy red wool coat, and she had a rosy aura. We smiled, exchanged quick hellos and no more, and then went on our ways. I must have blushed. Lucy said, "I think that is someone very important to you."

CHAPTER 5

You know you're near or at the end of therapy when you can't stand to say the word *I* any longer. This may take years.

In the early 1950s entering psychoanalysis—for those of us with money to blithely spend on books, records, theater tickets, lipstick, hosiery, and assorted knickknacks—was as much an initiation rite as pledging a sorority was to another kind of girl. In order to qualify for analysis you didn't have to be mad, unable to get out of bed in the morning, or self-mutilating—simple malaise or anomie would do it.

Nor was analysis as concerned with helping the female patient find herself (how about looking behind the couch in the study?) as with her forming a lasting relationship with a man. In this it was behind feminism by half a century. For years I had been dating men about as wholesome as deviled eggs left out beneath a midday sun. Only when the men with whom I went to movies and hockey games, Village bars and fancy Midtown restaurants, Fifty-second Street jazz clubs, Fire Island weekends, and boat rides on Long Island Sound, only when they had a nasty streak or an unchecked urge to squeeze me into a skin designed for someone else was I drawn to them. Otherwise I found them far too nice; niceness meant erotic voltage so low as to not give off any appreciable heat or light. I couldn't be bothered with them, was rude over the phone, sent them packing with the dispatch of a train conductor slightly behind schedule. All my female friends, intellectual, artistic and/or professionally ambitious, were also looking for mates. That's what you were expected to do and that's what you did. You got educated, you married, you had children. To reach your late twenties without being at least engaged was to face a future as "spinster." Not much had changed in the nature of the man-hunt since Jane Austen dramatized it in her novels.

Aged twenty-one, a senior at Barnard, and watching one classmate after another tie the knot, I was sufficiently aware of my tropism for pain to appreciate it but not strong enough to stop it. Psychoanalysis? Why not? Everyone else was doing it. I assumed—correctly, as it turned out—that my father had a direct line to the American psychoanalytic Vatican, and so it seemed logical to ask his help in finding someone to straighten me out, to get rid of the kinks and convert conflict into resolution. He seemed pleased to be consulted about something so private and profound as another person's psyche. Within a week he had produced a list of names. This man had done such and such, that one was one of his uncle's favorite pupils, a third was president of the New York Psychoanalytical Society; all were M.D.s, all were credentialed up to the ears. I shut my eyes and touched the piece of paper with my index finger. "I'll try him—Edward Kronold." On what other basis could I possibly have made a decision? "I'll let him know that you're going to phone him," my father said. I realized that one of my problems was the very act of applying to my father for help with my problems. He, at least, liked it that way.

My father offered to make the telephone call; I politely declined and made the initial call myself. A man with a soft voice and fluid Viennese accent told me to come to his office on Ninety-sixth Street and Madison Avenue on Wednesday at two o'clock. He didn't ask me how old I was or what kind of time I had at my disposal, assuming, I suppose, that if I was in turmoil I would stop whatever I was doing when summoned by a healer. I wrote down his address, although it was immediately inscribed into my memory.

Other than that one peculiar visit to the office of Dr. Kubie, I had no clue to how to behave in a shrink's office, and this made me extremely nervous. Dr. Kronold's office was in the sort of kempt apartment building I was accustomed to visiting. A uniformed doorman stood beneath a canopy stretching across the sidewalk. He touched his cap to me as I entered the building. (Did he know where I was headed? Of course he did.) An elevator man took me silently up to the ninth floor, a well-lit, odorless hallway, no peeling paint or tiny creatures scurrying into cracks. No cracks. I pushed the buzzer and a medium-tall, mostly bald man with sincere eyes and a slight stoop opened the door. This was the healer. He showed me into a tiny waiting room—two Scandinavian-type chairs, a table with a few magazines, a bathroom, a box of Kleenex—and said he would be with me in a minute and disappeared through another door. I sat down, picked up a current issue of *Holiday* magazine, and tried to focus, but I was too agitated and put it back on the table. The gears had started to grind in the deliberate and planned mystique of this arcane branch of medicine, the process of entering one quiet chamber after another, of—willingly or otherwise—relinquishing the deepest secrets of the heart, of being entirely in the emotional hands of someone you will never know as a flesh-and-blood person but only as a vague presence. I was an instant postulant.

Dr. K was back. "Come this way, please," he said and led me into his office, which, after a brief inspection, I decided was the family living room. It had two windows that gave out over Ninety-sixth Street, a large desk and desk chair, and The Couch, with several pillows piled at one end. Over the pillows lay a soft paper napkin, the kind dentists pin around your neck before they start in on you. Two low armchairs forming a V with a table between them were upholstered in light gray, the same pale, nonthreatening shade on the walls. Directly above the couch in this inmost sanctum, from inside a frame and behind glass, my father's uncle Sigmund's dour countenance looked out, or rather down, the Moses of the religion I was about to become a dues-paying member of.

"Please sit down," Dr. Kronold said, indicating one of the two armchairs. I was so relieved not to have to lie down on the dread couch that I almost, but not quite, smiled. He sat in the other side of the V and asked me why I was there, what had gone on during the previous twenty-one years of my life, what I expected to get from the treatment. None of his questions was sharp enough to disturb the crust over my unconscious. But that was the whole idea—a gradual and benign introduction into the maze that was at once both the contents of my head and the course of the therapy.

Soon enough I was on the couch. Dr. K was of the old school, the one whose driver's manual insists that the doctor never initiate a conversation. Three times a week, then twice, I showed up at Ninety-sixth Street, sat for three or four minutes in the decompression chamber—the waiting room—entered the inner sanctum, walked over to the couch, lay down on my back, and stared at the ceiling. No one who hasn't gone through it can imagine the strength of two purple currents—boredom and rage—that meet inside you as you lie on the couch trying desperately to find something to say. There were entire blocks of fifty minutes—time I was paying twenty-five dollars for, each block draining a trust fund my father had set up for me—when not a single word emerged from either my mouth or Dr. K's. "Your time is up," he would say, not recognizing the ambiguity.

During one "session" I told Dr. K that I would like to move into my own apartment, get out from under my parents. No big life changes during treatment, he said, nixing the relocation, the idea being that you had first to work through whatever it was that made living at home so aggravating; after you stopped minding the arrangement so much, *then* you could move out. No-big-life-changes-during-treatment notwithstanding, there came a day when Dr. K told me that I had a choice: either stop seeing Anatole, or stop treatment. Basically it was one of those *him or me* situations—without the jealousy. When I asked him why, Dr. K said my sick, dependent relationship with this man kept me from doing the hard work that analysis demands. That afternoon I called Anatole from a pay phone at Barnard. "Dr. K says I can't see you anymore," I told him. Anatole—who was in analysis himself—said, "I had a feeling this would happen."

This was very hard. Within twenty-four hours I went from total dependence to total solitude. Surprised that I possessed the muscle to make the right choice—Dr. K over Anatole—I was also surprised that I didn't feel at all good about it. In fact, it pretty much robbed me of any feeling at all for half a year while I went through the process of surrendering a heavy drug habit. Numbly, I sat in front of the television set watching Ernie Kovacs in the morning and *Mr. Peepers* in the evening. Sometimes my mother would watch with me; *Mr. Peepers* was her favorite program. She never asked me what was the matter.

I finished my senior year at Barnard, even managing to ace the final, seven-hour exam in English literature, starting in the Middle Ages, and ending in the twentieth century.

All through this dead time I kept my appointments with Dr. K, telling him my dreams as if they were short stories. They often featured a beach with a tidal wave and a blue-black sky. Each telling was followed by a sincere attempt to uncover buried meaning in the people and objects that filled the dream narrative. Nothing was what it felt or looked like. A baby wasn't a baby, it was an idea; a car, wasn't a car, it was a weapon, and so on. I had a hard time coming up with interpretations Dr. K wasn't skeptical of. How did I know this? From the sound of his breathing or of his lighting up yet another cigarette and securing it in its holder, or of his recrossing his legs behind my head. I was certain that, one day, he would kick me with one of them.

It went on and on. Sometimes I talked, sometimes I didn't. Where were we going with this expensive journey into the maze? At last impatience found my father. "How much longer are you going to see that man?" I had no idea; the twists and turns seemed to be moving no nearer the exit. Maybe he saw no change in me, at least nothing sufficient to justify the time and money it was using up. "I'm going to write the fellow a letter," he said.

A few days later Dr. K reported that he had received a letter from my father asking for a report on my progress. "You know," Dr. K said, making me feel good, "that I can't write back to him without your permission." His driver's manual said so. What would happen if he talked to my father without asking my permission? Would the whole edifice—the silences, the enforced neutrality, the insidious transference—come tumbling down, and would trust then fly out the window? Would the analysand, betrayed, curse the analyst and leave in a huff? But I gave my permission, figuring that during this meeting I too might find out how I was doing.

Dr. K wrote to my father, inviting him to come to one of my sessions. He read me the letter. "It is impossible to discuss your daughter's progress over the telephone. And, in any case, I cannot speak with you without Anne's being present."

This lit my father's fire. He thought he was going to get the word over the telephone, short and sweet, like a report of "benign," from pathology. "I'm not going there. I don't have the time," he said. Then, to my mother, "Doris, you go."

Later I asked my mother why my father wouldn't go himself. "Is he scared?" She wouldn't answer directly, which made me think he was; the idea that my father could be intimidated by Dr. K would have struck me as funny if it hadn't raised questions about my father I didn't feel like dealing with. You don't want to think your father isn't up to dealing with a little unpleasantness. This was not a new idea, but each time there was new evidence it stung me again.

Like a lot of women who, whenever they find themselves on uncharted waters, resort to a nervous flirtatiousness to keep themselves from being swamped, my mother did this now as she sat down in Dr. K's office and lit a Parliament cigarette. The three of us sat in a semicircle, each within an arm's length of the others. Dr. K asked my mother one frontal question after another while I remained largely silent. What did she think a mother's role consisted of? Had she found genuine satisfaction in her work as my father's professional partner? Had she ever considered having more children? Could she describe her emotional life with her husband? Her eyes were getting watery when he asked her if she might consider the notion that she had tried to do too many things at once and that had she focused on being a mother her daughter might not be so conflicted today. . . . The tears spilled out.

Had he overstepped? After all, this meeting was supposed to be about me, not my mother. She pulled an embroidered handkerchief from her purse and began to sob into it, stunning me. I had seen her cry only three times before in my life. Once, before I was old enough to understand that people sometimes enjoy hurting each other, when I found her weeping on the porch of a summer house soon after my father had slammed the door and left. Another time was when I came home from school and found her sitting at the kitchen table with the cook, both of them crying over President Roosevelt, who had died of a stroke that afternoon. Dr. K looked at her benignly, a doctor who has lanced the boil and is interested in the pus that oozes out. He was blaming my mother for my troubles, and instead of defending herself she caved. First he had stuck it to my father and now he was sticking it to my mother. While I felt sorry for her as the target of his polite attack—he neither raised his voice nor used charged language—I was also experiencing my first spell of *schadenfreude*, that half-guilty state in which you find yourself enjoying someone else's pain. Hard lines on her—she shouldn't have gone out to work from the time I was an infant, leaving me and my older sister in the care of first nannies, then governesses, and finally "companions," college girls recruited to take us for walks in Central Park and trips to the dentist. My mother never wore a housedress or apron, never plunged her fingers into a gob of dough, never wielded mop, dust rag, or broom. She worked on a typewriter in an office. Now my analyst was implying that she had made a fatal mistake. She was smart and didn't have to have this spelled out letter by letter. Thus

121

the tears—as well as my surprise. It hadn't occurred to me that she was even partly to blame for my poor taste in men, my dead-end romances. I would have to think it over. My mother wiped away the last of her tears as we rode down in the elevator. "He's mean," she said. "I never heard him talk that way," I said. "So opinionated."

"Am I such a terrible mother?"

"Of course not," I said, using the same words and tone I did whenever she asked me if she looked fat. Truth was, I had no one to compare her with.

My analysis seemed to borrow one of my great uncle's deathless phrases: "Analysis, Terminable and Interminable." Somewhere along about the third year I said—I thought casually—"Generals should have sons." Dr. K pounced on this as if waiting a long time for it, a pig smelling truffles in the forest. I meant that men seem to like having their male offspring go into their father's line of work. Dr. K then nudged me toward the ultimate confession: I wanted a penis. I told him I had never found the penis all that attractive, that it was as if a man's insides were hanging outside, making him both vulnerable and droll. I preferred a woman's body, its smoothness and symmetry. He didn't believe me.

Nor did he believe me when I assured him I had never seen my parents making love. These impasses prolonged the therapy while we danced around each other, Dr. K quietly trying to get me to spill the Freudian beans and I resisting because what he wanted me to say—I wanted to be a man, I wanted to sleep with my father, I was jealous of my mother—seemed far more ludicrous than plausible.

Dr. K bristled one day when, for lack of something better to say, I speculated aloud that I might try to write a story. Instead of the silence with which most of my remarks were greeted, he landed on me with both feet: "You didn't come here in order to learn how to write." At that moment I realized that yes, this desire was one of my secrets, but up until then, it had been so deeply buried I hadn't detected it myself. I construed Dr. K's response to be a taboo: "Do not write; it will interfere with your life as a woman." The bud was firmly nipped. It would be three years before I brushed away my misgivings.

CHAPTER 6

For better or worse, Sigmund Freud was the Pied Piper of my generation. We believed in him. He promised us self-knowledge, self-realization, forgiveness, freedom from the shocks and chimeras of our past, and if not a chicken in every pot and a car in every garage, at least a clearer view of our prospects. We fell into line behind him, like the children of Hamelin. Along with the grave cadences of T. S. Eliot's *Four Quartets*, Freud's gospel shaped our thinking and feeling. He had become, as Auden wrote in his great memorial poem, "a whole climate of opinion."

In my circle of friends, most of them graduate students at

Harvard, one of the effects of this ambient psychic weather was to make neurosis almost fashionable. It was a mark of distinction, not a stigma or impediment. In Boston in the late 1940s, before many of us left for New York to look for work in the real world, we often got together evenings in the cat-infested apartment on the wrong side of Beacon Hill that I shared with two other students. Several more lived upstairs. During World War II the building, near Scollay Square, the city's combat zone, had been a brothel. Now the only live vestige of the old flesh trade was a blowzy professional, Sally, on the top storey. Nailed to the outside of her door was a wooden sign painted pink, cut out in the shape of a teakettle, and bearing an invitation: COME ON IN, IT'S ALWAYS BOILING. One night after she moved away three juiced-up sailors came looking for action. In their rage at not finding it they ripped out four flights of banisters and threw them down the dark stairwell. A few days later, the landlady, Mrs. Annie Cohen, put the whole thing together again with baling wire, giving the sagging staircase a hallucinatory, expressionist look, like a set for Robert Wiene's film *The Cabinet of Dr. Caligari*.

Over pink gin and Ritz crackers, disaffected graduate students like me weighed one another's need for "treatment." We recited the traumas of childhood and adolescence, the roles—neglectful, villainous, or smothering—of our parents, and so forth, the whole psychic megillah, but, despite our shallow immersion in Freud, we never talked about sex. The homosexuals were silent on the subject—the closet door was only slightly ajar—and the rest of us were too demure or too repressed to bring it up, although no one's orientation or pattern of pairing off was a secret. Sex aside, an unspoken challenge—Can you top this?—drove our confessional marathons. We heard sad tales about heartless fathers, possessive mothers, the stigma of bastardy, the narrowness of adolescent life in a Nebraska parsonage. My best turn in these performances was to say that by the age of thirteen, having by then lost both parents, I was a double orphan. I felt guilty about the modest inheritance my parents had left me. "It's a goddam shame," one of my friends said. "People like me have the brains, and people like you have the money." I should have been angry, but I let this pass and went on to tell about how the still perceptible shock of being orphaned could be rendered in a cry of five words—"What's to become of me?"

We scarified our psychic topsoil and hoped someday to dig deeper. Meanwhile, just as the intellectual generation of the 1930s joined Marxist study groups and read *Das Kapital*, we read Freud's *General Introduction to Psychoanalysis*, his *Civilization and Its Discontents*, and other books with alluring titles like Karen Horney's *Self-Analysis* and *The Neurotic Personality of Our Time*. We assumed that neurosis was so bound up with creativity that it was virtually a prerequisite. If you weren't neurotic—that is, if you were "normal"—you were probably cut out to be a worker ant, moderately well adjusted but dull. On the other hand, if the goal of psychoanalysis was to help adjust patients to middle-class behavior norms, wouldn't it undermine "creativity" and turn a potential Dylan Thomas or Marc Chagall into a worker ant? There was a contradiction here that we weren't able to resolve. The adjective "sensitive" was a mild palliative—it fell considerably short of suggesting you needed "help," while "normal" had even more dismissive voltage than "nice," a euphemism for "harmless." My friends called me both "normal" and "nice." One, an editor at Little, Brown on Beacon and Joy Streets, a few blocks away from my apartment, gave me a copy of E. B. White's story about a mouse born to human parents, *Stuart Little*. She inscribed it, "Two delightful people: Justin, meet Stuart." I bore the stigmas of alleged niceness and normality in a resigned way.

Nevertheless, once back in New York I went into psychoanalysis, driven by career anxiety and what romantic novelists used to call a broken heart. Beatrice and I had been going together for over a year. She wanted to be married, to someone, for stability and direction, she said, while I, an unformed ex-graduate student wandering around the edges of New York book publishing, wasn't remotely ready even to begin thinking about marriage. On her wedding night she phoned me from the bridal suite at the Plaza to say that she was thinking of me, a gesture that combined tenderness and cruelty. There was little comfort in the notion she meant to hold me in reserve against (what proved to be) an uncertain future with the man she married. I felt orphaned once again— "What's to become of me?"—and spent a terrible summer racked with dermatitis and flaying my skin practically down to the raw flesh. I read Proust for the first time, thought of moving to France, and even packed a trunk, although I had no idea of what I would do when I got there. One day Lena Levine, a psychiatrist I met at a weekend party on Long Island, took me aside and said, "I think you're letting yourself go to waste. You ought to get some help." This was depressing but also reassuring: at least I had something worth saving and nurturing. My gratitude for her instant recognition of my deep-down misery swept away inhibitions. In the gentlest way possible Lena, who was more than twice my age, fended off my clumsy attempts to get her to go to bed with me—I had never before wanted to be so close to another person. My behavior was probably an extreme, and not to be anytime near equaled, case of instant "transference."

Lena arranged for an eminence in the New York psychoanalytic and psychiatric establishment, Dr. Carl Binger, to have me "evaluated" with Rorschach, IQ, and other such tests. If it turned out that I needed and could make good use of "help," he was to recommend a therapist who was compatible as well as affordable.

127

Personality aside, I wondered, could a European-born analyst recognize shades of idiom and American style, instances of non-Viennese "joke-work," and those famous slips of the tongue—parapraxes, in the jargon of the profession—Freud found so revealing of turmoil in everyday life?

Dr. Gustav Bychowski, number one on Binger's referral list, instructed me, in heavily accented English, to take a position on whether Fyodor Dostoevsky had been a lunatic or an idiot as well as an epileptic and a compulsive gambler. I foresaw hundreds of hours of such idle gassing, on my nickel, to indulge his hobby, which was psychoanalyzing dead writers in order to reduce them to the obligatory one- or two-sentence abstract printed at the head of professional articles. Bychowski, as I learned a few years later, was the author of "Walt Whitman—A Study in Sublimation," an article that disposed of *Leaves of Grass* as a product of narcissistic isolation, gnawing loneliness, and homoerotic libido. For clinical material Bychowski plumbed Whitman's "Song of Myself," a masterpiece in world literature, as if it were a free-associational, artless monologue from the couch, raw meat for the analytic grinder. Poor Walt! Anyone following this line of interpretation could not have guessed he was a poet, only a remarkably voluble sort of wacko with sex on his mind.

My search took me to the consulting rooms of several other bigwigs on Binger's referral list. When I arrived a few minutes late to see one of them, Dr. William Silverberg, he decided not to lose time on preliminaries and plunged into Topic A. "Young man, to begin with, let me ask you this: When did you last have sex with a woman?" I answered, quite truthfully, "About half an hour ago—that's why I'm late. She lives around the corner from you." He acted as if I had vomited on his shoes and practically threw me out of his office. His bill for this consultation—fifty dollars—arrived in the mail a few days later.

Finding the right dermatologist, although there were hundreds of skin doctors in New York, was even harder than finding the right analyst. According to the standard joke, what passed for a diagnosis in the skin trades consisted of one question, "Have you had this before?" and one answer, "Well, you've got it again." The "it," variously called eczema, atopic dermatitis, and psoriasis, consisted of unremitting hostilities between my skin and its occupant. In early adolescence I had been under the care of a medical autocrat in the Squibb Building off Fifth Avenue. Several times a years Dr. Lapidus examined my flayed and abraded skin, the result of uncontrollable bouts of scratching, and invariably said, "I see you've been having a good time." His remark had the instant effect of sending me into a fresh paroxysm of scratching. In addition to the pungent tar ointments and mineral oil preparations that constituted the entire armamentarium of the profession, Dr. Lapidus prescribed daily home treatments with a carbon-arc sunlamp. A medical equipment outfit delivered to our apartment an immense apparatus (when not in use it occupied its own closet) with a reflecting bowl the size of a locomotive headlight. Naked and goggled, I lay in the glare, splutter, and fumes of this satanic machine. Another skin guru dispensed a private brand of tar ointment that he formulated in a back room and gave me five minutes of his attention; his receptionist demanded payment in cash. Yet another put me on a diet of rice and canned peaches. A third sent me uptown to Columbia-Presbyterian Hospital for sessions of X-ray therapy—he was concerned only with immediate but short-lived relief from itching and scaling: long-term radiation effects were not his department. Dr. Clarence Greenwood, a benign Harvard Medical School dermatologist—his distressing academic title was "Professor of Syphilology"—was honest enough to say that whatever it was I had, it was something I'd have to learn to live with, preferably in a gentler climate. We talked mostly about his cat, who ate coffee beans while the doctor had his breakfast. Finally, the same year I went into analysis, cortisone and topical steroid therapy came to the rescue. At a time when almost any ailment was construed as "psychosomatic" or "psychogenic," dermatology and analysis were symbiotic.

I finally signed up with an American-born psychoanalyst—Roman Catholic, I guessed, because he had gone to Georgetown, a Jesuit institution—who was either unwilling or unable to haggle Dostoevsky or Proust and so, supposedly, would make the most of our time together. Dr. Hughes appeared to be new to a then over-booked profession because he was able to fit me in, a sort of scholarship student, at a compassionate twenty-five dollars for each of my four weekly visits. After a year or so, prospering like other psychoanalysts in their professional heyday, he moved from a dismal apartment off Third Avenue and Sixty-fifth Street to one facing the Morgan Library on Thirty-sixth Street. Once, by accident, we ended up sitting next to each other at a drugstore lunch counter where we were both having coffee before our fifty-minute session. We had nothing to talk about, except the weather (it was raining) and a sports headline in the *Post*. We might as well have been total strangers, except that total strangers meeting on neutral ground were not likely to be so halting and uneasy with each other. Freud's talking cure made no allowances for extracurricular encounters.

Even after four years of analysis with Dr. Hughes I failed to get any message from his bland, inscrutable presence. He smoked his pipe and just listened. "Transference" was not in the cards, but neither this nor the notorious element of "resistance" seemed to bother him as we plowed my psyche and my shaky sense of identity. I rehearsed the trauma of orphanhood and the contrary responses left in its wake: resentment and anger at having been abandoned (as it seemed), a sense of unworthiness, as if I had done something to deserve being abandoned, fear of competition and success, guilt about money, guilt about almost everything else, including the freedom, unrestrained by parental authority, to do and live as I wished. Like the orthodox Freudian that he was, Dr. Hughes rarely said anything and was almost impossible to provoke. "Your wife must have been a student at Mount Holyoke when you married her," I said for want of a more consequential opening for the day's session. I detected in his response a tiny tremor of distress at this violation of impersonality—"Why do you say that?" I explained, as if to say, You should be more careful in the future, that she had written her married name and college on the flyleaf of a copy of *Anna Karenina* I had found at the bottom of a bookshelf in his waiting room. There were few such tiny triumphs.

About midway in my analysis, my brother made me the gift of a trip to France with him. A friend, the artist Anne Truitt, introduced me by letter to Barbara Herman, a Bryn Mawr classmate of hers living transiently in Paris on the Rue Vaneau. Barbara was beautiful, with glossy black hair and high cheekbones, but even more striking, as I recognized in an instant, was her unflinching glance of appraisal, probity, and intelligence that made me call myself to account. We had dinner together, went for a long walk along the Seine, and agreed to meet again in Villefranche, on the Côte d'Azur. One late afternoon, hiking the winding hillside roads to the high village of Éze, isolated like an eagle's nest on a peak over the Mediterranean, we were caught in a pelting rainstorm and found shelter for the night in a villager's house. We huddled like children. Barbara stayed abroad, I went back to New York, and through our letters during the fall, winter, and spring we arrived at an intellectual and emotional intimacy of a sort I hadn't known before—in my head I carried on daily conversations with her. As deeply as I loved her for herself alone, she remained inseparable in my mind from the romance of "Europe," the great good place many of my generation had been reading about and longing for despite the fact it had only recently been a cauldron of previously unimaginable horrors. The next summer I went back to Europe to see Barbara again. She was then living in Ascona, a resort town at the Swiss end of Lake Maggiore.

In the aftermath of the Allied victory of World War II and of the Marshall Plan sent to rebuild Europe's devastated economy, Americans were welcomed, even admired. Liners of half a dozen and more nations sailed from slips along the Hudson, their departures and arrivals among the spectacular sights and sounds of New York. *Queen Mary, Queen Elizabeth, Île-de-France, United States, Andrea Doria, Stockholm, Mauretania*—the largest of these were almost a fifth of a mile long and among the most majestic, luxurious, and visually impressive things ever made in this world. The speediest crossed the Atlantic in only four and a half days. Even so Europe by ship remained a far-off place, and going there like dying into a new life. Eastbound, a few days out of New York you might begin to notice an occasional land bird flown off course; then clumps of floating vegetation, bottles, bits of lumber; then the sound of distant church bells and the smell of grass and cows even before you passed the green flank of Ireland. Europe smelled different—Gauloises and Nazionales, beer, fresh bread, and diesel fumes; pulses ran faster; colors were more vivid.

The journey to Europe was loaded with literary associations and as a result was both exotic and familiar. I stayed for a night in a Paris hotel, the Ambassador, on the Boulevard Haussmann, not far from Marcel Proust's apartment and cork-lined bedroom at Number 102. On the platform at the Gare du Nord, bound for Switzerland via Bern, I felt like Thomas Mann's Hans Castorp starting his ascent to the Magic Mountain—he entered a "primitive, unattached state" of consciousness liberated by space and time. In a second-class compartment of the Paris–Istanbul night train (Somerset Maugham's *Ashenden*) I sat next to a gaunt woman dressed all in black (*The Lady Vanishes*); the swarthy man opposite belonged in Eric Ambler's *A Coffin for Dimitrios*—he pulled his fedora down over his eyes, smoked continually, and clutched a briefcase on his lap. No one smiled or exchanged a word. Domodossola, the name of the Italian frontier town where I got off, projected its own mystery. In two hours the little narrow-gauge train from Domodossola chugged over the mountains and around Lake Maggiore to Locarno (*A Farewell to Arms*). I took the bus to Ascona.

For almost a century this town had been a haven for artists, bohemians, composers, remittance men and women, and societal

J.K. and Barbara Herman,
Nice, 1948.

resisters of all sorts: anarchists, pacifists, vegetarians, free-love advocates, and millenarians. Occasionally I'd see a band of Tolstoyan Christian-love disciples, the men bearded and dressed like muzhiks in long leather-belted white blouses and baggy trousers tucked into their boots. They had come down from the hills to replenish their stores of buckwheat flour, cabbage, and yogurt. The actress Paulette Goddard, née Marion Levy and once married to Charlie Chaplin, kept to herself in a lakeside villa left to her by her last husband, the novelist Erich Maria Remarque, author of *All Quiet on the Western Front*. Mysterious people, mainly Germans with mysterious sources of wealth, occupied other villas. Barbara and I had lunch with one of them, reputedly a *Baronin*, who took us on a tour of her house. She showed us a swastika banner on the wall above her bed and, on a side table, a silver-framed photograph of a uniformed Wehrmacht officer. "My father," she said. "He lives in Rio de Janeiro." Barbara and I left as soon as we could.

Ascona was also the summer capital and annual conference site of the Jungian psychological establishment, Carl Jung himself favoring it as a seasonal alternative to Zurich. Recently the lone Freudian analyst in town (and one of the few Jews) had taken a week off to go fishing; while he was away a patient of his went berserk, killed his wife and children and then himself. Among the Jungian professionals sipping coffee and aperitifs in the cafés one could sense a mildly compassionate gloat of *schadenfreude* as the poor man walked past.

Barbara was working on a translation of Lautréamont's surrealist poems, *Les Chants de Maldoror*. Her essay on the poet Hart Crane had recently been accepted for publication by *The Sewanee Review*, a distinguished literary quarterly founded before the turn of the century. Together we read Rilke, Proust, and Martin Buber's *Tales of the Hasidim*. Afternoons we bicycled along the lake, often to Brissago, the border town where Hemingway's Lieutenant

Henry and Catherine landed after their long row up the lake from Italy. Evenings we had suppers of bread, cheese, sausage, and wine and listened to radio broadcasts of concerts from Zurich and Barbara's records of madrigals, the Fauré *Requiem*, Ravel and Debussy string quartets. (She managed to move around Europe hauling her records, record player, radio, typewriter, and books along with the usual baggage.) Everything between us had a sweetness touched with sadness, like the music we heard. Sooner or later we'd both have to go home to another sort of life altogether. Perhaps the bond between us was too fragile, ideal, and untested, too lacking in perspective and irony, to survive removal from the psychic climate of "Europe" to the cross-grained realities of life in New York—getting ahead, the right clothes, a good address, parties: shallow values, but they were mine, however great my shame, and not Barbara's.

I was only a casual visitor to the Jungian lair and had left Dr. Hughes behind for the summer, but I was soon caught again in the web of psychoanalysis. It was a struggle to get out. Barbara was seeing a Jungian analyst, Aline Valangin. She had a house high above the town in which, before I arrived, Barbara had arranged for me to rent a room. A year-round Ascona resident, a handsome woman in her sixties, Mme. Valangin rarely smiled or unbent when we were together. I was uneasy with her from the start, partly because she radiated a professional authority that made me feel I was being scrutinized and evaluated even when it was just a matter of saying good morning over a breakfast of buttered rolls and coffee. In conversation with her, my stumbling French made me feel like a mental defective. Given our daily proximity to each other, she could hardly help trying to convert me to the gospel of Zurich. For me the Jungian ethos was fatally tainted by its founder's association with Nazi science and by the Teutonic solemnity that greeted his published pronouncements. Still, I admired his brand of analytical psychology, with its rich conceptual baggage of archetype, myth, symbol, and collective unconscious. It liberated and spurred the literary imagination in a way that Freud's relentless pursuit of slips, dreams, and hang-ups did not.

Twenty-four hours a day, awake and asleep, indoors and outdoors, of Jungian ambience soon became stifling. I sometimes told Barbara my dreams and concerns, and she sometimes repeated these during her analytic sessions. As a result Mme. Valangin took to asking me why I persisted in my plan to go back to my Freudian doctor in New York and recite what she, with a polite grimace of distaste, called *votre petites histoires*. Stay with us, she urged, and do yourself some good. She hoped I would pursue my interest in Jungian psychology and recommended I make an appointment with a Doctor Ernst Blumhard in Rome who supposedly spoke English.

Late one night, having lost the front-door key (it had fallen out of my pocket when I was bicycling), I entered Mme. Valangin's house by crawling like one of the local lizards through a tiny first-floor bathroom window and landing in the tub on my front paws. Surely this thing with the key told us something, my landlady said the next morning, when I explained what all the rattling and thumping had been about; surely it said something about reluctance and conflict and could not be dismissed as an accident. Literal-minded analysts back in New York would have gone to town with this bathroom window episode: it was a classic "bungled action," in Freud's terminology, furnished with all the symbols of womb, birth canal, and sexual entry one could ask for. But maybe this once, I argued haltingly, an accident was just an accident, to the same extent that a cigar, as Freud remarked, was sometimes only a cigar. She was certain, though, that I deep down wanted to enter Jung's enchanted forest and that inertia, stubbornness, and a closed mind were stopping me from facing up to the truth. Truth was, I felt pressured, tampered with, condescended to, and weary of being proselytized. I thought of Montaigne's image of marriage: a birdcage, with the birds on the outside wanting to get in and the birds on the inside wanting to get out. I wanted to stay out of this particular cage, and I did.

"Since you don't talk," I once challenged Dr. Hughes, "How do I know you're Dr. Hughes, the psychoanalyst, and not an uncle sitting in for him?" I should have known what the answer would be— "Why do you ask?" "Because you don't say anything," I repeated, and this, of course, prompted the rejoinder, "Why is that so important to you?" And so on—it was like a dog chasing his tail. Occasionally I would nod off—at first "resistance" may have been the cause, but later it was plain boredom with talking about myself and reciting my dreams—Freud's royal road to the unconscious. Some of these dreams I improvised in order to fill up the fifty-minute hour, and probably they were as valuable as the real thing.

Over the four years I spent in analysis there were no Hollywood-ish breakthroughs, no long buried traumas brought to light. Neither was there a "primal scene" to be revisited, although there was always the unspoken assumption hovering in the Freudian air that the patient must have seen his mother and father making love but blocked the memory of it. Sometimes, recalling a famous scene in Arthur Koestler's anti-Stalinist novel, *Darkness at Noon*, I was tempted, like Koestler's hero-victim, to make a false confession to his inquisitor—Yes, you're right, I remember!—just to get the primal scene out of our system and move on to something more productive.

Rather than any dramatic change, analysis—the goal of my generation—slowly eroded whatever it was that had been bothering me: unresolved issues with my parents, fear of abandonment and competition, guilt about money. Time and growing up might

137

have done this by themselves, but there was no way of telling—this would-be scientific experiment in gradual change had no "controls." But for all its lack of drama and its extravagant expense of time and money, Freudian psychoanalysis had been a great education, especially if one could shed its doctrinal baggage and implicit determinism and embrace the more dynamic and liberating view of human development that I was to find in Erik Erikson's *Childhood and Society*, when I read it in the mid 1950s. What psychoanalysis left me with in the end was a mode of forgiving along with recognition of the role internal conflict, symbols, fantasies, ambivalence, and unconscious motivation play in daily life: a run-up to biography.

A little while after Dr. Hughes and I "terminated" the analysis by mutual consent, I paid him a courtesy visit to thank him for his help and to tell him I was doing just fine in my work and would soon be married. "I think you might be especially interested to know," I added somewhat teasingly (Put that in your pipe!), "My fiancée, Anne Bernays, is Sigmund Freud's grandniece." This time Dr. Hughes abandoned his chronic composure and professional vow of silence. "Tell me," he said, "is she native American-born?" I stopped myself from replying, Why do you ask?

PART II

CHAPTER 7

The last office my father occupied was a three-storey, cinnamon-colored brownstone, once owned by the Auchincloss family, on Sixty-fourth Street between Fifth and Madison. Around the corner was the Chase Bank, its white-glove East Side branch. The Wildenstein Gallery, which had been a client of my father's years earlier, was directly across the street.

My father's desk occupied what once had been the front parlor. From this perch he could look out over the street and watch the quality passing by. He didn't do this very often; he was a man focused on his work the way a pathologist concentrates on the item on the slide. No time for daydreaming. Directly above my father's office was my mother's. Nominally his partner, she was kept in the background, like a new puppy whose bathroom habits are not quite jelled. She did not even appear in the firm's name— Edward L. Bernays, Inc.: followed, in smaller type, by "A Partnership of Edward L. Bernays and Doris E. Fleischman." Apparently, it did not trouble either of them that she was an unequal partner, the same paradox at work and at home.

While my father's office was furnished with heavy pieces, choice wood polished daily before he arrived, two enormous crystal inkwells with round brass covers, a leather armchair, masculine stuff, the woman's featured a pink faux-marble—but really wooden—table without drawers, flowered curtains, a light-colored rug, nonchallenging pictures, a fanciful chair, more like one you'd find in a drawing room than an office. She wore a hat to work and was hardly alone in this; ladies wore hats indoors except at home and sometimes even then. My mother wrote most of the firm's first drafts, speeches, articles, notices, triple spacing as she went. My father had persuaded his wife to stay in the background so as not to risk, he explained, being seen as a pushy female with ideas—a threatening and sometimes deadly combination, toxic to the male. She was not invited to conferences with clients nor was she invited along on his numerous business trips all over the country, places like Cincinnati or Chicago or Washington, to meet with presidents and sometimes lesser management of the companies who had paid for his public relations services. Once in a while he would take me with him, and while he was doing business, a woman, probably an executive secretary, would spend the day with me and show me the sights of the city we were visiting.

My mother—whom I never called anything but "Mother"— had plenty of ideas but was temperamentally a shy person; the arrangement was okay with her. On the way back from Barnard I would often stop in and pay her a visit before I walked home to the house on Sixty-third Street where we all lived together, they on the second floor, I on the third. There she was, in her custom-made hat, a small thing with tiny flowers and a veil, typing away at her IBM Model C typewriter. "Hello, ducky," she'd say, looking up. She was cheerfully energetic at work, docile at home. One afternoon in the spring of my junior year—1951—she told me that "Eddie would like you to work with us over the summer. We'll pay you." What would I do? "You're such a good writer," she said. "You'd be doing some obituaries and some press releases."

"Who died?"

"Nobody. But when, for example, Mr. Zemurray dies, we'll have his obit ready to send to the papers. Most of them will use it verbatim. Not the *Times*, though. They have their own obituary man."

"I don't know. . . ."

"Well, think about it. It would be a good experience for you."

So I did it—about six weeks that summer when I wasn't being a footloose New York girl. I went to my father's office every day and learned how to write a news release and an obituary. For Mr. Zemurray's I went to the New York Public Library and dug out the published facts of the life of the president—more like tsar—of the United Fruit Company. When I found statements somewhat less than flattering to Zemurray—the United Fruit Company, it seemed, had swallowed two Central American countries—my mother instructed me to soften them or leave them out. Obituaries—at least those that originate in a public relations firm—do not mention the unsunny hours. I learned that.

I also learned that you can't fudge details or guess in place of know; you can't make a mistake. My father was celebrated for firing people who got one thing wrong in a press release, one letter wrong in a word, a name misspelled, a date off by one day. No one who ever worked for Edward L. Bernays got a second chance. One of his former staffers told me a bunch of these men, all of whom had been canned for minor goofs, got together every so often to trade Eddie stories. They called themselves the "Bernays B'rith." My father's office manager, Howard Cutler, a laconic, unsmiling administrator of impeccable New England stock, did all the firing—and there was a lot of it—as my father could not face doing it himself.

And so I picked up some basic writing skills and at the same time advanced my knowledge of what sort of people my parents were, something I wasn't especially eager to do, suspecting that I would find holes and wrinkles—in other words (one of my father's cherished phrases) there was no guarantee that everyone was going to love them, especially my father. Children are supposed to recognize and absorb the grimmest truths about their parents—and then get over it—sometime before the age of puberty. Not me. It was as if I lived in a house whose cellar stairs I had never gone down, nursing a suspicion that there was something down there I would rather not see or smell.

A year or so after this my mother, settling into a voice range she used when serious and private, told me that she and my father had been talking things over, my father being at an age—sixty-two—when most men want only to retire so they can play golf in a world of perpetual sunshine. Well, of course Eddie wasn't about to retire—he had the look and the energy of a man in his early forties—but they had been talking things over, as she said, and since there didn't seem to be anyone within his circle of friends and acquaintances to whom he felt he could entrust "the business," they had decided to turn it over to me. I was a good, clear writer and I seemed to know what was involved in relating to the public. She beamed a smile at me, bestowing first prize on a contestant who doesn't even know she's in a contest.

I was stunned, surprised not only by what she was proposing, but that she also seemed unaware of how many hours she had missed the boat by. I had, apparently, hidden my distaste for my father's occupation as thoroughly as an alcoholic hides the bottles in the house. We were in my mother's office, a place that reflected someone else's taste, someone who liked frills and flowers—a postwar stereotypical version of a lady's working place, so distinct from a man's manly one. Manhattan's poshest neighborhood surrounded us quietly, without grime, with muted noise, with a sky that seemed brighter than that which hung over the Third Avenue El and those murky streets below Houston. Stirred by somewhat more primitive motives than my mother's and secretly mutinous against my father's equation, which placed perception and reality on opposite sides of the equals sign, I was horrified by her offer and just as horrified by having to decline it. I didn't want to have to hurt her feelings.

"I'll have to think about it," I said, honoring the way of the coward. "I'm not sure that it's exactly what I want to do."

My mother looked as if someone had poured ice water down her back. "You don't want to do it? Why not? Eddie thinks the world of you."

Yet another surprise; he had never told me this. He had, in fact, indicated from time to time that he thought women had not been endowed with a brain like a man's, ours being softer and less organized. But that wasn't the point. The point was I would rather have become a foot doctor than a public relations practitioner. I didn't want to have to mess around with the truth or tell people that Mr. Zemurray had done more for the people of Guatemala

145

than God had or sell someone the idea that they should buy something they didn't need. I loved my mother and father in a strange, powerful, and not especially happy way but I couldn't dream of placing my feet into the prints they had left in their stretch of the beach.

I didn't think it strange that Henry Sell, editor in chief of *Town and Country*, would invite a twenty-one-year-old girl with almost no work experience or proven talent to have lunch with him at Le Pavillon, New York's glitziest dining establishment. Moreover, I was too callow to imagine that he might want to have his way with me. The restaurant looked as if it had been decorated by the parents of a long awaited girl child. Everything but the flatware was pink—tablecloths, flowers, napkins, plates, carpet, curtains, waiters.

I was on time, but Sell was there before me, sitting at a choice table, a half-finished drink within reach. He stood to greet me. I was wearing a new gabardine suit—the jacket had a peplum, a kind of flounce just above the waistline—kid pumps, white gloves: a generic young lady of New York.

A transplanted westerner, Sell was remarkably good-looking for a man in his fifties. He had lots of thick silver hair, an open face, and the kind of extreme polish you acquire only by design and prolonged focus. While he mostly talked, I mostly listened.

"Your father says you might like to work for our little magazine." He speared a pink shrimp glistening with sauce and brought it to his lips, which opened and shut over it, leaving not a trace around the mouth hole.

"He does?"

"Well," Sell said. "How about it, would you like to come to

work for us? I can pay you twenty-five dollars a week—before taxes."

I asked what sort of job I would be doing.

"Marian, our beauty editor, could use some help," he said. "How does that sound?"

It didn't sound at all like what I had in mind. But it was a job in *publishing*. Dazzled by words but lacking the *sitzfleisch* for graduate work, I had been looking for a job for several months, had visited the headquarters of at least a dozen publishing houses, had stupidly turned down one job at *Newsweek* answering reader mail and another at the *New York Times* in their information department. When I wasn't looking for a real job I was at the Marguery Hotel, a huge place that occupied most of the block between Park and Lexington Avenues, Forty-seventh and Forty-eighth Streets, where Adlai Stevenson, running for president the first time, had his New York headquarters. Along with a lot of like-minded young people—most of them female—who could afford to volunteer their services, I stuffed envelopes and folded pieces of paper for hours on end. Once, the candidate shook my hand, sending me into a swoon.

I had just about given up landing anything but a job plying the telephone for a dentist when I broke down and asked my father for help. My main problem was that I had no useful skills, my feminist mother having persuaded me that I shouldn't learn how to touch-type. "If they find out you can type you'll get stuck there forever." She also persuaded me not to learn how to cook. Doubting, I nevertheless accepted Sell's offer and the following week started work at this swankest of Hearst monthlies. After a while it dawned on me that Mr. Sell must owe my father a hefty favor, for the so-called job for which he was paying me twenty-five a week did not exist; he had invented it. There was nothing for me to do. The office of the beauty editor, overlooking Madison Avenue, was a small room off the large bull pen where most of the other editors worked and chattered like birds in an aviary. On the shelves were dozens of empty perfume bottles: Joy—"the world's most expensive perfume"—Chanel No. 5, Femme, Shalimar. The beauty editor seemed surprised to find me in her office. "I don't know why Henry hired you," she said. "I don't need an assistant." She was perfectly nice about it. "Please call me Marian." Marian came in every morning around eleven, bringing with her clouds not of Chanel but of Johnnie Walker. She left before three, having gone out for a leisurely lunch in the meantime. There was nothing for her to do either.

At first, I was bored. I smoked dozens of Chesterfields, did the *Times* crossword puzzle. Phoned friends. Studied the perfume bottles. Paced back and forth. I was shocked to discover that idleness is worse for a person's amour propre than having too much to do. I wanted to quit but didn't have the nerve. What would Eddie say? "You don't leave a job until you have another one!"

Each month the magazine would "do" a city—Cincinnati, Louisville, San Francisco, Baltimore—that had retained something of an upper crust. Instead of employing models to pose in posh gowns, they used local debutantes, who posed for free, saving a good deal of money and, at the same time, making that issue of the magazine a must-buy for the families and friends of the models.

The editorial staff—all of them elongated and skinny—had an alarmingly high blue-blood count; several belonged to prerevolutionary Russian aristocracy. My father had unwittingly obliged me to equate Jewishness with shame and so, constantly aware of being Jewish, I wondered whether this exotic fact would automatically exclude me from their fun-loving, lighthearted, madcap, perfectionist company. I was like a recently pubescent girl, terrified that her menstrual blood has seeped through to the outside of her skirt. Hide it! These White Russian ladies, were they anti-Semitic or merely snooty? I couldn't tell. In any case, they never tried to talk to me, they never said hello in the morning or good-bye in the afternoon; they acted, in fact, as if I were invisible until the day I was vexed enough to ask if I could try writing some copy. "You mean," one woman said, staring at me as if seeing me for the first time, "you actually want to write that stuff?"

"That stuff" turned out to be precise but flowery descriptions of clothes and accessories fated to appear in the magazine's editorial pages. I soon discovered that *T&C*'s advertising and editorial departments were locked in a perpetual embrace, so that if, say, there was a full-page ad for a coat by the manufacturer Davidoff in the July issue, a Davidoff coat would show up in the editorial pages of the August issue. No one ever alluded in any way to this wicked coupling.

Toward the end of November dozens of gift-wrapped packages began arriving for the fashion editors. Whenever this happened all work would stop and the rest of the staff would gather at the desk of the recipient and shriek while she tore off its skin. Behold! A calfskin valise with brass fittings! A case of Chivas Regal! A fourteen-carat bauble to wear around the wrist! A pair of long white kidskin gloves! Squeals of joy. It was Christmastime at the orphanage. I wondered if it had occurred to any of these women to send the payola back?

The editor to whom I applied for work was absurdly grateful to me for taking the task off her hands, leaving them free to comb her hair, scribble thank-you notes to manufacturers who sent her costly presents, poke through piles of silk scarves at Bergdorf's and Bendel's.

When you compose descriptive caption copy you have to fit an exact number of characters into a space smaller than a stick of gum. Characters include every letter plus the blank spaces between words, plus punctuation marks. This exercise forces you to condense ruthlessly and to be willing to work hard on a project you wouldn't have picked, given the choice. But I actually enjoyed describing a froufrou dress or a pair of shoes I wouldn't be caught dead in. Describing perfume was more difficult because trying to put a smell into words is about as easy as rendering the flavor of roast lamb via music. You could get around this by comparing the smell to something else, but since this meant using more words rather than fewer, you had to pare down the rest of it with a lethal weapon.

Soon word circulated that the girl in the beauty department was eager to do this chore, and one by one the editors deposited stuff on my desk. "Thanks awfully, darling. It's such a bore." It kept me busy. Meanwhile, I had gone one morning into Mr. Sell's grand office to tell him, putting it into the most positive phrases, that I wished he had more work for me to do. The man's manner was so affable it was almost impossible to determine the nature of his true temperament. "What can I do for you, young lady?" he said. (Had he forgotten my name?) "Here, sit down and talk to me." With this, he glanced at his watch. "How are you enjoying our little magazine? How do you find Marian?"

I told him everything was fine except there didn't seem to be enough work to fill up eight hours a day. He took a moment to ponder. "What would you like to do?" he said.

"I'd like to read manuscripts. I was an English major. I did my honors thesis on Jonathan Swift." Did I imagine I saw a small smile sneak past Security?

"I don't see why that can't be arranged," he said, getting up. "I'll speak to my assistant. He's in charge of that operation. I imagine he'll be delighted to have you take this little chore off his hands."

Town and Country offhandedly published one piece of fiction in each issue, stories by international heavy hitters like Ludwig Bemelmans, Somerset Maugham, and a young Englishman, Denton Welch. Habit more than commitment to the life of literature kept this practice going, and agents sent enough stories to the magazine to ensure its continuing quality, though not its courage—everything published was by an author whose name would be known to even the most casual reader. Manuscripts began to appear on my desk, delivered there by the mail room boy. Whenever I wasn't writing captions or hanging out with Donald Gainor, the menswear editor, I read them and passed judgment. Eventually two of my picks made it into the magazine.

Donald Gainor was a slight man in his midthirties with half-inch-thick horn-rimmed glasses. Like the beauty editor, he had a separate office, and the moment I stepped into it I knew Donald had about as much in common with the other editors as I did. He kept poetry books on his shelves. He talked like someone who enjoyed reading more than being seen at Le Pavillon or Chambord. During our first conversation I realized, without his having to say so, that he wasn't exactly crazy about his job. This was something he communicated via subtle but unmistakable hints; his distaste for the kind of conspicuousness he helped promote lay just beneath the surface and came out in small bursts of frowns and groans, a raised eyebrow, a shrug, an assortment of body language and innuendo. I liked him for not ever bad-mouthing Mr. Sell or anyone else he had to work with. "Did you know," he said, "that Henry makes canned liver paste?" I assumed he was joking but he wasn't; we had a couple of cans at home, and now I connected the SELL on the label with the "Sell" who ran the magazine I worked for. "Sell's Liver Pâté," he said. "It's quite tasty for something in a tin can."

I took to Donald, he took to me, though it was clear he was not interested in girls qua girls. "There's not much for you to do here, is there?" he asked

I told him about the caption writing and manuscripts.

"It could be worse," I said.

"How would you like to go with me on a shoot this afternoon? You can be my assistant."

We walked over to Cafe Nicholson, a trendy new restaurant in the east fifties, one of the first places in New York to offer a prix fixe meal. It was suitably dark and smokey inside, and bored-looking guys in expensive suits stood around admiring one another and themselves. The photographer was fussing with lights and backdrop. Donald was telling everyone in the nicest way what he wanted them to do. We drank coffee out of tall cardboard cups. There was a lot of waiting. This was glamor, this was "backstage." But what was I doing except standing around and gawking? What was I learning except that many of the men who worked in the fashion industry were . . . you know?

I spent as much time as I could with Donald Gainor. He was the first person to talk to me about writing and writers as if I were not a moron. Before this, everyone, from Barnard faculty to book-ish boyfriends, had made it clear that they had a mission and that was to "educate" me; Donald credited me with some lurking judgment of my own. We went to lunch together. He took me with him to inspect the glove and tie counters at Saks Fifth Avenue. If it hadn't been for Donald I would have quit this job sooner than I did.

And how this happened was as inadvertent as are most "accidents." We are now about three months at *Town and Country*. Marian and I got along well, mainly because there were so few transactions between us that could have caused abrasion. She still seemed surprised to find me sitting at one of the two desks in her office. I did my captions, the exercise getting easier as my skill improved. It was just a trick, after all. One Thursday afternoon in early spring, just before leaving for the day, I straightened the papers on my desk as usual, dumped the butt-filled ashtray into the wastebasket, looked around to make sure all was tidy, put on my spring coat, shut the door and walked home, half a mile or so up Madison, across on Fifty-seventh Street, then up Lexington to Sixty-third. And down the block to number 163, the double house in which I lived uneasily with my parents.

The next morning as I got off the elevator Sell pounced. He'd been waiting for me.

"Good morning, young lady. Would you mind stepping into my office for a few minutes—no, before you take your coat off. There's something you probably ought to know."

This was the sort of frozen moment where the blood temperature plummets, the heart races, and everything bad you've ever done comes back to you in a toxic rush. I followed my boss into his airy office, with its greenery, its beige and chrome fittings, its odor of success.

"Sit down, please." As I sat, I noticed on the windowsill several small red cans: SELL'S LIVER PÂTÉ.

Sell went around to the far side of his desk, sat down and stared at me, his expression as inscrutable as a shrink's.

After a minute or so he said, "There was a little fire here last night. Are you aware of that?"

I shook my head.

"Yes," he said. "It seems to have started in your office."

What do you say—*I'm sorry, I didn't mean to do it?*

I started to say something that revealed my confusion, but he stopped me. "Yes, it started in the wastebasket—it's made of some sort of composition board, you know, very cheap—it caught fire. Someone [a piercing look in my direction] tossed cigarette butts in it without making sure they were completely extinguished. . . ."

"That was me. . . ."

"That's precisely how I imagined it to have happened. It 153 turned into a four-alarm fire. The fire chief called me at home at nine-thirty last night. Apparently it had been smoldering for some time."

"Oh my God . . ."

"A regular conflagration."

I scrambled through a slim repertoire of responses. Unable to read his face—was he furious or merely annoyed?—I considered several options: apologize (yes); offer to pay for the damage (no); offer to quit (maybe); jump out the window (maybe).

"How much damage was there?" I said, temporizing. "Four alarms?"

The number of alarms, it turned out, had as much to do with the location of the burning building as it did the extent of its flames. The Hearst Building was, relatively speaking, middle-aged, on a prime Manhattan site with tall, flammable neighbors. "Let's you and me go, shall we, and see just how bad it was. . . ."

Sell escorted me out of his office, down the hall, past the elevators, into the editorial precincts, where everyone managed to avoid staring at their resident arsonist, and into the beauty editor's office. It looked as if gray paint had been smeared over the walls and ceiling. The window pane had been smashed, leaving spikes of glass sticking out. Bits of it sparkled on the carpet, alongside puddles and streaks. Most of the empty bottles had been knocked over, the desk was a mess, the wastebasket consumed.

"Mostly smoke damage," Sell said. "We'll get the place cleaned up pronto."

Marian arrived, out of breath. "I just heard," she said.

"I'm terribly sorry," I said. "If there's anything I can do. . . ."

"What did you have in mind?" she said. "Henry, I hope you haven't been giving this poor child a hard time. It was an accident, could have happened to anyone. We're insured, aren't we? Well then, what's all the fuss? The place needed painting anyway."

Through my humiliation, I recognized the irony: I was a good girl not a careless or inadvertent one. I had never caused real damage or put anyone at risk. Although addicted to daytime and nighttime fantasies involving sex with dangerous men, in living color I was as prudent as a vestal virgin. Moreover, I had never shoplifted, cheated on an exam or at cards, never told more than a white lie.

After the fire, the editorial ladies, who, since I had taken the caption chore off their hands, had warmed up a couple of degrees, let their temperature drop again, and I felt the chill of their contempt. Accident or not, I had set fire to the premises, something not likely to endear me to its inhabitants. In an attempt to cheer me up, Donald tried to turn the fire into a joke, but to me it wasn't funny, suggesting that perhaps I was more in the thrall of my unconscious than I cared to acknowledge. Less than a month after the office was repainted, the perfume bottles restored, a metal basket installed under the desk, I wrote a note to Sell telling him how much I had enjoyed working for him but that I intended to quit. He didn't try to stop me. Marian gave me a jet-black bottle of Joy, the world's most expensive perfume, along with a whiskey kiss. "It's been nice knowing you," she said.

While trying to figure out how to leave my job at *Town and Country* with at least a whisper of grace, I met Vance Bourjaily at an after-dinner party given by Sue Kaufman, a woman slightly older than me in years but eons in worldliness. I had been introduced to Sue by Donald Gainor—both of them seemed to know everyone and were sturdy elements of the social net covering the city, people in glamor jobs connected one to the other all over town. Sue had published a couple of stories. Her friends were in publishing, fashion, the theater, and television, still in diapers. Sue's style was allover gloss, serious lipstick, cashmere sweater sets, a pageboy haircut. She wore long, low-heeled Italian pumps and a lynx coat. She was smart and caustic and taught me to hold my head up. Sue was bossy, but this didn't bother me; in fact, everything she recommended to me I eagerly accepted. I wasn't exactly an innocent, but Sue was both worldly wise and wise in the kind of subtle negotiation you do with men and with those you want something from.

Vance was a slight man with a round head, shiny brow, sea blue eyes, and skin so delicate and pale it might never have been exposed to the outdoors. Somehow, he reminded me of a turtle. Vance and his wife, Tina, were friends of—well it didn't matter, everyone was connected. In introducing me to Vance at one of her soirees, Sue told me that he was the editor of a literary magazine about to be published, called *discovery*. "We're going to give *New World Writing* a run for its money," he said, mentioning the competition, a softcover magazine of original stories, poems, and essays, published by New American Library, a mass-market house. *New World Writing*'s circulation was over two hundred thousand per issue, a figure that eclipsed that of any other literary magazine extant. *Discovery*'s publisher was Pocket Books, Inc., a lucrative limb of Simon and Schuster. Pocket Books started the mass-market revolution in 1939 and was, in the words of Herbert Alexander, its editor in chief, mainly committed to continuing "acts of commerce" rather than "acts of culture." This is what surprised me when Vance explained what he was up to. Pocket Books didn't expect to make money with this project, he explained, but to fish for and land new authors with blockbuster potential.

Shamelessly, I told Vance I'd love to work for something like *discovery*. I hated my job at *Town and Country*, and besides, I had just set fire to the place. I think this admission increased my value for Vance, far more than my fancy Barnard diploma, my English major, my knowing Sue Kaufman. He said he would speak to his coeditor, Jack Aldridge, a critic who lived on a New Hampshire farm with his wife and their six or seven children. Aldridge had recently published a book called *After the Lost Generation*, in which he commended the work of several World War II novelists, among them Norman Mailer, John Horne Burns, James Jones, Gore Vidal, and Vance Bourjaily. The hero of Bourjaily's novel *The End of My Life* was a Hemingwayesque wartime ambulance driver. Aldridge's book, his first, transformed him and Vance from unknowns into a couple of hot items, and on the basis of their newfound celebrity, he and Vance had persuaded the higher-ups at Pocket Books to help them launch a literary magazine. Pocket Books would produce and distribute; the critic and novelist would edit. Vance said he didn't think Jack would object to taking me on to read manuscripts, maybe do some editing. They needed help. "We'll make you assistant editor." There was just one little thing. "Until the money comes through, there won't be any salary for you. You'll have to work for nothing for a while. Sue says you live with your parents? By the way, your father knows my father."

"How long is a while?"

"A month or two at most," he said. "And just for now, we're running the magazine out of my apartment on the West Side. They're getting a place ready for us downtown. You don't object to the West Side, do you?"

The job as Vance described it was the one I would have invented for myself. I went home giddy and the next day wrote to my boss, Henry Sell, saying sayonara.

That undertaking was a snap compared to dealing with my father when I told him about the job. Saving the worst till last, I said, "There's just one little thing. They won't be able to pay me anything for about a month. They're waiting for funding from Pocket Books."

My father erupted. He assured me that no one in America respects work done for nothing or the person who delivers it. He said that such work has no value. I didn't need his permission, but I wanted his approval; my mother didn't figure in my calculations: my father was head man, my mother a timid assistant. I tried an assortment of arguments: he knew Vance's father. "Monte Bourjaily? Sure I know him, he's a good newspaperman." I tried to persuade him that this was a dream job, a job where I would be doing editorial rather than scut work, filing or answering the telephone. I told him that Vance practically swore that the money to hire me was in the works and would be forthcoming in a month or two. So I had nothing to lose and the experience would be invaluable. . . .

Scowling and jiggling his foot, my father said, "You're too smart to work gratis. Only dopes work for nothing."

"What about the volunteer work I did at Lenox Hill?"

"That was different. You were still in school. I wouldn't let you do that now."

"Do you know how old I am?"

"Twenty-one?"

"Twenty-two, but that's okay."

We both went away mad. I was determined to take this job no matter what my father said (knowing that, bleak as his judgments might be, he would not cut me off), and I called Vance and asked him when he would like me to start.

I went straight from *Town and Country* to *discovery* without missing a beat. Giving myself plenty of time, I took the Sixty-fifth Street crosstown bus and transferred to the bus that plies Central Park West, where I got off at 103rd Street. Twenty minutes early, I walked up and down in front of the apartment house until just before nine. The building was crummy. Sheltered and rendered timorous by my wealth and security, I had never known anyone who lived in an apartment house where the lobby tile was cracked and split, the walls dirty, and the smell like that of a hardworking institutional kitchen and a much used bathroom. I went up in the creaking elevator with its accordion gate, got out at the eighth floor, and rang the buzzer. Vance pulled the door open immediately. He was wearing soft moccasins, like the sole-less ones you wear at summer camp, a pair of chinos, and an oxford, button-down shirt.

I tried to get a fix on the apartment. It was small and darkish with a slim hallway. I couldn't see the "office."

"Tina's out grocery shopping," he said, helping me off with my coat, one of his pale hands lingering on my right shoulder. I wondered why he was telling me this but it didn't take long to pick up on his meaning: *Tina's out. Why don't you and I retire to the bedroom?* He smiled in that scampish way men do when they're trying to screw a new person.

The phrase that came to me later, namely, "I'll sleep with you or work for you—but not both," was too acute to occur to me at the precise moment I needed it. Instead, nervous and awkward, I told him I would much rather not, that it wasn't my understanding of what this job entailed. I was counting on his need for free labor, a need more urgent than getting laid. I could almost feel the pill of rejection in my own throat as he swallowed, taking it like a man. Vance never tried anything funny again. Maybe it was just one of those nothing-to-lose gestures that men exercised more out of habit and attitude than out of lust. We got down to work within a few minutes. Tina came back with two armfuls of groceries and greeted me warily. I guessed she guessed what he might have been up to.

After about a month, *discovery*'s funding was approved and I began to receive a salary of thirty-five dollars a week, before taxes; we also moved out of Vance's apartment. Working on *discovery* was like being at a perpetual party. Vance turned out to be an ideal boss—energized, funny, inventive, kindly. He didn't like telling me what to do or ragging me when I made a mistake. *Discovery*'s berth 159 was now in a building on Forty-seventh Street between Fifth and Sixth Avenues, a Pocket Books annex housing the mail-order department. It was a bare-bones setup, one large room with a screenlike partition on one side of which was Vance's desk, mine on the other. There was nothing on the walls but a coat of drab, streaky paint and no carpet, the sort of office a private eye down on his luck might rent until things turn around. Pocket Books' main office was three blocks up Fifth at number 630, the building with bronze Atlas down on one knee, shouldering a bronze world. Forty-seventh Street between Fifth and Sixth was the heart of the diamond district in the New World. Orthodox Jews in long black overcoats whatever the season, black hats and payess, transacted business on the sidewalks, their sparklers carried inside folded and refolded squares of tissue paper. It was like working in the Old World.

Vance had a mission. This, in part, is what he wrote in the preface to the first issue of *discovery:* "We began by rejecting the cynical portrait of the American reader as a juvenile oaf" and "The magazine will be governed by none of the editorial taboos, so enormously destructive to creative work," along with other high-minded sentiments suggesting that the reading public craved good, literary stuff in an inexpensive format.

Vance had designed the magazine's cover himself, an ersatz Mondrian with a different color scheme for each edition. Within the squares were printed the names of contributors. The idea was to present the reader with something vaguely but not in-your-face contemporary, modernism without threat, similarly the lowercase *d* in the magazine's name.

These are some of the writers who sold us never-before-published stories, essays, and poetry: Herbert Gold, Norman Mailer, William Styron, Anatole Broyard, John Hollander, John Clellon Holmes, Evan Hunter, Muriel Rukeyser (with a rare short story), Roger Shattuck, Winfield Townley Scott, May Swenson, Saul Bellow, Norman Rosten, Harvey Swados, Hortense Calisher, Otto Friedrich, Kenneth Koch, Bernard Malamud, Adrienne Rich, Louis Simpson, Harold Brodkey, R.V. Cassill, Richard Eberhart, Leslie Fiedler, along with a score of other writers in the six semiannual issues eventually published, from 1953 through 1955. I got to know several of them well: Muriel Rukeyser, an ardent woman with a wild sense of humor; she had a son whose father was reputed to be a celebrated American poet, but no one knew for sure. Winfield Scott, the first Yale Younger Poet. He was gentle and troubled but a generous companion. Bernard Malamud, a former schoolteacher, a fabulist with a deceptively reticent exterior.

Officially I was managing editor—or man-eating, as Vance came to call me. This meant that I was keeper of the records and manuscripts that poured in by the hundreds, about a third through literary agents. I read each one in the order it arrived, sometimes cheating if I saw a name I recognized. Vance trusted me to go through the slush pile and make decisions. The nos I sent back either with a printed rejections slip or with a note of encouragement. Those I thought good enough to consider publishing, I passed on to Vance. Then we'd talk about it, along with Robert Pack, a kid who appeared, unannounced, in our office one day and said he'd just graduated from Columbia College and would like to be *discovery*'s poetry editor. Jack Aldridge would have to be consulted. Robert Kotlowitz, a Pocket Books editor, fresh from the training program, was on the *discovery* masthead. I wasn't told this, but I figured management wanted to keep an eye on us to make sure we weren't going to slip something obscene or seditious over on them. From the day we met, Bob and I slipped into one of those platonic friendships men and women sometimes, but all too rarely, form. I also wrote the contributors' notes at the end of the book, an operation that involved both the telephone and the U.S. mail. 161

Vance's friends Norman Mailer, Louis Auchincloss, Hortense Calisher, Norman Rosten, and several others turned up from time to time to shoot the breeze and hang out. This was my first exposure to literary people, and I never got over the belief that, among mortals, these were the elect. Vance began to call me Rosy-pal.

"Rosy-pal," he said one day, apropos of absolutely nothing and coming from God knows where, "I hope when you marry the guy will be Jewish." Vance was Armenian, born a Catholic but, as far as I could tell, not at all religious. My link to my European roots was about as strong as Tarzan's were to those upper-crust English who were his forebears. "The Jewish race shouldn't be allowed to dry up," he said. "You people have been around too long to disappear."

I was too surprised to respond, but that Vance was more concerned about ethnic tradition than my own parents struck me as both curious and sad. In fact, my parents didn't give a hoot for most traditions and that was what had made them both energized and detached. They were unbelievers in a sea of firm believers. Something of a rascal, Vance loved executing practical jokes and maneuvering people like chess pieces. A young journalist, Leslie Felker, had been hanging around Vance and his literary moths for weeks, planning to write an article about *discovery*. One morning Vance called to me from the far side of the partition. "Rosy-pal," he said. "I've got a terrific idea. Jack's coming down this weekend. Why don't we introduce him to Leslie?" "Isn't Jack married?" I said. Jack's wife, Vance said, was even as we spoke in a New Hampshire hospital, having just produced their whatever it was, number six or seven. I asked him if he was serious. He got up and came around to my side, stuck his hands in his pockets and, grinning, told me that Jack was one of those men who couldn't resist the scent of a girl, a major cocksman. "I don't think I like this," I said. I wanted to be as cool as Vance, but his plan struck me as off-the-wall—and mean-spirited. I thought he should save this sort of choreography for his fiction. That Sunday Vance introduced Jack to Leslie; within weeks Jack had left his wife and six or seven children. He and Leslie married, settled in Princeton, New Jersey, and eventually divorced. She was awfully pretty.

My life beyond five o'clock and on weekends began to bleed over into Vance and Tina's. By this time, the Bourjailys had moved to an apartment in the West Village, a place that Tina's employer, the magazine *Woman's Day*, had renovated for them, then displayed as a before-and-after job in the magazine. Vance and Tina gave a party every couple of weeks, very informal, lots of beer and booze, usually starting after dinner and going on forever. Several times I heard that Norman Mailer had taken off all his clothes after I'd left and done the cha-cha, probably one of those early urban myths. A couple of the elect were always on hand. Dawn Powell, spidery with age. Kenneth Fearing, who wrote *The Big Clock*. Calder Willingham, a redheaded southerner, author of *End as a Man*, a violence-drenched novel about life in a military school, later turned into a play and then a movie. Sometimes Jack Aldridge, who would come down from the North for a sampling of the wicked life of the big city.

On Sunday afternoons Vance and his chums met in the White Horse Tavern, a modest bar with white tile walls made famous by Dylan Thomas a few years earlier. Calder Willingham played chess there with Herman Wouk—an odd couple. Norman Mailer dropped by for some brews. Shy to the point of paralysis, I mainly looked and listened. I hadn't yet learned how to start a conversation.

Vance grew restless. One time he went to Mexico for three months, putting me in charge. "Buy whatever you like," he said. "Even poetry?" "No, you better leave that to Packo." Then Vance and Jack began to growl at each other. From afar, Jack objected to this story or that poem. He was carping at Vance's taste. The two men couldn't have been more dissimilar in temperament and style, and it's no doubt a fluke that they could ever have worked together without beating each other up. Cool Vance was ironic, spontaneous, playful, bawdy; uncool Jack, a very tall man with thick yellow hair and a super aquiline nose, was literal-minded, grave, and cautious. You had the feeling that before Jack spoke he had already formed the complete sentence in his head. Jack's main critical thesis was that, with the breakdown of rigid class categories after World War II, the novelist had little left to write about. I imagine Vance thought this was nonsense—as indeed it turned out to be. One day Jack announced, via the mail, that he was through editing *discovery*. Vance had done by far the most work on the magazine, and he seemed relieved that big Jack was no longer on the scene to hassle him. Someone threw a fancy party uptown to bid Jack farewell. We ate off plates balanced on our laps, as there were too many people for a sit-down dinner. I ended up next to Jack on a low couch in the living room. Fueled by a couple of drinks, Jack unloaded a bursting heartful of grief and frustration, mostly having to do with the sorry state of literature, with the evils of the modern world, and the rampant commercial forces that deliberately baffled The Artist, etc., etc. It was hard for me to keep a straight face. Finally, he said, "Don't let them get to you, kid," at which I nodded solemnly and determined to stow this astonishing phrase in my permanent memory file.

It wasn't all beer and skittles for me at *discovery*, for Vance was quixotic, especially when he had had a couple of drinks. Twice a year Simon and Schuster and its satellite publishing operations held a sales conference, a two- or three-day event designed to whip up enthusiasm among a sales force that spent most of the year visiting bookstores and talking up the properties, hot and otherwise. Big-name authors like Walt Kelly, father of the comic strip possum, Pogo, and J. K. Lasser, the tax guru, would show up to plug their own books. After the last working sessions S & S threw a lavish party in a hotel for all its employees, from president to mail room boy. During the winter of 1953 the party was held at the Barbizon Plaza, a neutral sort of hotel with an enormous ballroom filled with tables for eight. Food and drink in Lucullan proportions appeared. A band played. Editors danced with their secretaries, management flirted with serf, people began stumbling around. And there was Vance, dancing by himself and removing his clothes, first his jacket, then his shoes and socks. He was unbuttoning his shirt when some kind soul escorted him from the dance floor. Then he spotted me and came over to where I was sitting. "You're fired," he said through his teeth. "I don't want to see your face again."

"Come on, Vance, let's go get some coffee," said his friend, pulling him away.

The following morning I had a choice: either take Vance at his word and start looking for another job or bury his remark, along with any others uttered by him in a mist of alcohol. Reasoning that he had been too drunk to remember firing me, I decided to show up for work. When I walked into the office, Vance told me he had a doozy of a hangover. Then he wanted to know if I had had a good time. "Did you meet anybody interesting?"

When Vance had his heart in it, *discovery* was a first-class product. The stories were fresh and smart, not one of them giving off even a whiff of pretension, a quality that sent Vance around the bend. Few of our writers had gone through MFA programs like Iowa or Virginia, and occasionally you could hear the gears grinding, but you never had the sense that the writer was composing according to a set of rules learned from a master in the classroom.

No stories in which every word is asked to carry extra weight, every detail fraught with hidden meaning. Each story was sui generis; each delivered, at the final sentence, that tying-up moment so you don't have to ask "And then what happened?" Vance was a wonderful, instinctive, and disciplined editor; whenever he worked over a story or essay, he made it better. The poetry was equally strong. The essays carried the same sort of weight. Vance made one big mistake: after holding on to the first chapter of an untitled novel by an unknown writer named Joseph Heller, he finally turned it down. Heller's novel was published a year or so later as *Catch-22*.

Discovery's éminence grise was the editor in chief of Pocket Books, a man who looked more like a boxer than a dealer in words. This was Herbert Alexander, an ex-army sergeant whose chest must have measured more than fifty inches. He spoke with what some misidentified as a Brooklyn accent but which was pure Manhattan. Not quite, but almost pronouncing *th* as *d*. Herb Alexander was the person responsible for bringing *discovery* under Pocket Books' aegis, though, in conversation, he usually returned from where you were headed straight back to "commerce." A book he considered too slow, pretentious, or cerebral, he would dismiss as "too much talking, not enough fucking." Because whenever he talked about "belles lettres" he grew almost weepy, I suspected that he would much rather have been doing Vance's job than buying blockbuster novels from hardcover publishers. But no, if he really would have rather been editing literary work for a pittance, he would have. He wasn't trapped—he had willingly made his bed, and now he was lying in it, luxuriating. He kept a plush-seated barber chair in the bedroom of his Riverside Drive apartment overlooking the Hudson River. Once a week a barber would appear to trim Herb's hair and give him a shave. I was there once when this

happened; he went right on talking, a royal personage being prepared for a ceremonial rite. Was he going to give these things up
for the sake of "art"?

Herb was a nonstop talker—about almost anything; he had
read everything, thoroughly digesting the lot. He had opinions the
way beer has fizz. He would get an idea into his head and nothing,
no evidence or protestation, could dislodge it. Once he had
decided that I hated my father, that was it. "I know you hate your
father, but . . ."

Each time you visited Herb in his ample office with its grand
desk and stylish auxiliary furnishings, you knew you would be
there at least an hour, mostly listening as wit and brilliance frothed

off his tongue. He had stories (some suggesting that after his stint as an army sergeant he had operated a black market of spare tank and aircraft parts), tales of youthful indiscretions, gossip about people you knew and people whom you'd only heard of. He could be passionate and dismissive at the same time. Herb kept several white shirts in the office because he sweated so profusely that he had to keep changing them. If you were there, he'd do it right in front of you, flashing that swollen chest. Whenever his glasses needed cleaning, he would ring for his secretary, who, answering his summons, took the specs from his outstretched hand without his looking at her, and returned with them minutes later, washed, dried, and polished.

After a visit to Herb's office I would walk, somewhat giddily—for he had an effect on those who loved him of strong drink on an empty stomach—down the hallway of the twenty-seventh floor, trying but unable to recall any but the tiniest scraps of the conversation just over. And this happened to others who confessed to the same thing: "What the hell did Herb say?" Some thought of him as a hugely warm and generous man; other saw him as a kind of devil, a tyrant, and a bully.

When I was twenty-three, I met Justin Kaplan, the Jew whom Vance wanted me to marry. Justin was an editor at Harry Abrams, the only really good American publisher of art books, a field that, until Abrams started his operation, had been completely dominated by European houses. Justin, or "Joe" as his closest friends called him, had done some freelance editing for Herb Alexander—a Pocket edition of Plato and an assignment to do a similar edition of Aristotle. And so it seemed natural that when I was trying to decide whether or not to marry Justin, I went to Herb, rather than to my father or mother. Herb said that

Kaplan was one of the smartest people he'd ever worked with, adding, "He's very quiet."

"I know that," I said. "I'm trying to thaw him out."

"You have my blessing," Herb said. This was like being touched by a seraph.

CHAPTER 8

An official letter in June 1947 put an end to my time as a graduate student in English. "The department has again been considering your excellent course record," it began, pleasantly enough, "and wishes me to convey its decision that you should not register for further English courses until you have passed your reading examinations in Latin, French, and German." The writer, Professor George Sherburn, an authority on Alexander Pope, was kind enough not to say that beyond these deficiencies, which would have taken several years to remedy, I had racked up three incompletes, something of a high-water mark for delinquence, according to Miss Helen Jones, the department secretary. It was a relief to have others make up my mind for me and so ease my escape from a Ph.D. program that I had begun to see as a dead end. Egyptians took three weeks to turn someone into a mummy; the English department, as the joke went, took three years, and I had already spent two of them.

At twenty-one, and without regrets, I left Harvard and academic life and went back to New York, in my mind and speech simply and always "the city." I had spent the first sixteen years of my life there, but now I felt as if I had just arrived from Omaha or Toledo and was seeing and hearing New York for the first time. The clacking of traffic lights along Fifth Avenue late at night made my blood race. I had been allowed to reenter a Promised Land where, for someone my age, almost anything wondrous and unexpected could happen.

At the party for Somerset Maugham I ran into Beatrice, a girl I had met briefly a week before. We left the party together, took a cab downtown, and stood on Brooklyn Bridge. When we kissed she asked, "Did you know this was going to happen?" I said, "I hoped so," although no would have been the honest answer, because one only dreamed about such a thing.

Beatrice wore her dark silky hair in bangs. She had beautiful skin and a penumbra of privilege: good dentists, Henri Bendel, Bergdorf Goodman, and expensive schools—Dalton and Sarah Lawrence College. She was luxuriantly, possessively, radiantly at home in the city. She had a high girlish laugh set off by whatever she found "hilarious" or "hysterical," which was most everything one generally took too seriously. I felt lifted in spirit by her apparently untroubled view of the world, her openness and emotional generosity. That spring and summer Beatrice transported me from comfortable, socially drab West Ninety-sixth Street to the relatively glittering world of the Upper East Side of Manhattan and the North Shore of Long Island. She lived there—in the former Pulitzer mansion on Seventy-third Street and at Cow Neck Farm, a country estate at Sands Point—with her formidable mother, Ray, and Ray's second husband, the publisher M. Lincoln Schuster.

We spent most of our time together, even playing together like children—we walked along the rocky beach at Sands Point and the seawall by the Guggenheim mansion, sent Slinkies down Pulitzer's marble staircase. Her family appeared to approve of the affair. They also assumed that having left graduate school in literature I was cut out to be an editor, an occupation I had never thought of until then but now seemed the right thing, although no one seemed to want to hire me. Partly to meet social and professional norms, at least as I understood them, I shed my Cambridge fatigues—chinos, ratty tweed jacket out at the elbows, faded, fraying blue oxford shirt, and dirty tennis shoes—and began to buy my clothes at Brooks Brothers and J. Press: Egyptian cotton shirts, gray flannel suits, the darker the better, with practically stovepipe trouser legs, black string ties—the overall effect of this uniform was both snappy and funereal as well as reassuring, that is, if you wanted to blend in at parties. For winter: a reddish tan Harris tweed overcoat from Abercrombie's, wild peccary gloves from Mark Cross, and, a gift from Beatrice's mother, a green cashmere scarf long enough to go twice around my neck.

Max Schuster was no one's idea of what a rich and powerful book publisher should look like. His hands and lower lip trembled, he wore heavy glasses, his head was too big for his torso, and he had the goggly, slightly bewildered look of a schoolboy chess prodigy who happened to stray into the football team's locker room during a session of towel snapping. One could easily imagine him in knee pants. He had a disconcerting habit of clicking ball-point pens and chewing on their barrels. When he had to take a phone call he held the receiver away from his mouth and ear, as if it were a live lobster. In his nervous and initially reluctant way—having been prodded by his wife, at whose bidding he would jump—he allowed me to use him as a reference when I started hunting for a job, although it would have made sense for any potential employer to ask why Max himself didn't hire me. Aside from my knowing something about books but nothing about book publishing, the answer may have been that I had become a pet of his wife and he minded that.

Ray Schuster pampered me with Scotch, smoked salmon, sturgeon, and late-night omelets she made herself. She joked about adopting me and, on no evidence at all, especially since I was often tongue-tied when alone with her and Max, introduced me to their friends as "brilliant." When Ray praised me as "brilliant" to Joseph Barnes, a legendary newspaper editor who had come to work at Simon and Schuster, he responded with a chilling, properly skeptical "we'll see." Ray Schuster applied such extravagant terms rather promiscuously to many people but, for once with some justice, to her husband as well. Hiring me, Max must have thought, would be like hiring an agent of a foreign power, a threat to independence and internal security. To Max's regret, his wife had recently talked him into taking on one of her sons-in-law. This one was not notably competent, but largely because he tended to run to her for support in his dealings with Max, he did not last. Max bucked him to the sales department.

Although muffled by a flurry of endearments and compliments, tensions between Max and Ray tended to mount during dinner. By the time the chocolate soufflé with hard sauce arrived she might be teasing him: about his partner Richard Simon ("the piano salesman"); about the firm's "little bookkeeper," the third *S* of S&S, Leon Shimkin ("belongs on Seventh Avenue, selling *shmattes*"); about the current list ("mostly dreck"). Her teasing was sometimes so cruel that he left the table and locked himself in the

Staged photograph of party chez Schuster, late 1940s. *Used by permission of Pearl London.*

bathroom. We could hear him sobbing. I was ashamed to be there. Perhaps another reason for not hiring me was that I had witnessed too many such scenes of humiliation.

On my own, and through a loose Harvard network, I managed to find a couple of temporary jobs, one a summer stint with Random House on the *American College Dictionary*. Working in former maids' quarters on the top floor of the Fahnestock mansion on Madison Avenue and Fiftieth, about a dozen young men and women with no particular qualifications for dictionary work beyond a basic literacy pounded out definitions. During July and August we sweated away in our airless coops to meet a daily quota of definitions that the editors, Clarence Barnhart and Jesse Stein, would regularly ratchet up, from forty to fifty and beyond. As I learned when admonished for what they considered slacking off, to keep up the pace they kept track of worker visits to the water cooler and the bathroom. Presumably they were going to up the ante until we reached the limits of our capability. There were timely parallels here to the much discussed Stakhanov speed-up system Joseph Stalin promoted for Soviet coal mines and industry. Our taskmasters discouraged us from wasting time in so-called research, for example, consulting the *Oxford English Dictionary*. Our job was to produce definitions sufficiently rewritten to disguise their prime source, an old *Century* dictionary to which Random House had bought the rights. Bennett Cerf, cofounder and public countenance of Random House, boasted to the press that the *American College Dictionary*, representing an investment of over half a million dollars, was his cherished baby and he kept a paternal eye on it each day. The one time Cerf came to visit the harmless drudges defining away on the airless top floor of his building he got himself lost on his way back to the elevator and ended up in an office supplies closet. I saw Cerf in the corridor trying to find his bearings, and that was the closest I came to meeting him.

In my wanderings in the world of work I had a temporary job as one of several editor-ghostwriters on a medical textbook about psychosomatic diagnosis. The author, a psychoanalyst, drank gin throughout the day from a silver cup and masked the aroma with drenches of Chanel No. 5. By closing time she was sometimes stuporous. For someone in analysis, as I was then, this peek behind the curtain of professional authority and inscrutability was like meeting the Great Oz face-to-face and discovering him to be, as he conceded, "a very bad wizard." On two or three occasions, after our employer had left, we helped ourselves to the champagne in her refrigerator, ordered in fancy dinners from Casserole Kitchen, charging them to her account, and with the connivance of her secretary, listened to tapes of the day's analytic sessions. Two years later I ran into a middle-aged corporate lawyer I recognized from his voice and upper-class New York accent as the patient whose taped recitals of physical afflictions (hives, chronic nervous diarrhea) and sexual frustrations I had heard: he complained that his wife's sole communication during his spells of sexual need had been, "Go take a cold shower." I fled from him like the guilty creature I was.

Max Schuster eventually summoned me to see him at work in the U.S. Rubber Building on Sixth Avenue. His glossily designed offices there, a marriage of elegance and efficiency, had been featured in *Architectural Forum*: surrounded by decklike balconies they gave me a sense of being at sea on a *Titanic* without lifeboats. He had relented to the extent of assigning me to do outside work on some of his publishing projects. For what he had in mind he offered fees so tiny I was virtually paying for my apprenticeship, but I thought this was fair. (I managed to get along on my brother's generosity and what was left of my inheritance after paying Dr. Hughes's monthly bills.) One project was a 1,200-page edition of Thoreau, with chronologies, bibliographies, and a selection of critical comment, from Emerson and Whitman to Mohandas Gandhi and beyond. (Max allotted three to five weeks for my full-time research and offered a fee of $250.) Another project was a Bible so encrusted with marginal commentary incorporating the latest scholarship that the text practically cowered. Max also had me work on a series of single-play editions anachronistically titled (a vestige of the United Front 1930s) *The People's Shakespeare*. As planned, the People would buy the Bard's work through the Sears Roebuck catalog along with garden tools, BB guns, ladies' foundation garments, and other mail-order merchandise. All three projects died on their way to the delivery room, but not before I had put in several months at the Forty-second Street library, typing out hundreds of pages of material on my Royal portable.

More consequentially for my future, Max farmed me out as research assistant to Louis Untermeyer, a famous anthologist. An accomplished poet, translator (from the German), and public wit as well, he had so far produced nearly ninety collections and was reputed to be always ready to turn out another one, needing only a publisher to propose a title and financing. He had fallen behind in putting together an apparatus-heavy edition of Walt Whitman's poetry and prose for Simon and Schuster and needed help right away.

Untermeyer educated two generations of readers with his perennial *Modern American Poetry* and its British counterpart, doing a great service to the poets as well. Snobs preferred to overlook this and make fun of him as a sort of carnival barker. The Village poet E. E. Cummings, one of the beneficiaries of the exposure Untermeyer had given him, skewered him in a quatrain:

> *mr u will not be missed*
> *who as an anthologist*
> *sold the many on the few*
> *not excluding mr u*

Mr. U riposted with a smilingly viperish thank-you postcard to Cummings—"Dear Estlin: It's the best thing you've written." You had to admire Louis for that alone.

In his middle sixties when I worked for him, Louis had a day job writing liner copy for Decca Records and lived on the upper floors of 88 Remsen Street in Brooklyn Heights. Philip Van Doren Stern, an editor and prolific author of books about the Civil War, owned the house and lived downstairs with his family. The place was the center of a little commune of like-minded, left-leaning writers who lived in the neighborhood, among them the poet and playwright Norman Rosten. Louis's resident companion, whom he was to marry in Cuernavaca as soon as his Mexican divorce went through, was Bryna Ivens, an editor for *Seventeen*, a glossy magazine for girls who had reached the age of rampant consumerism. Counting Bryna, Louis was married five times to four women (twice to one of them, the poet Jean Starr). He was not in the same league with the much married movie star Mickey Rooney and the playboy Tommy Manville, heir to an asbestos fortune, but his marital history was enough to make him easy copy for the *Daily News* and *Mirror*. Like Bluebeard, as Dickens's Sam Weller said, Louis could be called a "victim of connubiality."

By normal standards he had married to excess and not always wisely. "Bigamy is having one wife too many," he liked to quote. "Monogamy is the same." But he continued to value hope over experience. One of his wives, a judge, took him to the cleaners in their divorce settlement and made off with his farm at Elizabethtown in the Adirondacks, his pet donkeys (Isadora Donkey and Don Quixote), a personal library that included presentation copies from his close friend Robert Frost, T. S. Eliot, and other poets of the day, and the better part of the money he inherited from the Untermeyer family's jewelry business. (Like Captain Carpenter in John Crowe Ransom's poem, one of the staples of *Modern American Poetry*, Louis was shorn "of his goodly nose and ears, his legs and strong arms at the two elbows.") When I asked him what compelled him to marry such furies instead of just living with them, he answered, "My Jewish conscience."

He was clearly besotted with Bryna but not so much that his infatuation and Jewish conscience blinded him to attractive women. At the spring reception of the American Academy and Institute of Arts and Letters, of which he was a member, Louis kept sending me off to fetch drinks and tea sandwiches while he flirted with my date, the beautiful and brilliant literary scholar Aileen Ward. According to Louis, whatever Bryna did, no matter how trivial, called for medals and a hallelujah with chorus and consort of trumpets. "That ham and cheese sandwich she made for you," Louis said. "Wasn't that the best goddam ham and cheese sandwich you ever ate?" Over uninspiring suppers—canned soup preceded the historic sandwiches—Louis and Bryna extended my political and literary horizons with readings from the poems of Mao Zedong, soon to be leader of the People's Republic of China. "Listen to this," Bryna said, as if favoring me with another ham and cheese sandwich:

> The Red Army fears not the trials of the Long March,
> Holding light ten thousand crags and torrents.
> The Five Ridges wind like gentle ripples
> And the majestic Wumeng roll by, like globules of clay.

I said that was very fine, but as a travel poem I preferred Edward Lear's "The Owl and the Pussycat." Out of clearly strained tolerance Bryna and Louis let this remark pass as a juvenile indiscretion, the opinion of a "paper tiger" (as Chairman Mao might say).

Louis was a socialist from way back and a rebel against conventional literature and manners. He had been a contributing editor of *The Masses*, a radical journal suppressed as seditious by the government during World War I. He was now a passionate supporter of former Vice President Henry A. Wallace, the Progressive Party candidate for president in 1948. For Louis loyalty to Wallace was the crucial test of one's liberalism. That autumn, a time of terrible simplifiers, one was either a Henry Wallace progressive or a capitalist running dog, whether Democrat or Republican it didn't matter. The need to argue out the choice put a strain on friendships. For people like me, who thought of themselves as political realists, a vote for Henry Wallace, a third-party candidate, whatever your ideological loyalties, was a form of electoral masturbation. Since third parties had only subtractive power in general elections, you might just as well give your vote to the Republican candidate (and clear front-runner) New York governor Thomas E. Dewey because you were taking it away from his underdog opponent, President Harry S Truman.

On election eve Louis, Bryna, and I went downstairs to Stern's apartment, where a number of neighbors had assembled to hear Wallace's campaign-closing radio speech. I lighted a cigarette and was scolded for this sign of inattention—I felt myself back in the synagogue, being shushed. "Truman's managers know he will lose," Wallace declared. "They are running him only to confuse millions of progressive-minded Americans." I muttered—to myself, I thought—the word "bullshit." Stern pulled me from my chair, said, "Get your coat," and ordered me out of his house. By the time I returned to Remsen Street a week later Louis and Bryna had cooled down, and appeared to be resigned to Wallace's defeat and his return to the study of hybrid corn—he had failed to win a single electoral vote. We avoided the topic of Truman's surprise victory.

As well as being a victim of connubiality Louis suffered for his uncompromising political loyalties. His name came up in congressional hearings, where he was denounced as a Communist sympathizer who in addition led an unsavory domestic life and set a bad example for the young people of the nation. Some libraries removed his anthologies from their shelves. Along with the actress Arlene Francis and other celebrities, he had been a panelist on the popular television show *What's My Line?* Pressured by sponsors obedient to blacklisting, the producers fired Louis, replacing him with the ideologically clean Bennett Cerf, who had the same sort of ready wit. From then on—he also lost his job with Decca Records—Louis earned part of his living on the lecture circuit.

Louis's ticlike punning on any topic or occasion could easily get wearisome. "At best she's a matzo-soprano," he said of one performer. And he was irrepressibly playful. I once heard him compliment a friend's black cook on her roast chicken—"Flora, it was so delicious I'm going to give you your freedom." She played along: "Yassuh, Mr. Untermeyer, yassuh." A young man in Louis's lecture audience once asked, "How much do you get for a lecture like this?" "More than it's worth," Louis replied. He always had an answer or witticism at the ready. "Of what?" was his scribbled comment on the sign, SIMON AND SCHUSTER, PUBLISHERS, that the partners had put up on their office door when they started their business in 1924. (Years later it was still an open question—one answer could be, "Everything and anything.")

At one of Max and Ray Schuster's power-packed, champagne and smoked sturgeon parties Louis introduced me to Amy Loveman of the Book-of-the-Month Club—I had been hoping they'd hire me as a reader. He told her I was "a demon researcher" but had been advised by doctors to relax and take up basket weaving, this being one of the standard diversions for mental patients. What was behind such mischief was the old battle between age and youth. I fed this by reminding Louis from time to time he had been born during the first year of the first administration of Grover Cleveland, one year before the internal combustion engine, and three years before T. S. Eliot. (This sort of information was to hand because we were working on a chronology of Whitman's life and times.) I also put over on him an article I claimed to have turned up in my research: it argued that certain anguished entries in Whitman's notebooks referred not to his crypto-lover Peter Doyle, as commonly supposed, but to the number identifying the Washington Street railway car on which Doyle worked as a conductor. Louis should have been tipped off by the title alone: "A Note on Walt Whitman and a Horse Car Named Desire." He did not take kindly to being on the receiving end and pretended my hoax never happened. But mostly we got along well and moved ahead smoothly with the Whitman project, executing it in line with Max Schuster's detailed editorial "blueprint." Among other features of this massive edition was a thirty-thousand-word biographical introduction.

During the day I took notes on Whitman biography and criticism in the reading room of the Forty-second Street library. Tuesdays and Thursdays I rode the BMT to the Borough Hall station, a short distance from Cranberry Street, where in a little printing office on the corner of Fulton Street Whitman had helped typeset the first edition of *Leaves of Grass*. After a kitchen supper at 88 Remsen Street with the happy couple I went upstairs to Louis's study to work. It came as a terrifying surprise that he expected me not only to supply the research for the introduction but also to take turns with him in writing it on the spot. I told him I wasn't ready, didn't feel in the mood. He said, "Mood doesn't matter. Just do it. If you're going to write, then *write!*" I was grateful to Louis for this kindly and corrective lesson, even though I felt that his own fluent professionalism and wit—his ability to turn out polished and sprightly prose on short order—sometimes left the heart out of his work. I sent him an affectionate telegram on his eighty-fifth birthday celebrated at a gala dinner at the Tavern on the Green. Louis's editor, Henry Simon, who was to read the bundle of congratulatory messages, collapsed at the table and died of a heart attack during the dessert course before he got to mine.

Meanwhile I continued to canvass magazine and book publishers, hoping someone would hire me full-time. For a month or two I attended rehearsals and trained as a scriptwriter for Worthington Miner's *Studio One*, a live television drama show featuring hour-long adaptations of novels like Walter van Tilburg Clark's *The Ox-Bow Incident*. My main achievement was to get out of the actors' way without tripping over camera and lighting cables.

Motivated by curiosity of a self-punishing sort I managed to wangle a job interview with Merle Crowell, a senior editor at *Reader's Digest*, even though I had heard there wasn't a single Jew on the editorial payroll. Just the place-name of the *Digest's* Westchester headquarters, Pleasantville, was irresistible: so bland, so white bread, so in keeping with the magazine's spectacularly popular American chop suey platter of uplift, consolation, conservative politics, practical knowledge, spoon-fed science, and picturesque speech. The *Digest's* chaste Colonial-style headquarters, perched on a hilltop far in from the highway, looked like an expensive mental institution. You half expected to see patients walking the immaculate grounds under the eye of burly attendants in white. But the grounds were deserted, the editorial occupants of the building presumably busy rummaging through other publications in search of digestible material.

We had all heard that the founder-owners of *Reader's Digest*, DeWitt Wallace and his wife, Lila Acheson Wallace, ruled over their domain like benevolent despots. For a brief period, on the advice of either nutritionists or efficiency experts, the Wallaces had ordered peanut butter and wheat germ sandwiches distributed to everyone in the building, from management to mail room staff. (They abandoned the experiment when filing cabinets and desk drawers began to overflow with rejected sandwiches in advanced states of decay.) The reception room—one of several similarly furnished—could have been a parlor in a high-class mortuary. The air was heavy, almost stifling, with the scent of gardenias—Mrs. Wallace's favorite flower, I was told, the blossoms personally selected by her each morning—floating in porcelain bowls on a cherry-wood tray table. It was almost a relief to be taken from this visitation room and into the astringent presence of a senatorial-looking man with white hair, down-turned mouth, and modified Down East accent. After some disturbingly irrelevant questions about the car (my brother's black Pontiac) I had driven to Pleasantville—Model year? Color? Hydra-Matic or stick shift? Miles to the gallon?—Crowell got down to business. "I see from your résumé you've worked for Louis Untermeyer," he began. "All those wives! What do you know!" He seemed almost amused but reverted to his more natural grimness when he quizzed me about Louis's political leanings. Did I think he was a Communist? It was all too clear, as I had known it would be, that I was in the wrong place and with the wrong credentials. "Let me ask you this," Crowell said, getting up from his desk and nodding in the direction of the door, "was Maine one of the original thirteen states?" I hesitated. "Well, if you've learned anything today, it's that the answer is *no*. Maine was not one of the original thirteen states. It was part of Massachusetts until 1820. Thanks for stopping by." I waited in the parking lot for a few minutes until the trembling stopped enough for me to start the car.

By the time of this encounter things were beginning to look up, somewhat. I had met Herbert Alexander, editor in chief of Pocket Books, and started doing freelance work for him. Alexander represented a relatively new style in New York book publishing—Jewish, brash, impatient, and splashy. At about the same time, an editor in all ways antithetic to him, Edward Dodd Jr. of Dodd, Mead, and Company, invited me back to his office, having apparently, to my surprise, remembered me from a job interview a month earlier. Dodd was a third-generation principal in a thrifty old-line family business that had its first successes in the 1870s with Sunday school books. His company now published George Bernard Shaw's *Complete Prefaces and Plays*, Winston Churchill's *History of the English-Speaking Peoples*, and a torrent of books, with more to come from a cache of manuscripts in the company safe, by the late Frederick Schiller Faust, better known as Max Brand, "king of the pulps." Dodd took me out to my first publishing lunch—tuna fish sandwiches and Cokes at a drugstore counter on Park Avenue South—and proposed that I edit an anthology of misogynist writings, eventually titled *With Malice Toward Women: A Handbook for Woman-Haters Drawn from the Best Minds of All Time*. This depraved idea must already have been turned down by any number of prospects Dodd had approached. But he was offering me a real publishing contract, even though it was for the commission of a low editorial deed.

When it came to discussing contract terms, Dodd Junior took me into another office and handed me over to Dodd Senior, chairman of the board. There was something Dickensian about this intergenerational arrangement, a musty air of the counting house with clerks on high stools wielding asthmatic quill pens. It wouldn't have been altogether surprising if Junior called Senior "Aged P." Without a word of comment on the book itself (you could hardly blame him for this), Dodd Senior put a question to me. "Would you like an advance?" I told him I didn't know. "Well, let me tell you about advances," he said. "An advance in a book contract is a sum of money the author takes from the publisher for work he hasn't done yet. Taking an advance from a publisher is exactly like borrowing money. Are you in debt to your bank? Do you have a mortgage or car loan? Are you behind in your bills?" I said no, of course not. "In that case, you don't want an advance," and that was that. I had a lot to learn about book contracts.

In six months of intermittent library work I put together an anthology of misogynist writing that included classical sources and the more repellent church fathers as well as Nietzsche, H. L. Mencken, and D. H. Lawrence, all of this brightened in spirit and appearance by James Thurber's drawings for his *War Between Men and Women*. In my painfully composed introductions I tried to stand above the issue, a fatal error in a book of satire. Duly published in the United States and in England, banned for some reason in the

Irish Republic, my book slipped out of sight almost instantly. I never again heard a word from either Dodd Junior or Dodd Senior.

For almost five years, starting in 1950, I worked for Harry N. Abrams, formerly a board member, advertising manager, and production manager of the Book-of-the-Month Club. A long way back, he had hoped to be a painter and had enrolled at the Art Students League. Now he was willing to stake every dollar he owned on a bold and risky venture: to publish quality art books, and art books only. No American publisher before Harry had dared enter into head-to-head competition with prestigious European firms like Phaidon, Hyperion, Pierre Tisné, and Albert Skira. Harry was Napoleon-like in drive, temperament, and vision—he went forward with his idea in the face of doom predictions by nearly everyone in the publishing business. He was something of a bully as well. His editorial director, Milton Fox, who had moved from Cleveland with his family to take this job, often left Harry's office after one of their set-tos with tears in his eyes. Harry's moods at work shifted without warning from sweet reasonableness, cajoling, and arm-squeezing wheedle to red-faced abusive rage and a self-absorption so intense that for a moment you doubted your own existence. In one of his fits of inadvertence he handed me the Christmas bonus envelope intended for the elevator man. He wasn't the least bit embarrassed when I handed it back to him.

When level-headed, Harry was capable of shrewd and imaginative decisions. One of these was to recruit as advisory editor the legendary art historian, critic, and polymath, Columbia University professor Meyer Schapiro, then in his midforties. I spent Saturday mornings with him in the cramped and cluttered little study of his house on West Fourth Street. Several times I found him on the floor hidden behind his desk—doing exercises for back trouble—

but he carried on as if he were in the lecture hall at Columbia. We were supposed to be editing the introductory essays Harry had commissioned from scholars and museum directors for his first wave of books, to be published under the grand series title *The Library of Great Painters*. Whatever their eminence and store of scholarship most of his writers couldn't write at all and needed drastic remediation.

We also worked over Meyer's own essay on Van Gogh which, he said, would not discuss the famous mutilated ear, the only thing the general public seemed to know about Van Gogh biographically except for his dementia and suicide. For all Meyer's brilliance and dazzling fluency as a lecturer he tended to cramp up when it came to putting ideas down on paper. Presumptuous as this was, and he was invariably patient with my suggestions and tolerant of my ignorance of the visual arts, I tried to get him to relax, let a little breathing space into his densely packed arguments, and doff the "Indian suit," as we called it, that he put on to address other big chiefs instead of simple braves. Please write for me, I said, and he did his best. We sped through the working part of these Saturday sessions, leaving the rest of the morning free for what turned out to be an extraordinary free-ranging tutorial. Meyer could hold forth on practically any subject in the world, except maybe ice hockey and tropical fish, and out of memory supply reading lists in a couple of languages. He considered Bernard Berenson—like him a native of Lithuania—to be something of a fraud, both as an art historian and as a celebrity who occasionally referred to his "Puritan forebears" and Anglo-Saxon extraction: Berenson's ancestors, Meyer commented dryly, must have been "rabbis on the *Mayflower*." In ten minutes he gave me more ideas about Jules Verne and nineteenth-century technology, for example, than I had been able to accumulate in months of reading on my own. Time spent with the great Meyer Schapiro was that pot of gold at the end of the rainbow—a reward suddenly and extravagantly bestowed—that the New York of the 1950s promised and delivered.

Harry's fledgling company was always undercapitalized (he had put most of his own savings into it) and shorthanded, even when established enough to be moved from his East Seventieth Street apartment, where we did layouts on the living room floor, to offices downtown. In emergencies he sent me out to supervise expensive four-color printing runs at plants in Manhattan and Philadelphia. I did my best to fake an air of confidence and command with press foremen who of course realized right away I knew nothing about color printing and paid no attention to me when I told them to lighten up on the yellow or offered similar shaky advice. I was even somewhat color-blind in the green-blue range. These outings, for all the anxiety they generated in me, still felt like a vacation from the daily office routine of composing, often on Harry's capricious demand—"I need you right away to put on your Renoir hat"—the prose commentaries, gray blocks of print, that for potential consumers filled up the page opposite the glorious, hand-tipped color plates, the reason for buying the book in the first place. "One's eye keeps wandering back to that lovely face," I wrote in one of my excursions in art appreciation, "its doll-like perfection set off by playful wisps of hair which keep this beauty from cloying. If painting can be compared with music, surely this canvas is Mozartian."

Harry was even less qualified than I to write this sort of fluff, and I think he put a low value on all prose except for direct-mail and advertising copy. Having once hoped to be a painter he was now a collector of sorts, starting with the work of an immigrant Russian artist whose men and women all looked like freshly dug baking potatoes. Harry moved on from him to minor and affordable works by major contemporary painters. Subsequently, obedient to trends of the late 1950s, he traded everything in for pop art.

He once called me into his office to translate for him a letter he had just received from Paris. The writer identified himself as an artist who years earlier, destitute then as now, had painted a number of pictures that he signed and sold as the work of the French expressionist Chaim Soutine. At this point, seeing the expression of growing consternation on Harry's face and remembering what traditionally happens to bearers of bad news, I was tempted to fudge the rest of the letter, but it was too late. The writer went on to say he understood that one of these so-called Soutines occupied a place of honor in Monsieur Abrams's collection. He wished now to inform Monsieur Abrams of his willingness, for a price and with his travel expenses covered, to come to New York, sign his name to the work in question, and in doing so free the distinguished collector from the embarrassment of harboring, and in a sense abetting, a forgery.

Poor Harry! Instead of raging he looked as if he was going to cry. In the jargon of dealers and collectors, his "Soutine" had been "attributed down," way down, lower even than the Russian potato master, whose work was at least authentic. I felt sorry for him then and another time, when the battery fell out of his rust-eaten Buick as we were driving along Tenth Avenue in heavy truck traffic. It was hard not to feel a twinge of sympathy for a bully who was accustomed to winning, but even this had limits. My work space was a rickety table that looked out on a dark air shaft; mounds of pigeon droppings covered the outer windowsill. Harry ignored my appeals for improvement in these conditions, and one day I simply walked off the job and said I could be reached downstairs at a local bar, the Gamecock, on East Forty-fourth Street. I had a couple of beers, watched some soap opera television, and waited until the office manager came down to tell me Harry had caved and a con-

189

tractor finally called in. Harry remained distant from me for several days, as if I had betrayed him by extracting such a concession.

But even with this token victory it was clear to me that working for Harry and ghosting prose for his "sumptuous" (the obligatory advertising adjective) picture books was a dead end. Maybe I ought to get out of publishing altogether, I thought, and go into social work, where I could do some good by alleviating misery and want. I consulted my friend and adviser, Herbert Alexander, who told me the way to flush such goofy career ideas from my system was to sign up for the vocational testing program at Stevens Institute of Technology, across the river in Hoboken. I worked my way through a month of six-hour Saturday sessions—written tests, spatial puzzles, and interviews that probed and supposedly measured every imaginable aptitude and interest. The results, presented to me in my final session at Stevens Institute, showed that my helping-other-people impulses barely registered while my verbal-interest scores went off the chart. For better or worse, that was that, as far as service to humanity was concerned. I later learned that Jack Goodman, a top editor at Simon and Schuster, had gone through the same testing program only to be told he was cut out to be a civil engineer.

PART III

CHAPTER 9

Soon after Annie and I became engaged, a psychologist we met at a party told us we were the worst imaginable marital risk. Each of us was the younger sibling in a family of two same-sex offspring, and younger siblings, he said, being as a rule demanding, dependent, and self-centered from infancy on, proved unable to meet the needs of similarly disadvantaged partners in marriage. We had heard that more than one of every three American marriages ended in divorce, and that was bad enough. But this prognosis, supported, the psychologist said, by statistical evidence gathered in his researches at Brandeis, appeared to be as dire as if he had identified in us a rare blood disease. The 1950s was "the age of psychology," according to a series of articles in *Life*, a time when the mind and behavioral sciences, as popularly understood, had an almost scriptural weight. We listened politely and even respectfully as he handed down his verdict, accepted his sardonic, slightly Vienna-accented good wishes, and went on our way to what he believed was certain disaster.

We had met in the fall of 1953, saw each other almost exclusively during the winter, became engaged in the spring, and married in July; in September we went to Italy and England on our honeymoon. It had all happened much faster than most of the marriages we knew of among our friends. Early on, maybe after our third or fourth date, I had invited Annie to dinner at my apartment on Thirty-seventh Street. I wanted the evening to be just right. Georgia Edwards, the West Indian woman who had brought me up from infancy, agreed to cook the dinner, shrimp creole with rice. The day before I bought six place settings of white Arzberg chinaware along with proper wineglasses and linen napkins. The other guests—Fielder Cook, a television director, and his actress wife, Sally; an art historian, Sam Hunter; and his fiancée, Edys Merrill, a painter—supplied a plausible setting for an evening that might otherwise look like a prelude to attempted seduction. (I had in mind, as suggesting a precedent to be avoided, a cartoon that showed a leering host greeting his date at the door of his apartment: "*We're* the party!") A few nights later Annie came over alone and, as we talked, picked up from the coffee table a little bronze horse figure, supposedly Etruscan, that I had bought a few years earlier from an antiquarian in Rome. She asked me for some metal polish and a cloth, applied herself to the horse and, as I looked on, went about removing perhaps two thousand years of verdigris. What she was doing was so intimate, spontaneous, and innocently abstracted that I couldn't say "Stop!" I even felt a sort of somber delight as I ran my fingers over my denuded horse.

Annie still lived with her parents. In February we went away for a ski weekend in New Hampshire. Caught in a snowstorm on the way, we spent our first night as a couple in a Manchester commercial hotel after decorously registering for separate rooms. Soon after, we were together almost every evening and often on our lunch hours. On Sunday mornings she would come over with a bag of croissants from a French bakery around the corner from her parents' house. One evening she announced that her analyst had told her it was all right for her to think of getting married. It had all happened so naturally.

We were caught up with each other, with overcoming our shyness, discovering our capacity for play and humor, and with being young, healthy, and at home in the city. We went to the New York City Ballet, to Ralph Kirkpatrick's harpsichord recitals at Town Hall, to the movies (rarely to "films") as often as we could—*Shane, From Here to Eternity, Rear Window, On the Waterfront, Stalag 17, Roman Holiday*. We didn't have much time for reading. We didn't think a great deal about the future or about careers (we both had editorial jobs in publishing), never discussed money or (except jokingly) the old status tussle between German Jews (her people) and Russian Jews (mine). Even after we decided to marry we gave no conscious thought at all to the prospect of children. Children were so remote from my own experience—I had never touched or held an infant much less ministered to one—that for me they weren't even conceivable.

Annie had a core of sweetness, shrewdness, and merriment. She was my idea of the fully realized 1950s Girl of the City (and of no other): immensely attractive, a proto-feminist, self-assured, easily amused, wary of anything pretentious, street-smart, privileged without ostentation or snobbery, comfortable with luxury but unspoiled by it, and professional minded: she had been Barnard campus correspondent for the *New York Times* and was

195

now managing editor of *discovery*, a quarterly of new writing published by Pocket Books. I thought she was near perfect except for her initial reluctance (quickly eroded) to joke about "serious" things; her objection (also transitory) to "bad" language; and her looking askance at my drinking martinis before dinner (her previous boyfriend, a writer for television, had been a lush). My record of promiscuity, if she was at all aware of it, didn't seem to bother her.

Of more concern to her, although briefly, were my male friends, many of them homosexual or sexually indeterminate, relatively dissolute, or, as was the case with my college friend Bernard Winebaum, all of the foregoing in addition to being preoccupied with giving and going to parties. She and Bernie adored each other at first sight. She minded that I couldn't dance, was a Yankee fan, did not admire Adlai Stevenson (I thought he was a snob and a born loser), and was mostly silent instead of casually communicative when we looked at pictures in museums and galleries. We had made up our minds to marry with little recognition of the demands of living with another person: patience, humor, and flexibility tempered by resignation and inertia. Maybe it was not love alone that defied normal prudence and caution but the psychic climate we lived in. Our outlook had been formed by a collision of forces: the postwar, almost utopian exuberance that made all good things appear possible, and the nuclear arms race, pursued to the brink, that transformed the city's subways and basements into one big fallout shelter. We seized the day, hoped for the best, and took short views.

Annie's parents had no patience with short views: for them a life not planned ahead in at least five- or ten-year units was a life abandoned to chaos and irresponsibility. As a prospective son-in-law, when Annie first told them about me, her parents probably would have preferred a (high-caste) Hindu to a Russian Jew, Harvard apart, from the other side of Central Park. Their first response to a potential wrenching of their social order was plain disbelief. "You must be joking!" Annie's mother told her. Over a few weeks their incredulity declined into wariness, cautious acceptance, and even a degree of warmth. But they were formidable and exacting, and I broke into a sweat whenever I entered the Gothic mahogany-paneled foyer of their double house on East Sixty-third Street. At dinner with them one night, placed with my back to an active fireplace, I could as well have been a planked shad ready to be deboned. Whether placing me close to a pile of burning logs, to roast there like a heretic, was mischief or accident I couldn't tell.

Although polite, Edward and Doris Bernays voiced powerful opinions that combined moralism and hair-trigger disapproval with a fiercely practical view of how the world should work. According to Annie they had recently expunged from their guest list a lawyer who had got tipsy at one of their dinner parties as well as a doctor and a *Newsweek* editor suspected of carrying on an adulterous relationship. Edward and Doris exerted force in tandem, like a span of matched horses, and were used to being in command and equally unused to being challenged. Eventually I

A.B., New Hampshire skiing
weekend, winter 1954.

devised sly and oblique strategies for putting them off balance—by answering their questions with questions, for example, or dealing in deliberate non sequiturs. In Doris, but not her husband, I found a congenial element of irony. When apart from him she eased up on their collective rectitude and allowed herself cigarettes and more than one cocktail. She took Annie and me out to a festive lunch at Carlton House on Madison Avenue and congratulated me on winning the hand of "the last remaining virgin in New York City." We all drank to that.

When Annie and I first met I knew nothing about her father, Edward L. Bernays, except his name, which I had often noticed in the credit line—"Courtesy of Edward L. Bernays"—whenever the *New York Times Book Review* ran a picture of Sigmund Freud holding a cigar. I learned right away that Edward was not simply the proprietor of rights to the official portrait that scowled down at patients from the walls of nearly every orthodox psychoanalyst's office. He was also Freud's double nephew, a genealogical knot that took a deep breath and slow-motion untying whenever it was explained to me: brother and sister from one Viennese family had married sister and brother of another, an arrangement that sounded unholy but was 100 percent kosher once you understood it. Sometimes mocked as "a professional nephew," Edward was justifiably proprietary about his uncle: as a young man he had arranged for the first translations of Freud's work to be published in America. He regarded Freudian theory as a historically important intellectual commodity that offered valuable insights into mass behavior, but he had no use at all for it in his own life and could barely tolerate the fact that he had permitted his daughter to see a psychoanalyst. He himself would as soon consult a gypsy palm reader to find out which way the wind blew. His unconscious was nobody's business, not even his own.

In Edward's view, and that of his disciples, he was the Father of

Public Relations, a profession I knew nothing about. When I did learn something about it from Edward it was a little like being told there was a secret government. Edward believed that the counsel on public relations (a job title he invented) acted as the guardian of capitalist democracy, a behind-the-scenes philosopher-king and wizard who, supported by opinion and policy experts, told governments, corporations, and societies in general what was good for them. Public relations introduced corporate giants to benevolent, enlightened, and endearing policies, thus maintaining their interests, and the public's as well, in gainful equilibrium as they walked together along a two-way street of "information, persuasion, and adjustment." Edward was a passionately sincere believer in the social value of public relations, possessed brilliance, flair, and imagination in practicing it, and was extravagantly rewarded for what he did. He insisted that nothing had value unless it was visible and publicly acknowledged. The title alone of one of his books, *The Engineering of Consent*, chilled me to the bone because it treated democratic society like a big child. He refused to consider himself Jewish in any binding or meaningful way, dismissing as "the higher hokum" all religion, however disorganized. We argued about these things, sometimes heatedly, and kept our juices at a healthy boil.

Because of Edward's horror of clergy and of any taint of religious ritual Annie and I were married in the living room of 163 East Sixty-third Street by a New York State judge recruited for the task. My brother was my best man. A hundred people wilted in the late July heat and waited for the bar to open while the judge carried on, inexplicably and at exasperating length, about William Shakespeare. As arranged by Edward and Doris without consultation with either of the principals, this was a full fig wedding, from the policeman stationed on the street outside to the tailcoat that encased the bridegroom and the tossing of the bridal bouquet.

CHAPTER 10

Every week or so I left our *discovery* office and walked up three blocks to where our parent, Pocket Books, Inc., occupied the entire twenty-seventh floor of 630 Fifth Avenue, posh premises. I was there, in Bob Kotlowitz's office one late fall day in 1953, when I noticed a young man standing in the doorway of Bob's office, peering in at us. The man was wearing a Harris Tweed overcoat and a long green cashmere scarf he had wound once around his neck, leaving most of it hanging gracefully down his back. I was transfixed by the arrangement of scarf and body and wondered, for the briefest moment, whether this display said something I might not want to hear, for instance, that he liked boys better than girls, or that he was hopelessly in love with himself. I hardly bothered to look at the face above the scarf.

"It's cousin Joe," Bob said. "What are you doing here?"

This Joe said, "You haven't heard?" and went on to explain that Pocket Books and Abrams were collaborating on a series of art books. Cousin Joe, it seemed, was its general editor.

Bob introduced us. "This is Justin Kaplan," he said. "His friends and relatives call him Joe." Justin—or Joe—said hello in a surprisingly light and gentle voice. I asked him how he was related to Bob. Bob answered for him: Bob's wife, Billy, was a first cousin of Joe's cousin Jerry's wife, Eleanor. Did that make Bob and Joe cousins? I didn't think so. This answer reminded me of the way my father insisted I was related to James Joyce: "Your mother's brother's first wife's second husband was the son of James Joyce." The beads were not on the same string, and yet if you were proud of any connection at all, you could, for the sake of the pride, pretend that they were. I had recently met Justin's first cousin Leon; the two men looked so much alike, they could easily have been taken for brothers: both had assertive jaws and noses, dark hair, and emphatically intelligent expressions. The Kaplan genes were evidently powerful.

I stared at the scarf, amazed at its pulsating green-ness, its softness. Its owner seemed shy and not especially forthcoming, but there was something about him that adhered, like the smell of strong perfume on a woman who has left the room.

My current boyfriend, Paul, and I had, without consciously admitting it, come to a fork in the road of life from where he was about to take off one way and I another. The main problem was that I wasn't sure that he wasn't more attached to the bottle than he was to me. We endured a prolonged and painful severing, like pulling a Band-Aid off slowly so it won't hurt so much, and of

201

course it should be done in one swift yank, but we really loved each other and couldn't bear the idea that we might never see each other again. As all this was going on I felt, buried in my brain, a fragment, a pun based on Mr. Kaplan's name, that would not be dislodged: Just-in case—just in case I'm cast on the shore alone again.

It took me and Paul several months to pull the Band-Aid all the way off, and when it was done, a stinging raw spot was left underneath. Melancholy, I asked Bob if he could arrange a lunch date for him, me, and cousin Joe. I couldn't figure out any other way of seeing him again without looking desperate and aggressive; a girl could wait until she turned into Miss Havisham.

The lunch date was swiftly accomplished. On the day and time agreed upon, Bob and I walked over to the Golden Horn, on the northern border of Rockefeller Center, where Joe was waiting inside the door. This was one of the first upscale Middle Eastern restaurants in New York, a cavernous room entirely fitted in white: white curtains, tablecloths, napkins. The waiters wore knee-length white aprons. It seemed as if the air was white with a kind of dry mist. There were only a few other customers in the place, one a man by himself, reading a book. We had plenty to talk about. A week or so earlier two young men, Dennis Wepman and Harlow Fraden, had dispatched Fraden's parents by forcing them to drink an arsenic-laced daiquiri. The two boys had taken what money there was lying around, booked a room in the Essex House, and holed up there until serious bickering began and Wepman tried to stave in Fraden's head with a telephone he'd ripped from the wall. Wepman had worked briefly in Pocket Books' mail room and Bob knew him—Bob had actually talked to a cold-blooded murderer. Their story kept the three of us afloat through my sudden and Joe's seemingly permanent reticence.

Halfway through the meal, the ambient sense of drama abruptly escalated when a waiter, serving the book-reading diner, upturned a large platter of gummy white soup into the man's lap. It was like a silent movie: Man rises to his feet, looks down in disbelief as the stuff dribbles over his front while waiter tries to brush soup from man's pants with napkin. Man angrily pushes waiter's arm away. Headwaiter rushes over, points to kitchen door, banishing waiter. Soup victim stalks out of restaurant without paying. It seemed as if the episode had been performed solely for the three of us, although its message was unclear.

There was no way to top this incident; we finished our exotic meal, somewhat unnerved but sated, not so much on the food—*baba ghanoush*, salad with chopped mint, spiced lamb—as on the tableau of the overturned soup plate.

"What kind of soup was that?" I said to Bob as we walked back to our office. "It looked like library paste."

"It must have been tapioca soup," he said. "Good thing it was cold."

"Do you think he's going to call me?"

"Who, Joe? You must be kidding," he said. "Cousin Joe is smitten."

"What makes you think so?" I said.

"Enough," Bob said. "Just wait and see."

Cousin Joe called me less than a week after the Soup Lunch and asked me to meet him the following day. I usually ate lunch with one of my friends, Francine or Marian, or alone at a hamburger place or, if he was free, with my boss, Vance Bourjaily, at a cafeteria on Forty-seventh Street west of Fifth that Vance called the Tel Aviv Café for its almost exclusively Hasidic clientele. Once a week or so, Bob Kotlowitz and I walked around the corner to the American Bar and Grill on Sixth Avenue, where I had convinced our favorite waitress that Bob was Glenn Ford, the movie star, whom he eerily resembled. But a lunch date with a prospective boyfriend put things at a different depth. It meant dressing up. It meant being careful of what you said and what you revealed about yourself. Joe asked me to meet him at Maison A. deWinter, a French place, on the southern border of Rockefeller Center, our hub. The restaurant was on the second floor, in what had once been the front parlor of a milk-chocolate-colored brownstone house, very subdued. I was nervous; cousin Joe was perspiring and ashen. He focused on the menu. "The calf's brains are very good here; they're cooked in black butter and served with capers," Joe said. "Would you like to try them?"

Unaware until that moment that I was weighing him in as a possible mate, I decided right then that I could never marry a man who ate brains for lunch—or, as far as that went, for any other meal.

"I think I'll have the salade niçoise," I said.

Like a car with transmission problems, we had trouble keeping a conversation moving forward. Question, followed by answer, followed by silence. I did manage to learn that Joe's mother had died when he was six, his father when he was thirteen, both of cancer, and that he had been raised by his aunt Frances, his older brother, Howard, and Georgia Edwards, a woman from St. Kitts who had come to work for the family Kaplan when Joe was an infant and was still working for Howard.

When the brains arrived—via a dumbwaiter—I had to admit that they looked almost edible, something like sweetbreads or pale scrambled eggs. Cousin Joe dug in.

The lunch dragged on, my mind adrift. Although Joe was undeniably sweet, smart, and sexy, he seemed too private and cov-

204

ered to divulge anything a woman could use to build on. As we said good-bye at the bottom of the brownstone's stoop, cousin Joe's pallor had deepened and sweat poured down both cheeks.

"You're not feeling well, are you?" I said.

"Not really," he said. "I think I'll just go home and go to bed."

When I got back to *discovery*'s office, Vance asked me how it had gone. I told him that cousin Joe was a mute. Also, there appeared to be something wrong with him. Malaria? Something more dire?

When Joe called me a few days later he said that he'd gone straight home after the Brains Lunch, taken his temperature, which turned out to be 103, and lay in his bed with the flu, shivering and spiking a fever for the next three days.

I asked him why he'd kept our lunch date when he was so sick. "I couldn't bear to break it," he said.

The next time I saw Cousin Joe was at the apartment he'd been living in for a year or so on Thirty-seventh Street off First Avenue, near the East Side Airlines Terminal. I'd never been that far east before except to leave the city. The apartment was in a pale brick postwar building devoid of any architectural character whatsoever, hastily put up, aesthetically careless. Joe had invited me to a small dinner party in his home, number 303. About to push the buzzer, I was abruptly reminded of a recent *New Yorker* cartoon: a leering older guy opens the door to a ripe young thing and says "Party? Why, my dear, *we're* the party!" I took a deep breath and pushed anyway. Cousin Joe answered. I looked past him into the living room. It was a space so small it could have fit into my house's downstairs foyer, with room left over. I thought it was adorable. Two couples were already there when I arrived, a TV director, Fielder Cook, and his wife and an art historian, Sam Hunter, and girlfriend, to whom I was carefully introduced by Joe, who said my name in a way that had it dripping with honey. The director's wife, Sally Chamberlain, was a soap opera actress, delicately pretty. The historian's girlfriend, Edys Merrill, was an energetic painter, larger than her husband. There was a woman in the kitchen, cooking, I supposed, our dinner. Joe introduced us: "This is Georgia Edwards," he said. "She's the woman who raised me." Georgia administered a psychic X ray, unsmiling.

For most of the evening I listened. A good deal of the talk was about people I didn't know and had never heard of. Edys told a story about how her mother, snooping, had found her diaphragm in a suitcase and, apparently never having seen one before, asked Edys what it was, and Edys told her mother it was a paint strainer and her mother believed it. We all laughed like crazy. Every so often Joe would fill in a missing piece of exposition. He smiled at me as if he couldn't quite believe I was there. We ate shrimp creole with rice and a sweet dessert. Then there was coffee in Arzberg cups of porcelain. This was, I figured, cousin Joe's nod to ordinary middle-class props.

Just-in case was slowly becoming Just-in time. Playing with the words this way made marriage seem more a game than what I recognized as an appalling decision. I knew myself well enough to recognize that, when it came to most men—with a couple of notable exceptions—I was a regular firefly, never staying still long enough to adhere. I fell in love at least once a month, desperately in love. After a few weeks of infatuation, the sting of love would start to wear off. What, if anything, distinguished Justin from the others? Why shouldn't I tire of him just as quickly? I hesitated. He was too quiet, too baffled by reticence. But he was adorable— sweet, a little sad, greatly humorous, generous, and blessed with what teachers call "character," and Jews call *Menschlichkeit*.

206   I told my mother I had met someone I liked, telling her his

name, saying it in a tone that would signal he was not like my other boyfriends. My mother immediately asked me about what she called his background, without having to explain that she wanted to know what sort of Jew he was—the acceptable German kind or the unsuitable others. She was playing solitaire in my parents' bedroom while my father slept, a scene so familiar as to seem ordinary. I told her Joe's father had landed on Ellis Island, via steerage from Hamburg, and that his people were originally from Russia. How I enjoyed presenting her with this unsavory morsel. She frowned at it. "By the way," I said, "what's the difference between a Galitzianer and a Litwak?" two words I had learned only recently. She said, "They're both bad." I told her Joe had been orphaned very early. This didn't seem to please her either. "When do I get to meet this Joe Kaplan?" she asked.

"How about dinner next weekend?"

"I'll have to ask Eddie," she said, but I could tell it would happen.

When he arrived at our house for dinner, wearing his best suit, he began to perspire like a runner at full throttle. My parents were polite but wary, house cats to whom a new dog has been introduced. For his part, Joe wasn't used to being examined so finely and the sweat flowed on, his discomfort not improved by the fact that my father had seated him at the dining room table with his back to the fireplace, where a wood fire burned merrily. Later, he told me he felt like a planked shad being slowly immolated. And what did he think of my parents? "Formidable."

A couple of weeks went by during which I kept rubbing the magic bottle while the genie remained stubbornly inside. How to get him to fly out? I figured that since he worked for an art book publisher, he must like or at least know a lot about painting. "Where would you like to go on Saturday?" Joe said over the phone. "How about the Met?" I said.

He picked me up at my house on Sixty-third Street and we walked up Fifth Avenue in silence to the museum, where we left our coats in the cloakroom and climbed the wide marble staircase—in silence—to the second floor. There we began to tour halls containing some of the world's most celebrated art. Silence surrounded us. Every so often, I would say, "Look at that." Joe would look at that. At last, feeling as if I too were sealed inside a bottle, I said, "What are your enthusiasms?"

I had never before asked a question remotely like this one, and as soon as it left my tongue it rang stupidly in my ears, a donkey braying. Embarrassed, I said, "What do you like?"

"I like that," he said, pointing to a landscape by Cézanne. He seemed to be as embarrassed as I was. Why was he so shy? Why did he turn his eyes from my face when talking to me? Was I willing to work hard enough to pull out the stopper?

Well, I was, for I had already formed a strong idea of who this person was, and he was unlike anyone I had known. He had the brains of Anatole but not his vanity; the style of Ian but neither his chill nor his social imperatives. Joe wasn't cut from the same bolt of cloth as the men my parents wanted me to go out with—lawyers, businessmen, doctors, people not about to question their own certainties. Joe wasn't buying the line that leads inevitably to a "successful career." How I knew this is part of the story of the two of us, a continual revelation, some secrets never disclosed at all, the sweet, musky scent of the mysterious. He certainly didn't say anything remotely like: "I set my own metronome, use my brain where and when and how I want; like what I like, reject what I don't—and make gentle—and sometimes fierce—fun of almost everything." He would never have articulated any of this, but I heard him say it silently and I was very much drawn to it; I would soon became as iconoclastic as Cousin Joe, while maintaining the skin of a well-tempered middle-class wife and mother. I loved our disguise.

Cousin Joe and I were married in the house I had long considered a temporary residence, first, and obviously, because I hoped to move away as soon as I had a good reason to, but also because it was branded indelibly by my parents' taste and style, neither of which I wanted to duplicate. Not that I didn't appreciate money, but I wanted my life to be less grand and gaudy than my parents', quieter, more covert.

As if imitating Sergei Diaghilev, the Ballet Russe impresario he had worked for as a press agent in his youth, my father produced the entire wedding, relying on his assistant, my mother, to supply the less important props, like menu, flowers, tablecloths, and hors d'oeuvres. Together they worked out how the drama was to be played, failing to consult me on a single detail, except to make sure I wasn't going to be menstruating on Thursday, July 29. The day they picked turned out to be the hottest day of the sum-

After the ceremony. *From left to right:* Richard Held (Doris Bernays' husband), Doris, Justin, Anne, Edward Bernays, Doris Fleischman, Howard Kaplan (Justin's brother).

mer of 1954; the humidity almost matched the temperature, both in the high nineties. The living room was plastered with banks of white flowers tied up with wide satin ribbon, enough for the funeral of a minor movie star. I wore my sister's fitted satin dress with a score of tiny, satin-covered buttons up the back and a long slippery train. Joe rented a formal outfit with striped pants, its black tailcoat cut from the sort of heavy-gauge wool used for cold-weather overcoats. Rivers of perspiration, inspired by heat and terror, coursed down his face and soaked the rented suit. My mother's cousin's husband, Erich Leinsdorf, conductor of the Metropolitan Opera Company's orchestra, sat down at our Steinway Baby Grand and played the traditional wedding march. This startled me as my father and I entered the cavernous living room. Folding chairs held sweating guests bathed by warm air circulating in front of two huge standing fans. This musical flourish was a last-minute touch that no one had told me about; so was the plan to have Erich's red-haired five-year-old daughter, Hester, carry my train. She followed me, clutching it like a life preserver, to the far end of the room, only tripping once and nearly pulling me over backward. My father had asked a municipal judge named Irving Ben Cooper, a dapper self-important person with a salt-and-pepper Errol Flynn–type mustache, to perform the ceremony. It never occurred to me or Joe to question my father's selection of Judge Cooper, or any other arrangement. To do so would have meant a loud, accusatory argument, which my father would win anyway. I figured his money and pride trumped my own misgivings about having a complete stranger marry us, and unable to come up with an alternate—certainly not a clergyman—I kept my mouth shut. Joe, I found out later, didn't want to make trouble, nor did he think it important enough to object—though given the opportunity he said he would have preferred almost anyone else so long as he had talked to at least one of us before our wedding day.

Judge Cooper stood with his back to the fireplace and married us, using a secular text. He glowed, he expanded in this minuscule limelight, reminding Joe that "you love Shakespeare," and evoking yet more drops of embarrassment. When the ceremony, such as it was, was over at last, the judge kissed my hand. Then the new couple, their families and guests went downstairs to the wood-paneled dining room, where a buffet of crabmeat and chicken salad, asparagus and individual ice cream bombes catered and served by Sherry's was awaiting us. Tables had been set up in the backyard. The party lasted all afternoon.

The new couple spent the night in the bridal suite of the Sherry-Netherland Hotel, where the Bernays family had lived for two years and whose manager, a White Russian emigré named Serge Obolensky, was a tight friend of my father's. A basket of flowers and fruit was waiting for us in the suite. We went to Martha's Vineyard for the weekend and were back at our respective jobs the following Monday.

For us, 1954 and 1955 were the years of the honeymoon. My parents had given us a trip to Europe as a wedding present, and in early September we boarded the U.S.S. *Constitution* and sailed to Italy. We had a room in a small hotel on Capri near the sea with a balcony where we gazed at the water and had our morning espresso and croissants. One night Joe went for a solo walk after I'd gone to bed. Instead of falling sleep, I was gripped by a breathtaking spasm of anxiety, absolutely certain he would never come back—a fear irrational enough to be terrifying. This had not happened to me since I was nine when, over a period of a couple of months, I was obsessed with the idea that my parents were planning to put me in an orphan asylum in upstate New York. When Joe walked into the room an hour later I was too scared and relieved to talk. From that moment, the long buried fear of being taken to a strange place and there forsaken came out of its hole and ate into my pleasure when-

211

ever we went somewhere new and I was left alone for more than a few minutes.

We made our way up the Italian boot, stopping for a few days in Rome (my first exposure to the sound of the Vespa, a small motorized two-wheel vehicle that thrummed through the streets like a giant bee night and day), where we gaped at the Coliseum. We stopped at the usual tourist places, traveling in relative luxury, thanks to my parents—Florence, where we spent hours in the Uffizi and picked up a rented Fiat (whose pedals were too close together for Joe's feet), in which we drove, hair-raisingly, over the Apennines, visiting the medieval hill town of San Gimignano, where we took soulful pictures of each other sitting on a stone slab next to a stone tower hundreds of years old. In Bologna we ate a gourmet lunch in a restaurant someone back home had recommended, telling us that if we failed to eat there we would miss the meal of a lifetime. I ordered half a chicken disguised as poulet Margaret-Rose. It was pretty good. Following an imaginary tourist's primer, we were oared up and down canals in a Venetian gondola and fed the pigeons in St. Mark's Square. Milan was our

J.K. and A.B. on honeymoon, Rome, 1954.

last Italian stopping place. Here we read in the *International Herald Tribune* about the pope's worrisome hiccups which had lasted more than a week, and the latest municipal scandal: the architect of the brand-new Milan airport had forgotten to put a staircase between the first and second floors. From Milan we flew frighteningly over the Alps to London, where some of the Freud family lived. My father had armed me with a small book of telephone numbers, among which was that of Ernst Freud, Sigmund's oldest son, an architect. Over the phone, his wife, Lucy, a naturally affectionate woman invited us to dinner with their son, Lucien, whom she said was a painter. Lucien, a thin and pale man a few years older than me, had darting eyes. He was handsome and offhand, in a haunted-artist kind of way. I hadn't been aware of it, but breakneck traveling to places where you don't know the geography or the language, with a shy man you have never lived with, draws heavily on reserves of nerve and stamina that need some respite. Once inside the large Freud house in Hampstead, I fell into Lucy's arms as if she were a mother and was reminding myself that my mother was neither warm nor affectionate, even as I knew, from the way her eyes had always followed me, that she wanted desperately to be both and simply didn't know how.

We stayed in England for about a week, visiting Oxford on a chill and gray day. The university, where we knew no one, seemed merely an ungiving, rain-streaked cluster of gray stone. I was anxious to get home. On the trip back, the *Île de France*, the French equivalent of the British *Queen Elizabeth*, hit rough North Atlantic weather. The ship rolled, pitched, and yawed, clearing the dining rooms and promenade decks; no one could walk without holding on to something; unsecured items crashed to the floor, young men in white uniforms scurried around battening down every loose item. As I left the game room to go down to our cabin, where I intended to die of seasickness, I had to sidestep a stewardess

213

throwing up on the staircase carpet. In the habit of reading signs and portents into ordinary events, it was hard for me not to view this sickening voyage as ominous. But it turned out to be just another ordinary crossing for that time of year. My parents met us at the dock, and after a short visit with them, I entered 303 East Thirty-seventh Street, relieved to be home.

A second honeymoon, in April of 1955, sent us to Santa Fe. For ten days we stayed at the Rancho del Monte, a dude ranch run by a couple from the East, the Hootens. Bill Hooten was a former New York advertising executive, a self-declared fugitive from Madison Avenue. Barbara did the cooking. We were there over the Easter holiday, during which I demonstrated a recurrent spasm of idiocy by coming down to breakfast and, seeing vases of lilies all over the place, asking, "who died?" Joe was speechless with laughter. The day we arrived in Santa Fe, Joe had telephoned Mabel Dodge Luhan, the self-promoting hostess of a New York "salon" where, shortly before World War 1, men of intellectual voltage—along with a scattering of women—gathered to discuss the world's most pressing matters—people like Lincoln Steffens, Walter Lippmann, John Reed. When Dodge tired of New York and its stresses, she moved to the Southwest, where she met Tony Luhan, a beautiful, craggy-looking, non-English-speaking American Indian. She also made friends there with D. H. Lawrence and his fat German wife, Frieda, who had a house down the road. By the time Joe telephoned, Luhan was in her eighties. Could we pay her a visit? She was oh so sorry, she told him, but she was going to Texas to visit her grandchildren for a few days. That was okay, Joe said, "We'll be here for ten days."

"And when I get back," she said, as if she hadn't heard what he'd said, "I think I'm going to be sick."

PART IV

CHAPTER 11

When Joe and I were in Italy on our honeymoon, I had picked up a letter with *discovery*'s return address on it at the Rome office of American Express.

"It can't be good news," I said.

"What makes you say that?" Joe said.

"Just a feeling," I said. "Let's sit down."

It was as I suspected: Vance was leaving the magazine for good; he wasn't getting the support he thought owed him by Pocket Books. I handed the letter to Joe.

"He doesn't say it's final. It's says right here—this is only temporary."

"I know Vance," I said. "*Discovery* has lost its charm. So he blames Pocket Books. Herb loves the magazine; it makes him feel like he's got if not a hand, at least a finger or two, in belles lettres." If I hadn't been on my honeymoon I would have howled in fury. For the rest of our trip I tried not to think about Vance's letter and what it meant in my life. When we got back to New York two weeks later, Vance had left town. No one knew where he was, though Mexico was suspected.

"I'll never get another job like that," I said.

"Probably not," Joe said. "It was a dream job."

Discovery's death had made me grieve, more for myself than for the future of literature. American writing could limp along without me, but what was I going to do with myself all day for the rest of my life?

Herbert Alexander summoned me a day or two after I got back to work tying up the last of the magazine's chores. *Discovery*, he said, was only sleeping; it didn't have to die. "How would you like to be editor?"

"Editor of what?" I asked.

"What do you think?" he said. "Editor of *discovery*."

"But I'm only twenty-four."

"What's that got to do with it?"

"Do you really think I could do it?"

"Why else would I be asking you?"

I told Herb I would let him know in a couple of days. I wanted to accept but was terrified of making bad decisions, worried that my judgment was insufficiently developed, uncertain that I would be able to deal with balky, cocky, or pissed-off authors, certain that the responsibilities would crush me. Justin said I should go ahead and give it a try. This was the first time I had been faced with a major choice involving other people. Over a weekend I struggled, trying to decide whether or not to take the job. Part of me, having apprenticed for two years, felt I could do it, I knew perfectly well how to drive this car. Another part, employing a fainthearted and timorous voice said, Your feet don't reach the pedals. Forget it. This was a man's job. Faintheartedness prevailed and I told Herb I didn't think I could meet his expectations—which, in a sense, called his own judgment to account. He was not at all pleased, disgusted really, and told me I was a foolish girl. Then he offered me a job in the Pocket Books publicity department. I accepted this paler offering and for a while turned out news releases and an in-house newsletter.

While not especially demanding, my job was agreeable enough; it took me into the offices of other Pocket Books workers, where I interviewed them for the newsletter and traded office gossip. The older men were almost invariably flirtatious and jokey, the women more subdued, often walking around with their eyes downcast. I had an office to myself with a window looking down twenty-seven floors to the skating rink in Rockefeller Center. No one checked up on me; I sometimes took a very long lunch hour, eating with my new husband (my ring was still shiny and unscratched) who worked seven blocks away; we'd go to the American Bar and Grill on Sixth Avenue or one of several little Italian places he'd discovered. Occasionally I had lunch with Bob Kotlowitz or Sue Kaufman or a Barnard friend, Marian Magid, who worked for Norman Podhoretz at *Commentary* magazine and who had a sardonic sense of humor. Always at least half an hour late, Marian would show up breathless with an assortment of ingenious excuses. After work I picked Joe up at Abrams and the two of us walked home to 303 East Thirty-seventh Street or, after we moved, to 242 East Nineteenth Street. Sometimes we had a few people in for dinner, sometimes we got dressed up in our finery and went uptown to a party given, usually, by one of his friends.

When Bob Kotlowitz set me to writing back-cover copy, I figured they must be grooming me for an editor's mantle. The first of these was for a reissue of the Raymond Chandler thriller *The Lady in the Lake*. Bob explained that my copy should tease the reader with just enough plot to hook him without giving away the whole story. At the same time, it had to make an instant pitch. I took the book back to my office and dug in. The more I read, the more lost I became; following the narrative and keeping track of who was doing what to whom and why was about as easy as following an overgrown trail through a dense forest, and I felt like the child I once was, confronted with a math problem whose theorem I had forgotten. After finishing the novel and taking extensive notes, I typed a draft and brought it to Bob. "This doesn't do it," he said. "It limps. I want it to dash." I could feel tears gathering. After several more drafts, in which I managed not to reveal that I never *had* unraveled the plot, I gave Bob something he could accept, while he confessed that he had deliberately given me a task formidable for even the most experienced copywriter; Raymond Chandler, he said, was justifiably known for his labyrinthine plots. Should I take that as a compliment? Everything else from then on, he assured me, would be a breeze.

A few days later Herb asked me to select poems for and write a preface to a new edition of Ogden Nash verse, a book that had done extremely well. Ogden Nash was probably the most read, the most popular composer of light verse then going—and oh so mid-century polite, giving matters sexual the tiniest little tweak:

> *The turtle lives 'twixt plated decks*
> *Which practically conceal its sex.*
> *I think it clever of the turtle*
> *In such a fix to be so fertile.*

Compared to writing a précis of *The Lady in the Lake*, doing the Nash edition was a piece of cake.

My brassy presumption—that I deserved to do, day in and day out, the thing I most enjoyed—made me restless at Pocket Books; we were not a perfect match. I wanted something with a mouthful of very literary teeth; my brain was dozing. When I paid Herb my farewell visit, I was close to tears. He didn't seem to understand why I chose not to stay on and become a full-fledged editor—something he assured me would happen sooner rather than later. Unable to identify the true source of my restlessness, I couldn't give him an answer that satisfied either one of us.

More or less by default, I enrolled in Columbia's graduate school, department of English, and managed to stay there for three months. The only class in which I couldn't help dozing—more from boredom than fatigue—was Gilbert Highet's classical literature, mainly because he was more a very smart actor than a teacher, gesturing, pacing, yelling, reading long passages of Homer aloud; some people whose devotion to serious matters was more profound than mine dismissed him as a "showman." A good teacher didn't need to carry on as if he were Laurence Olivier. In my other courses everyone (all headed toward professorships) took

221

down every word the teacher uttered; all you could see was the tops of their heads. Another mismatch.

Mainly by default my next job brought me to Park Avenue South and into the New York office of the ancient and decorous Boston publishing firm of Houghton Mifflin Co. HMCo brought out sure-fire sellers like Winston Churchill and grand literary writers like Carson McCullers and the debut stories of Philip Roth. They "discovered" Rachel Carson. Since the early 1930s they had been publishing the English-language edition of Adolf Hitler's *Mein Kampf*.

I had heard about an opening in the editorial department from someone who knew someone, the network functioning as it should. I showed up in the office on Park Avenue South for an interview with Jack Leggett, the New York editor, who told me I was overqualified, which I was, but it didn't matter because I couldn't seem to find anything else. A cheerful Yale man with a well-tempered literary sensibility and an enthusiasm that was constantly being thwarted by the top editor in Boston—a fierce woman married to the poet Robert Hillyer—Jack too was an ideal boss; every instruction was issued as a request. "If you feel like it, why don't you. . . ." On paper I was assistant editor; in actuality a peon whose principal labor was reading manuscripts. Some were so rotten you could smell it by the second paragraph. But since you were supposed to write a report for every manuscript submitted, coming in either over the transom or through an agent, you had to go far enough past paragraph two to write a report that sounded as if you had read the whole thing. I felt like a Dickens character, forced to sit on a stool rubbing blacking into gentlemen's boots from morn till night. During the switchboard operator's lunch hour I was often asked to fill in for her, routing calls by inserting what looked like miniature fire hoses into round holes on a panel and then holding back a small Bakelite lever, causing the phone in someone's office to ring. "Houghton Mifflin, good afternoon." I understood that this midday task was a kind of mortification and that they wouldn't have dared ask any man in the editorial department to work the switchboard. But in a mindless way that I wouldn't have admitted, it was a relief from the eye-watering, disheartening work I did during the other seven hours in the HMCo office.

When an editorial position opened up in Houghton Mifflin's Boston headquarters I told a friend, Bob Gutwillig, about it. Bob already worked in publishing, had edited his college literary magazine, and wanted to edit books as a career rather than make money—there was no question of doing both at the same time. Jack agreed to interview him. After Bob left I asked Jack if he was going to recommend him. He shook his head.

"Why not? I thought he was just right for the job."

"They'd never go for anyone with a last name like that," Jack said. I didn't ask him why he had bothered to interview Bob at all. Maybe he wanted to see if Bob looked Jewish—which he did.

I thought Jack was joking, but he wasn't. Soon after the Gutwillig episode I went to Boston for an HMCo sales conference and realized, while surrounded by other employees, that I was the only Jew on the payroll. I hadn't felt so conspicuous since the second grade at the Brearley. All these Yankee blue bloods, a retired naval commander, a nature freak who wore boyish rubber-soled shoes that squeaked like a threatened bird, assorted brahmins and social register-ees, and not a single Hebrew—with the exception of me, and I worked in New York so I didn't have much chance to spread contamination: could this possibly be legal? The phrase "they prefer to be with their own kind" came swimming up from somewhere in my unconscious. I had already decided this was true and untrue in about equal portions, and that there's always a part of you that simultaneously yearns to belong and to remain outside, each part pulling against the other like two dogs fighting over a grease-soaked pot holder. Looking around at the perfect American faces with perfect New England noses, outdoorsy cheeks, and long sturdy fingers, I knew exactly what Jack had been trying to tell me. Bob would have languished at wonder-bred HMCo.

CHAPTER 12

Like Dora, David Copperfield's child-wife, I knew nothing about the flesh, blood, and bones of a home, or how to maintain their health, my rich, arch-feminist mother having warned me away from the kitchen and from doing any chore that didn't require a college education. In effect, I was helpless and hadn't the faintest idea what went into a stew or a cake, how to iron a blouse, or how to get rid of a stain. Paradoxically, I was helpless while continually waited on by what my mother called "the help"—governess, cook, maid, laundress, and sometimes butler. This was all very well when I lived at home, but as soon as I married and moved out of the big house on Sixty-third Street, and into Joe's three-room apartment on East Thirty-seventh Street, my ignorance caught up with me. Dora didn't seem to mind—or even to notice it; but I wasn't at all sanguine about my incompetence. I felt stupid and didn't like it that my husband knew more about keeping house than I did.

I don't know how we would have managed—probably not as well as Dora—if Joe hadn't been living alone for almost a decade before we met, in which time he had become adept at shopping, cooking, and cleaning up after himself. The day we started back to work he picked me up outside my Forty-seventh Street office at five o'clock and told me we were going to stop at the Grand Union on Third Avenue, where he would begin my lessons on how to buy and prepare food. Never had I felt so binary. By day (like the Green Hornet) I was the hotshot managing editor of a classy literary magazine; by evening, hesitating outside the Grand Union, I was a domestic illiterate.

My mother shopped for the family's provisions while lying in bed and talking over the phone to the grocer and the butcher at Gristede's around the corner on Third Avenue. She knew both their first names and chatted them up in a time-honored faux-flirtatious manner. "I'll have eight of your lovely lamb chops, Stanley." She had, as far as I knew, never set foot in a supermarket, those wonderfully convenient new grocery stores I'd been reading about, where you wheeled a steel-wire cart in front of you and plucked whatever you wanted or needed from shelves arrayed down several aisles. Too bad—she was the sort of person who would have enjoyed shopping at a supermarket, where impulse is far more fun and creative than a list.

David Copperfield was optimistic about his bride-to-be, Dora: "I showed her an old housekeeping book of my aunt's, and gave her a set of tablets, and a pretty little pencil case, and box of leads, to practise housekeeping with."

Optimistic but dense: "the cookery book made Dora's head ache, and the figures made her cry. They wouldn't add up, she said; so she rubbed them out, and drew little nosegays, and likenesses of me and Jip, all over the tablets."

"This," Joe said, unwittingly imitating art "is the produce department. That means fresh fruits and vegetables." I was determined to learn fast—for both our sakes. "This"—he picked up a green ball with leaves—"is a cabbage. And that," he said, putting down the cabbage and pointing to a similar green ball, "is a head of lettuce."

He took my hand and led me past pyramids of raw carrots, beans, peas in the pod, squashes, potatoes, and apples, pears, and oranges to a hip-high case of chunks of raw meat wrapped in clear plastic. He explained the difference between two so-called roasts by saying that you cooked one inside the stove and the other in a pot on top of it. "How do you know which is which?"

"You learn the names and remember them. And if you don't remember, you can always look it up in one of our cookbooks." As a wedding present we'd been given five cookbooks by a second cousin who had correctly guessed the shallowness of my home-making skills. The books didn't make my head ache, they merely baffled me.

The lessons continued. Still, I felt as if I had been shoved into a chemistry lab with nothing more than a sixth-grade education, and instructed to create an explosion. Who knew what would melt together, burn to a crisp, or implode? I was fearful, not trusting my instincts—for I had none when it came to the kitchen—or my ability to follow the directions in a cookbook. How many cups in a quart? What does *blanch* mean? What's *tbs*; *sauté*; *parboil*; *fold*? I knew *boil* and *stir* and that was about it. My confidence was hardly bolstered when one of Joe's relatives informed me that, were Joe's mother still alive, "she would not have set foot in your kitchen," meaning I had broken ancient Jewish law and had defiled my house by preparing meat and dairy products in the same vessel. I asked Joe if he thought his nosy cousin was right. "That's silly," he said. "Honest to God. That bitch." She had stung me nevertheless and had started me wondering what it would be like to keep a kosher house and to focus on what is forbidden rather than on what I had now, namely an almost endless number of options. "Why does eating shrimp make you a bad Jew?" I asked my husband, who had been raised in a house where shellfish was considered a toxic substance. Joe said that wasn't the point; the point was not the shrimp but obedience to the law. I could understand this but could not take that final step into belief that following an arbitrary law is any better for you—or for the world beyond the front door—than experimenting your way through life.

It didn't take me long to realize that my mother had not done me any favors by advising me to let someone else do the household chores—"that's what they're being paid for." My mother was both rich and a feminist, which made it possible for her to act on her principles; she was like one of those 1930s American Communists who, on the Q.T., bought cheap land on Cape Cod or the Vineyard, trusting it to increase a hundredfold in value—which it did. If she hadn't been so well off she would have done the scrubbing and cooking, the scut work, whether or not she believed housework to be demeaning. In my case there *was* no one else—except Joe and Georgia Edwards, the woman who had raised him after his mother and father died. Georgia showed up at 303 East Thirty-seventh Street once a week to do some serious cleaning. She also cooked for us when we had people over for dinner. Her repertoire consisted of three meals, which she wisely alternated. One was shrimp creole, one chicken fricassee, and the third pot roast. When she cooked dinner for us she always brought along a package of hermits, chewy squares of ginger and molasses cookie from Horn & Hardhart.

While most housework involves getting rid of something—dust, grease, cobwebs, stains, spills, odors, smears, footprints and handprints, streaks, scum, wrinkles, sand, cat poop, and general disorder—cooking is the opposite. You've got something palpable—and, if you're lucky, even delicious—when you're done. But instead of treating the act of preparing a meal as a lark, a challenge, I was daunted by the idea of turning a chunk of bloody meat and a couple of carrots into a pot roast that tasted like Georgia's.

For the first three or four years of our marriage I trusted myself with preparing only one meal for company, certain that I would spoil, set on fire, or in some other horrible way render anything else inedible. This was an eye round roast, restuffed baked potatoes, "French-style" frozen beans, and a "bought dessert"—ice cream with some kind of gooey topping. The one time I tried a chocolate soufflé it ended up like a piece of blotting paper at the bottom of the casserole. This set me back another couple of years. Quite handy in the kitchen, Joe spent a lot of time there while I stood by his side.

We ate out about once a week; you could get a good meal for two, along with a glass of wine or beer, for around fifteen dollars. There was a steak house we liked on Third Avenue. It had green sawdust spread over the floor—God only knew what was underneath; the house specialty was mutton chops. The Three Crowns was a Swedish restaurant in the east fifties, with a smorgasbord arrayed on a round table that rotated; you selected your herring, cheese, potatoes, smoked eel, etc., as the dish moved toward you and made a grab for it before it whirled away. If you wanted to see friends in publishing, you went to P.J. Clarke's on Third Avenue; there was always at least one person at the bar whom you knew well enough to go up to and start a conversation. The only thing to order at Clarke's was a medium-rare hamburger. Neither Joe nor I liked the kind of restaurant featured in glossy magazines and the food columns of the *Times*, places like "21," Le Pavillon, Chambord, the Forum of the Twelve Caesars, pricey expense-account eateries favored also by out-of-towners and rich bachelors. Dinner for two—with wine—at one of these classy restaurants could set you back as much as thirty-five or forty dollars.

"Takeout"—with the exception of Chinese restaurants—had not yet embraced the urban imagination or appetite; you either cooked or ate out. One establishment brought precooked meals to the back doors of the rich, who ordered them over the phone. This was Casserole Kitchen, which delivered an entrée in a steaming earthenware container, picking up the empty next day. Casseroles were a streamlined way of getting your meat, vegetables, and starch in the same pot. In 1956 we bought, for $2.95, a cookbook

A.B. on Ninth Avenue, 1957.

entitled *Casserole Cookery Complete*, a revised edition of the original 1941 product. Its format was a ring-bound vertical that you stood up, like an easel, the easier to read and keep smear free. In her introduction, the bestselling book's author, Marian Tracy, urged her readers to drink wine with a meal—"the world looks rosier"—and to buy only fresh herbs. Some of her recipes were startlingly original, although you had to be braver than I was to try them. Others in this category suggest wartime shortages. A random sampling includes: no. 125: Brussel Sprouts and Tongue in Cheese Sauce; no. 126: Creamed Tripe with Onions; no. 117: Kidney, Heart and Liver in Soubise Sauce; no. 167: Sweet Potatoes Stuffed with Birds—quail is recommended.

The most celebrated food guru was Clementine Paddleford, who wrote for the *New York Herald Tribune*, the only newspaper that rivaled the *Times* in clout, style, and substance. In 1960, Ms. Paddleford published *How America Eats*, a book that had taken her twelve years to research and write. "In New York City," she wrote, "you eat around the clock." But not, it turns out, all that variously. Paddleford's journey across and through the United States made her appreciate regional cooking, but as for the city, she focused mainly on oysters, soup, lobster, and cheesecake. She also included Waldorf salad. Invented by a self-promoting maître d', known as "Oscar of the Waldorf," this salad was a medley of sliced apples, walnuts, mayo, and celery. One of Paddleford's more imaginative recipes tells you how to make Leek and Pig Tail Soup—and begins "wash six pig tails." Her Crown of Lobsters requires the cook to "parboil lobster for three minutes. Cool. Remove meat and run three times through fine grinder." What you get when you're finished is a kind of lobster mousse. Not one of Paddleford's recipes calls for garlic, sesame seeds, or cilantro; many of them ask you to include generous amounts of cream.

In 1956 Joe and I lived in an apartment at 242 East Nineteenth Street, on the corner of Second Avenue. All the other buildings on the block between Third and Second, both sides of the street, were the homes of Puerto Rican families. These were mostly brownstones, once lovely, now flaking, their stoops askew. For no reason other than strangeness, I was frightened of my neighbors when we first moved there; later, they seemed friendly if somewhat distant as I walked home from work. On Sunday mornings the street would sparkle with the glass of bottles tossed from windows during the night before in a frenzy of celebration.

Along Second Avenue homeless men lay curled up in doorways trying to generate enough strength to get themselves to Bellevue Hospital in order to sell their blood for a few dollars. A common night sound was the wail of an ambulance siren, not quite loud enough to wake you but which penetrated sleep and burrowed into dreams.

Our building had a doorman and an elevator man who delivered the mail every morning; the place was decently but sparely maintained—no frills. Our apartment consisted of a tiny one-and-a-half-person kitchen open at both ends, and a dining room that gave onto an alley. The middle-aged couple across this alley engaged in nightly afterdinner battles during which they screamed imprecations at each other and threw things. Married less than two years, I couldn't imagine what would bring a man and a woman to the point of such rage. The living room was long and thin and had three tall windows overlooking a skimpy garden, more brown than green. In the back was our bedroom, a bathroom, and an extra room Joe had put dibs on for a study. Pregnant with our first child, I figured that sooner or later he'd have to give it over to the baby.

232

We furnished the place with some of Joe's things but mainly with new pieces we bought on Saturday afternoons with the help of a painter friend, Alvin Ross, who had somehow wangled a pass to decorators' showrooms—an understuffed, hard-edged couch covered in pink velveteen, several Scandinavian chairs, a round, marble-topped table, objects of functional economy; this was our 1950s rejection of superfluous detail and design.

Even though Joe had been touted as a superhost, as a couple we didn't entertain much. Both basically shy people, I suppose that deep down we were afraid that if we sent out invitations no one would show up. We didn't have an event to trigger the party we decided to give at last, not birthday anniversary, holiday, or promotion. It could have been that our impulse to celebrate arose from a sense that, even if neither of us had pulled off a noticeable success at work, at least we weren't going backward; and also the dim awareness that, after the baby came, our partying life would be reduced to a very small item.

We invited our guests, about two dozen of them—among them my Barnard friend Francine du Plessix, editors Jason and Barbara Epstein, *New Yorker* writer Anthony Bailey—by sending out cards—"After 8." We hired a bartender, laid out a ham we had baked, some cold cuts and cheeses, and worried that no one would show up. On the day of the party, Jean Stein, a woman about my age with whom I had been producing a series of spoken word records for MGM Records, phoned me. Jean was the daughter of Jules Stein, said to be the most powerful entertainment agent on either coast. Jean knew all her father's stellar clients—movie stars, writers, musicians, publishers—but had retained a curiously girlish manner. When she spoke you had to get right up next to her to hear what she was saying, and she often asked questions that suggested a barrier between her and the facts of life. My alliance with Jean was characterized by her dependence on me—specifically for

233

what she believed to be my vast knowledge of books and literature but which was, in fact, only vast compared with hers. I did most of the editing for selections that were read by Carson McCullers and William Faulkner. The other records in this series had Alec Guinness reading from *Gulliver's Travels* and Ralph Richardson doing some Joseph Conrad. The series was too highbrow to sell well; but it had "class" written all over it.

Jean seemed to be in need of basic sex ed. One day when we were having lunch together she said, "I know it sounds stupid but would you please tell me where babies come out." Without missing a beat, I said: "They come out the same place they went in."

Over the phone on the day of the party Jean asked if she could bring a friend with her. Of course, I told her. "Do I know him?"

"It's Bill," she said. "Bill Faulkner. He's in town working with his editor." This was Albert Erskine, a lean southerner who had been briefly married to Katherine Anne Porter and who was famous all over town for his social polish, his old-fashioned manners.

"It's all right if I bring him, isn't it?" Jean said in her breathy, little-girl voice.

"I guess so," I said. "Sure, that's fine. Does he know where we live?" I knew Jean was Faulkner's New York girlfriend, I had heard this in the kind of whisper that gossip often uses to transmit delicate messages, though I could not remember who the messenger was.

"What difference does that make?" she said.

The idea of William Faulkner, winner of the Nobel Prize, walking into our apartment and shooting the breeze with our friends, mostly junior people in publishing, many of them wet behind the ears and brash, was as daunting as if I were the village priest informed the pope was about to show up for dinner and all I had in the house was cabbage stew and black bread.

The bartender—a graduate student not much younger than we were—arrived and set up the bar in Joe's study. I brought out

234

trays of cheese and crackers in a heightened state of nerves; I had some trouble holding the trays steady. Guests appeared and dumped their coats on our bed. By a little after nine Jean and her friend had still not arrived and I began to think that they would not come at all, had found another party at a better address, or had decided to keep the party a private duet.

Just as this thought occurred to me, bringing with it both disappointment and relief—because I really didn't want to deal with this daunting visit—they came in. Jean was wearing a blue taffeta dress, the skirt puffed out below the waist like a bell, her black hair brushed and shining. She was beautiful in a Liz Taylor sort of way. And, a step or two behind her, Himself, in a thick, impeccably tailored tweed suit, a slight man not more than five foot eight, with delicate features, a furry gray mustache, and melancholy eyes. With my heart pounding noisily against the back of my throat and my legs gone soft, I went over to greet them.

"This is Bill Faulkner, Anne. I just picked him up at the airport." They gazed at each other with hungry eyes. I said something about how nice it was that they could come. Faulkner bowed slightly and said it was a pleasure. I escorted them to the bar and left. I went back to that room only once during the evening, terrified that I might have to talk to him. But there was more to it than shyness. It was his aura, his scale—too large and bright, not the man himself, who was shy, to the point of reticence, but what he had done with his life. Our celebrated guest, I learned later, had backed up against a wall and talked rather formally and in a near whisper with those who were braver than I was. One of them pointed to a tiny rosette in his lapel and asked what it was. "That's the French Legion of Honor," he said, withdrawing a white handkerchief from his sleeve and patting his lips with it. "For service during the First World War. I was a pilot, you know."

Exceedingly famous people upset the psychic balance of a 235 gathering—unless everyone there is equally famous—making waves, creating a kind of draft. It may be thrilling to realize that the man standing next to you is a writer from Olympus, but the psychic space between you is as wide as if you had four legs and fur and he two and feathers. You can see nothing "natural" about William Faulkner or Laurence Olivier or T. S. Eliot, for it's almost impossible to get past the luminescence of the enormously gifted.

A few days later I had a lunch date with Marc Jaffe, an editor at New American Library. We met shortly after noon in an East Side restaurant with a French name and a clientele of publishing executives, literary agents, and a smattering of tourists—a place in which it didn't hurt you to be seen. The prime-cut customers were sent upstairs to the second floor; Marc was prime-cut. As we reached the top of the staircase I saw William Faulkner sitting at a table for four, a bottle of wine in a cooler his only companion. He had a plate of food in front of him and seemed quite content to be alone. When he saw us, he got up and, still holding his napkin, walked over to us. Bowing slightly from the waist, he said "How do you do, Mizz Kaplan." Trembling, I introduced him to Marc.

After we sat down at our table Marc said, "So that's William Faulkner. I'm surprised how shy he is."

I realized that this would be one of those frozen moments and that I would unashamedly think of it as "memorable" for the rest of my life. I transmuted Faulkner's unremarkable greeting into prose as indelible as his Nobel Prize acceptance speech.

"He is shy, isn't he?" I said and stopped myself from telling Marc he'd been at our house, since we hadn't invited Marc to our party. "And isn't he gorgeous?"

"Well I don't know about that," Marc said. "And I've heard he has something of a drinking problem."

"Nobody's perfect," I said.

In the 1950s, as in times long gone, the notion of "doctor" inspired reverent submission. The medical practitioner was viewed as part high-ranking army officer, part school principal, and the remainder, shaman. When you went to see him [*sic*] you asked no questions, neither about what he was doing to you—especially when you couldn't see what it was—nor what your chances for improvement were. By remaining beyond the obligation to report, he kept you emotionally at arm's length and conveniently out of his hair. Office visits were snappy and to the point. A tap here, a poke there, a tweak, an X ray, a swabbing, the shining of strong lights in small places, the hint of pain and humiliation enhancing the diagnostic process. The prescription he handed you didn't tell you much either, not even the drug's name or probable side effects (vomiting? purple spots on your belly? blinding headache?). You were afraid of bothering the doctor, and he liked it that way. In other words, what your doctor did to and for you was none of your business.

Incredibly, from the moment we met, Joe and I had not once talked about having children, the idea never having occurred—at least consciously—to either of us. This was our partnership: one and one make one—forever.

And then, along about our second year of marriage, everything changed, and I wanted a baby so badly the desire felt like a wound. Surprised at how, without any awareness, I'd made a 180-degree turn, I was a newcomer to the sort of profound transformation a person can undergo more or less overnight. The woman who drives you crazy in November becomes your best friend in December. You may think this is because she's changed but it's more likely you who has been able to see her through a cleaner window. From *I never want children* to *a baby is the only thing in the world I need*—this happened almost overnight. Although he didn't share my enthusiasm, Joe, a generous man, was willing to go along with it. I had no trouble conceiving—it took three months—but for no reason other than superstitious fear, I wasn't sure that it would ever happen.

Babies had played no part in Joe's life; he had never even held one.

My mother and father were doctor snobs. While a lot of non-Jews resort, when they're really hurting or fearful, to a Jewish doctor, figuring he or she is not only smarter but softer of heart, my parents consulted mainly WASP doctors, those trained at Columbia or Harvard, with offices on the Upper East Side of Manhattan.

As soon as I had missed one period, and, cavalierly, not having visited a gynecologist since Anatole had dispatched me, four years earlier, to get myself fitted with a diaphragm, unconsciously repeating, almost verbatim, the line in Mary McCarthy's novel *The Group:* "Get yourself a pessary," I phoned my mother to ask for the name of her doctor. The nature of our watery bond made it far easier for both of us to connect when there was something specific to talk about; I was, I suppose, using my request to try to warm up to my mother. There was a shadow across her that she almost never—no doubt because she didn't really know how— invited me to step in and share, and this phone call seemed to please her. "His name is Equinn Munnell," she said. "He's very handsome; all his patients are in love with him." I told her he sounded like horses and money. She assured me of his brilliance.

Women did not invite their husbands to come along to their medical appointments, and if they had, the likely answer would have been: "Are you kidding?" A man was expected to show up for work no matter what was happening outside the job; many bosses didn't know—and didn't want to know—when an employee's child was sick or his dog run over.

So I arrived, solo, at Dr. Munnell's Park Avenue office ten minutes ahead of time. There were seven or eight comfortable chairs in Dr. M.'s waiting room, and all but one were occupied by women reading up-to-date magazines like *Holiday, Town and Country, Yachting*. For most private doctors and dentists this let-the-patients-wait-forever policy was standard; they scheduled more patients than they had hours to see them in. What happened to those at the end of the line? Did the doctor stick his head into the room and say, "Sorry, folks, we're closing shop. Come back tomorrow"? Even when you showed up on time you often waited several hours to be seen—and these were not clinics where you would expect to sit on a hard bench all morning or afternoon; these were Park Avenue, top-of-the-line specialists.

Mom was right. Dr. M. was darkly good-looking, with sleek brown hair and a smile one notch below seductive. He wore a long white coat, open to expose an expensive three-piece suit beneath. The backs of his hands were very hairy. During a short interview I told him I thought I was pregnant. "Lets just take a look-see," he said, motioning for his crisp, middle-aged nurse to escort me to the examining room. She handed me a cotton johnny and told me to remove everything I was wearing, and then get up on the table. Briskly, Dr. M. inserted a speculum that felt as if it had been stored in a freezer and poked around while the nurse stood off to the side, staring at the wall. Back in his consulting room he told me he thought I was a month or so into pregnancy but they would test my urine on a rabbit to make sure. The rabbit test was positive.

Soon I was showing up once a month at Dr. M.'s office, setting aside a three-hour block of time for each visit. His affability factor was high, but I sensed that below it lay a chunk of ice not much subject to melting.

Dr. Munnell apparently liked his women thin. He instructed me to gain no more than seventeen pounds. This seemed like very little weight to me, but he assured me it would be best for me and for my baby. Unquestioning, I put myself on a punishing diet and for nine months was always ravenous. Meanwhile, from the fifth month on, the baby—gender unknown—moved about in its quarters almost constantly, kicking and twisting even at night while I lay in bed, too excited to sleep more than a few hours at a time.

Until just a few years after the war, women starting out in labor were doped to the ears or knocked out altogether, the idea being that they would find the pain of childbirth intolerable. Just in time, a new notion about giving birth took hold of the imagination of a lot of women who thought it would be invigorating to give birth the way peasants do, laying down their scythes when birth was imminent and having the kid at the side of the field, then going back to work for the afternoon shift. This was known as natural childbirth, without anesthetic, mechanical assistance, or episiotomy. It included a course of workshops where you and your husband, along with a dozen other couples, crouched on exercise pads in a gym while an instructor told you how to respond physically and psychologically to each of the three stages of labor and how to lessen the "discomfort" by panting and/or taking deep breaths. The instructor also showed you gruesome pictures and explained the risks to the unborn of any sort of anesthesia. When I told Dr. M. that I wanted to try giving birth by this new method, no drugs or painkillers, he was skeptical—"Well, Anne, if that's what you want. . . ."

There was no way of telling my baby's gender, so I thought of it as "it." On May 10, the day before it was officially due, I looked as if I had a watermelon inside my belly. My navel had popped out like a cork. Labor, however, had not begun, and my water hadn't broken, but Dr. Munnell had planned for this baby to arrive on the eleventh. My private room at Columbia-Presbyterian Hospital, on 168th Street, overlooking the Hudson River, had been reserved. "Come on in," he told me over the phone, "we'll induce you." He explained in his white voice that they would start dripping Pitocin into a vein in my arm by IV. Before the procedure, a young resident came into my room to take my history. He pulled up a chair and sat by my bed, a folder on his lap. There wasn't much to tell him—I was twenty seven and almost never sick. A medical frown accompanied his rebuke: "Why have you waited so long to have a baby?" he asked.

"My mother was thirty-nine when she had me," I said. "Mother and child are still doing fine."

The frown persisted. He made me feel as if I'd broken some rule no one had told me about. Before they wheeled me to the labor room, they made me take off my earrings and my wedding ring.

Designed to bring on the muscular contractions of labor, Pitocin packed a wallop: I went from zero to sixty-five in less than half an hour. I groaned politely. "Are you sure you don't want something for the pain?" Dr. M. asked, as he withdrew his head from between my legs. "Well, maybe a little something," I said. "But no Scopolamine." This was a painkiller we had been warned about in the childbirth class; it was a so-called truth drug that would make its victim say anything that came into her head and then, after it wore off, not remember a thing. We were also told that it was commonly used by torturers to loosen men's tongues. When we settled on a small fix of Demerol, I felt I had betrayed my sisters in the natural childbirth movement.

Sitting beside me, Joe insisted on reading to me from a book of S. J. Perelman pieces he'd brought with him. I could understand

241

single words but sentences were beyond me. "Isn't that funny?" Joe asked. I told him to shut up. The pain was ferocious, worse than anything I had ever experienced. It felt as if my insides were being ripped from their container. High-pitched shrieking in the hall outside didn't help. "Some women," Dr. M. said, with eyebrows raised significantly, "seem to need to express themselves more than others." Joe rubbed my back the way he had been taught by our instructor. That didn't help either. Did I see on Dr. M.'s face a look saying he'd told me so?

They didn't ask Joe to join me in the delivery room when Dr. M. announced that the last stage of labor had started, but sent him out to a fathers' waiting room to chew on his nails. Once on the table, my legs hoisted on steel troughs like two pieces of dead meat, I pushed so hard that I broke hundreds of tiny blood vessels in my neck and shoulders. Dr. M. announced that he was about to perform an episiotomy. "A little cut in your perineum. To make room for the baby." I didn't protest and felt it as he sliced into the tissue. "There," he said, like a seamstress pleased with a neat hem-stitch. "The head's crowning." Drained of every sensation but the need to get this hideous business over with, I said "Thank God." "It's a girl," Dr. M. announced. "She's got very large hands and feet." "Susanna," I said. She was just under six pounds.

I tried to nurse Susanna, but my milk was slow in coming, and she refused to suck, twisting her mouth away from my nipple while her body went rigid. I begged our pediatrician—the same man who had taken care of me from the time I was an infant until I went away to college—to let me try a little longer. But by day three he decided that Susanna needed food and had her put her on the bottle. From that moment she was hooked on the easier way and I gave up, crying for a week after I got home, and scrambling to see the bright side of things.

TWO years later to the month our second child was due to be born. On my last office visit to Dr. M., he had said, "Better not have it this weekend; I'm going sailing."

Did he know something he wasn't telling me? My water broke over my feet after dinner—a turkey leg at the Tip Toe Inn, a delicatessen around the corner on Broadway—on Friday night. I called Dr. M.'s office and was told by his answering service that he was away for the weekend and couldn't be reached. Dr. Wilson was attending to his patients. Who was Dr. Wilson? I'd never heard of him. Choiceless, I met Dr. Wilson when he came into the labor room to see how far along I was. He was so generic, his manner so impersonal and earnest, that I could not have described him two minutes after he left the room. During labor's second stage he showed up again. Saying that he wanted to make me "more comfortable," he asked me to turn onto my side and, without a word about what he was doing, inserted a needle into my spinal column and started injecting a painkiller that numbed everything below my waist. This dispatched the pain within minutes, for which I was properly grateful. It was only afterward that I realized that Dr. Wilson, like Dr. Munnell, was no fan of natural childbirth. If a patient had rights, they were locked away in a safe in the bowels of the hospital.

Hester was born a few hours later. On Monday, a tanned Dr. Munnell breezed into my private room and sat himself down, beaming at me. "I hope you're not going to wait too long to try for a boy," he said.

BY the end of year five in our marriage—I had stopped working at a job shortly before Susanna was born—I was a whiz at mashed potatoes, scrambled eggs, hot dogs, pancakes, Shake 'n Bake, and Junket. From time to time I still burned the toast. I heard about shallots on a radio cooking show, and one day as we walked up Broadway—we had by this time moved to a six-room apartment at 175 Riverside Drive—I stopped at one of those fruit and vegetable shops seductively spilling onto the sidewalk and asked the proprietor if he had any shallots. "Lady," he said, "I got enough trouble without shallots." Another time I asked the same man, "Are these eggs fresh?" He turned away, refusing to answer. Joe thought I'd hurt the man's feelings.

Our apartment was on the twelfth floor and if you stuck your head far out the bedroom window and looked north, you could see the George Washington Bridge spanning the Hudson River. Almost everything was done for you: Mail and newspapers were delivered to your door. Elevators took you quietly to your floor; garbage disappeared down a chute in the hall. Snow was cleared from off the sidewalk. The super arrived the same day you called him to take care of leaks and stoppages. Joe and I knew only one or two families who lived on the West Side. It was considered not quite up to snuff, somewhat seedy, giving off too strong an odor of the Old World; the opposite of the Upper East Side. On evenings and weekends, we spent a good deal of time walking, with Susanna in her English-made baby carriage, staring at the sky. The Broadway that Isaac Bashevis Singer writes about with inhuman accuracy and affection seemed to me the very center of an energetic cosmos, and the New York that made Singer skeptical—he said it had "all the symptoms of a mind gone berserk"—might have been there, lurking, but I didn't see it; my glasses were tinged with the pink of living where life's pulse and throb were on the surface, not buried under layers of rectitude and caution.

On a bitterly cold Sunday in November 1957, with the wind whipping around us as at the top of Mount Washington, Joe and I, with Susanna in her carriage, were walking in Riverside Park when a girl about six or seven emerged from the bushes waving a large pistol. Not pausing to figure out whether or not it was a smart thing to do, I went over to her and said, "Little girl, let me have that gun please." She obviously didn't want to, but my tone persuaded her. Having handed it over, she disappeared back into the shrubbery. What followed was a typical urban tale: we called the police from the nearest call box. Two cops showed up in a squad car and whisked Joe off to the local station where they made him sit for two hours in a kind of cage before releasing him with the neat send-off: "I guess you're legitimate," and as a coda, "Next time you find a gun, mister, toss it in the river."

"It apparently never occurred to them," Joe said later, "that only a lunatic would commit a crime and then call the police to announce he'd found a gun. All I need is to be seen throwing a gun in the river."

At a party soon after we were married I was asked by a woman devoutly and unhumorously feminist which one of us, I or Joe, made the family's "administrative decisions." Unprepared for this challenge, I couldn't answer. "Who," she wanted to know, "stops working when one of your children is sick?" "I do," I said. "I have softer breasts." She didn't like this answer and got up from where we both had been sitting and walked off to find someone more compatible to talk to.

Administrative decisions within a family struck me as a pretentious notion. Nevertheless, I was discovering that completing domestic tasks was a complicated business. In 1955 my mother published a book called *A Wife Is Many Women* in which she nailed it: we will play as many roles as we let society thrust upon us. It was assumed—even by my husband—a statistical freak by virtue of his doing any of the housework at all—that I would be in charge of the laundry, both clothes and linens; I became known as the laundry fairy. If the rug or floor needed vacuuming, I did it. Strict division: Joe became the garbage fairy. Decisions about the children's health and well-being were largely mine, although we were equally ignorant about caring for infants and toddlers.

Someone responsible should probably have overseen our child care. Within two years Susanna was hit above the eye by a swing, fell off a slide in the playground, giving herself a severe concussion, sucked on a camphor ball she found in a drawer of sweaters, and bit into a tiny flashlight bulb from God knows where. She also opened a floor-level cabinet door, found a bottle of vodka there, took off the top, and lifted it to her mouth just as I came 'round the bend. Any one of these "accidents," had they been upped one notch, could have killed her. I was so ignorant I thought they were normal mishaps of childhood, that every baby experienced something similar, and I emerged after each one shaken but inculpable, convinced that small children were less fragile than I could have imagined. One of my friends assured me that Susanna was accident-prone. Maybe she was, but by the time Hester arrived two years later, we no longer left camphor balls around to be mistaken for candy.

Every afternoon if it wasn't raining or snowing I wheeled Susanna in her carriage across Riverside Drive and down several blocks to the playground, where I sat on a bench talking to Maggie, a woman I had struck up a friendship with after seeing her every day for over a month without exchanging more than a cool smile. Maggie was a midwesterner whose principal trait was openness and sweetness, two qualities I wasn't all that used to. We talked only about babies and food and about how living in New York was so exciting and so hard at the same time; I heard from her that she and her husband were having a tough time adjusting to the city after Des Moines, a place so exotic to me that it might have been Des Moon. Maggie and I had almost no way of calibrating each other except as wife and mother; the only thing we had in common was two children approximately the same age who lived in the same neighborhood. As a basis for genuine affection it seemed as tenuous and unexpected as the fact that I had begun, more or less out of the blue, to write.

I was eight years old before I could extract any meaning from the marks on a page which, when combined, form words. Before this, my mother, alarmed because she seemed to have produced a dummy, took me to be tested for some physical explanation of my slowness. These tests came up negative except they did indicate that I was not only left-handed (surprise!) but severely left-eyed as well; they made me wear a black eye patch over my left eye for nearly a year. My mother, hoping to make me feel less miserable, told me I looked like a pirate, but I knew I looked like a cripple. When I was no closer to reading, she had me tested for mental capacity, the results of which reassured her but not me. I knew I was a dummy.

As an analog to this delay in reading, I was late to start writing. I had been an editor for years, but it never occurred to me that I could do it; writing seemed to me as remote, risky, and difficult an enterprise as taking Victoria Falls inside a barrel.

Writing was an activity that only writers engaged in. You couldn't expect just anyone to sit down at a typewriter and turn out a readable, let alone a publishable, piece of work. Like glassblowing or conducting an orchestra, writing involved an arcane initiation as well as exquisite, possibly painful, training. How did you make the turn from scribbling fragments in a notebook to having your words set in type for other people to read? What did you have to do to make it happen?

One day, shortly before our first child, was born, I ran into Ellinor, a Brearley School friend, whom I hadn't seen in several years. Asking her the obligatory—where did she live, what was she doing these days, how were her children—I soon found out that she was taking a fiction writing class at Columbia. As I walked home in a mood now turned sour, I was uneasily aware that Ellinor had triggered a spasm of envy. If she was writing, why couldn't I, who had been circling words for years? And so, shamelessly prompted by envy, I began the very next day to write a short story on a Royal portable typewriter set up on the dining room table. This was the first time since Barnard, where I had taken a one-semester writing class more or less as a lark, that I was trying to create something out of nothing, but bits and pieces of life, memory, radio programs, books, and movies stored somewhere far below the surface of my daily existence. Up until the day I ran into Ellinor, I had never dared to predict for myself anything as difficult or exhilarating as writing fiction. I had worked at a so-called literary job; now I thought that all I wanted was to be a wife and mother, like most of my Brearley, Wellesley, and Barnard classmates. Justin, tuned into my moods and shifting attitudes, let me know that he wanted for me what I did. That there might be something other than envy, that there might actually be a writer under the mother/wife skin, didn't occur to me at the time. I just had these stories in my head I had to write down.

The cover that Dr. Kronold, my therapist, had clamped down tight over the container flew off, spewing sensations, connections, and words that I quickly captured like butterflies in a net, and pinned on the page before they could escape. Words poured out of me. They came faster than I could type, faster even than I could think. Starting from scratch, my fiction was light on plot and imagination, heavy on feelings, sensations, nuances; overly dependent on metaphor, I was hesitant about leaving my own house for material—what did I know about anything but a soft life cut off from 99 percent of the world's population and its concerns? I was a hothouse flower, never having faced hunger, an empty purse, or genuine danger. So I stuck to my own life, as I suppose most beginning writers do, feeling their way, barefoot, across a lawn studded with broken glass. I was terrified and aroused at the same time, almost forgetting to eat. I managed to plow clumsily through to the end of a first story, then began a second.

Susanna's birth, in May 1957, wiped out any interest I had in producing another story, but after six weeks the pressure to write returned. My heroines—Virginia Woolf, Jane Austen, Muriel Spark, Mavis Gallant, Katherine Mansfield—all were either unmarried, childless, or unconventionally domesticated. The underlying message of this self-denial was not lost on me: it was unwise to try to be wife, mother, and writer simultaneously. The pressure, building daily until it became a distraction, proved irresistible. Each day I waited until Susanna fell asleep for her morning nap, shoved the telephone inside a drawer, and stuffing a couple of pillows on top of it, began to write. I turned out ten stories in one year, none of them any good, although one was sold by an altruistic agent, John Schaffner, whom I knew from my days on *discovery*. He sold it to a magazine called *Audience*. The story, "A Better Place," was about a young woman visibly pregnant with her first child. One day an old boyfriend whom she stopped going out with—high on pretension, low on sense of humor—sees her on the street and pauses to talk. After a few minutes of banal chitchat, he says, "What are you doing to make the world a better place?" This ticks off our heroine, whose defenses are galvanized—because she isn't doing anything at all except having this baby. She applies to her husband for comfort. He dismisses the man and his challenge as not worth thinking about, and then what's really worrying her erupts: she's terrified of childbirth. Knowing how small the cervix is, she wonders aloud how a baby can possibly squeeze through such a tiny opening. As I was writing this story I wasn't aware of how frightened I had been of giving birth and, subse-

249

quently, of being responsible for an infant. Only when I finished it did I realize how close I'd come to my own anxieties. The fiction writer is lucky if she's in touch with what's simmering inside her. My first published story was too long for its slender plot and clotted with meandering, self-consciously "literary" prose. Still, it was a start, my first published fiction. Once someone has bought something you have written you can call yourself a writer—but not before. This is the reality: a writer writes not for himself or herself but to be read by others—the more the better.

It never occurred to me that I was "juggling" anything. The feminist movement—at least this particular phase of it—was too soft to be heard and I considered myself incredibly lucky to be able to do the two things I most wanted to do, namely to write fiction and have children.

CHAPTER 13

Over the years I had stayed in touch with Max Schuster, gone to his parties, and visited him and his wife at Cow Neck Farm, his place on Long Island Sound. One Sunday we went sailing on the Chinese junk that Robert Ripley, originator of the popular cartoon feature *Believe It or Not*, had ordered built for his floating residence. Off Lloyd Neck Harbor we hailed and boarded *Sea Cloud*, the largest private yacht afloat, owned by Mrs. Marjorie Merriweather Post Davies, heiress to a Post Toasties fortune. And there were other bizarre encounters. I rarely saw the Schusters except when they were in glittering company. From time to time

Max had sent me books by authors he was especially proud to publish, among them Nikos Kazantzakis and Bertrand Russell. He came to our wedding in July 1954, and in November, doubtless swayed by the fact that I was now the son-in-law of the father of public relations, he invited me to work for him. Max was fifty-seven, chairman of Simon and Schuster's board of directors, and I was to be his personal assistant with a promise of promotion to editor. He set up a noonday meeting at his office in Rockefeller Center to "spell out," as he said, my "duties and privileges." Perhaps it was a matter of contagion, but even after knowing him for some time I was invariably twitchy and uncomfortable in his presence and expected to be more so with him as my boss. On my way to our meeting I thought it a good idea to stop off for a vodka martini at the bar of the New Weston Hotel off Madison Avenue—I might well have ordered a second drink if I had had more than an inkling of what the years to come would be like. But I thought better of this, made a final attempt at self-composure, passed the gilded statue of Atlas at the entrance to the International Building, and ascended to the twenty-eighth floor.

Max had written out the agenda for our meeting on a three-by-five pink slip and, as I noticed later, in a minuscule script that only someone as thickly spectacled as Max himself could read or write without a magnifying glass. Crammed onto this bit of paper were thirty or so headings, each of which, as he talked, he elaborated with tutorial verve, occasionally clicking his ballpoint pen for emphasis. His briefing notes covered the obligations of my job with him: to pursue "better books" and "younger authors" for the S&S list; to review the backlist with an eye to our joining the ongoing "paperback revolution" in trade publishing; to deal diplomatically with Kazantzakis, Russell, Bernard Berenson, and Will Durant, aging thoroughbreds in Max's stable of authors. Several times, interrupting the logic and continuity of his notes, he reminded me not to discuss internal affairs with his wife. At the end of our session, while Max was out of the room, I retrieved his crumpled briefing notes from the wastebasket.

And so I came to work in the office next to his, regularly seeing him open his door a crack and peer out to be sure that the corridor was clear of authors and employees before he scurried like the White Rabbit on his way to the elevator. As I discovered, he always appeared to be busier than he was and more remote from the editorial operations of his publishing house than he realized. Once, overcoming his ingrained reluctance to deal with literary agents, he called Sterling Lord to express interest in the autobiography of the boxer Rocky Graziano, *Somebody Up There Likes Me*. "But, Mr. Schuster," Lord replied, "You've already published that book."

My small room had a window that looked out over the Rockefeller Center skating rink. At the zenith—that is, at the beginning—of my career at Simon and Schuster, along with a private bathroom, Max and I shared two secretaries, both of them male. When they eventually left Max's employ, either out of exhaustion or despair at occupying a gender-anomalous role without much of a future, I was charged with interviewing and hiring their male replacements. The candidates were not, as a rule, an impressive lot. Mrs. Schuster had ordered this unbending arrangement—office romances leading to either marriage or the divorce courts were part of the firm's rich history of improvisation. Dick Simon, her husband's partner, had married the switchboard receptionist; one of Ray Schuster's sons-in-law had taken up with an editorial secretary. Ray saw no reason to test her luck by putting Max in the way of temptation. At least once during my time she ordered the purging of employees engaged in intramural affairs.

My first morning at work I found on my desk a message from Max. "Just a note to say Hello and greet you at the beginning of a creative adventure." The adventure got off to a soggy start with a

253

novel by a retired Chinese diplomat, Dr. Chang Hsin-hai, whom Max had met at someone's house on Long Island. Dr. Chang was at work on the story of a concubine named "Golden Orchid," who plied her trade during the Boxer Rebellion, married the Chinese ambassador to Germany and Russia, and became a power in the dowager empress's court. According to Chang, his novel-in-progress had everything—sex, violence, intrigue, exotic settings, historical authority, a journey on horseback through Poland, Russia, and Outer Mongolia, and similar episodes with great production values for a film epic. Without seeing a word but sensing he had made a great discovery outside of conventional publishing channels (he liked to bypass his editors and the agents they dealt with), Max decided *The Fabulous Concubine*—Chang's title—was a bonanza, with fabulous trade sales, book club, reprint, and movie potential. Violating one of his basic precepts, "Don't overstimulate authors," he made the mistake of telling all this to Dr. Chang over a festive lunch, practically unhinging him with visions of wealth and liberation from his academic post at Fairleigh-Dickinson University in Rutherford, New Jersey, an uncomfortable commute from his house in Great Neck. Out of esteem and personal affection, Max announced, without a flicker of hesitation, that he was going to ask for only 25 percent of the movie rights "instead of the usual 50." ("The usual 50" was purely imaginary; 10 percent was more like it.)

Duly delivered in person and with Mandarin ceremoniousness, Dr. Chang's enormous manuscript, hardbound in buckram so that the pages couldn't be removed and murkily typed on what felt like tissue paper, turned out to be a catastrophe, a train wreck of mangled plot, character, and storytelling. I reported to Max that anything short of incineration—certainly pencil editing, even paste-and-scissors editing—would be pointless. Unfazed, he gave me a little pep talk about "creative editing" and quoted (somewhat inaptly, I thought) Speaker of the House Sam Rayburn—"A jack-ass can kick a barn down, but it takes a carpenter to build one." He set me carpenter-wise to putting the entire manuscript through my manual typewriter. I did this over the course of a couple of weeks, all the while enduring Dr. Chang's daily and sometimes hourly phone calls, a Chinese water torture drip-drip of noodges, kibitzing, and second thoughts.

What the book needed, to cite an old joke, was not monkey glands but a whole new monkey. Chang's concern for his misshapen offspring became even more exigent as the day approached for its release. Max's "fiction event of the year" (one of the shopworn clichés of the book trade) passed in silence, unnoted by reviewers and booksellers, despite a fancy jacket reproducing a Chinese silk painting and Max's hypomanic promotion and advertising copy. Dr. Chang's awful novel, which Max believed should have been at least a *succès de scandale* because of its sexy story, wasn't even a flop *d'estime*. Max accepted its failure with an endearing mix of resignation and amusement, the response of a thirty-year veteran of a largely inspirational business notorious for its peaks and valleys. Dr. Chang's telephone calls tapered off into aggrieved silence.

With the exception of Nikos Kazantzakis's Dionysian and life-celebrating *Zorba the Greek*, fiction was not Max's best hold.

Warning that I was dealing with "one of the world's great analytic minds," Max had me, over his signature, negotiate royalty percentages, advances, scheduling, and the division of rights with Bertrand Russell, mathematician, philosopher, and winner (in 1950) of the Nobel Prize for literature. Russell had had a great popular and financial success with his *History of Western Philosophy*, published by Simon and Schuster in 1945. Since then Max had obediently issued a stream of Russell's books, most of them of minor importance, in the hope of eventually acquiring the rights to Russell's autobiography. Fidelity, marital and otherwise, had never been one of the philosopher's virtues—he eventually auctioned off his two-volume autobiography to Little, Brown.

Max also had me sweet-talk and haggle contract terms, this time face-to-face with the legendary financier, presidential adviser, and park-bench blowhard Bernard Baruch. "With my major enthusiasm and big best-seller campaign," Max cabled me from Palm Beach, "we can sell at least fifty thousand copies plus big reprint deal and excellent chance of book club selection." During one of my sessions with Baruch in his Fifth Avenue apartment, I heard him deflect a phone call from his mistress of long standing, Clare Boothe Luce. "Tell her I'm asleep," he instructed his assistant. Baruch wasn't any more forthright with us than Russell had been. He sold his memoirs to another house, having used our offer to bump up their terms.

Max's restless mind generated some queer, short-lived ideas, among them a children's book that floated in the bathtub and a three-wheeled vehicle that he proposed to the Ford Motor Company. With *The People's Shakespeare* laid to rest, he planned an edition of the plays and poems that would be "something different," he said, "an act of creative publishing." He had been won over by a book published in 1920, *"Shakespeare" Identified in Edward De Vere, the Seventeenth Earl of Oxford*, the work of an amateur scholar named Thomas J. Looney. Max decided this "something different" should be an edition giving full credit to the earl of Oxford and titled *Looney's "Shakespeare."* Title and author's name apart, I had to convince Max that although several other great minds, including Sigmund Freud and Mark Twain, had bought into the Oxford authorship theory, hard evidence—including textual references in the later plays to events that occurred after Oxford's death in 1604—suggested that Dr. Chang had only a slightly weaker claim than the earl to have written *The Tempest*. Subsequently, Max assigned me to deflect the trickle of Oxfordians, Baconians, religious enthusiasts, Bible decipherers, and possessors of the secret of the universe who showed up from time to time at the reception desk determined to be heard. I had to remind myself that if these monomaniacs insisted the moon was made of green cheese the burden of proof was on them.

Another of Max's back-channel acquaintances, a cultivated refugee businessman named Martin Lederman, had written a diet book called *The Slim Gourmet*. It argued that if you want to lose weight you don't have to give up the rich, fattening foods you love, just eat smaller portions of them. Lederman managed to spread this astounding one-sentence idea over a couple of hundred pages, demonstrating a bloat principle that he planned to apply, in a second book, to the subject of canned soup, inevitably Campbell's, since Campbell's accounted for about 80 percent of all canned soup sales. Max was taken with the prospect of selling thousands and thousands of Lederman's special soup book to Campbell's, who would offer it to soup lovers as a tie-in and promotional premium, the sort of thing you'd get for sending in fifty cents and the label peeled off a can. He assigned me to put together a prototype, to which Lederman contributed a watery text extolling the convenience and versatility of canned soup. It also explained the wonders of the book's gimmick (and sole reason for existence)—a windowed cardboard wheel showing which two or three or four canned soups could go together, with appropriate garnishes, in delicious, novel, and calorie-frugal combinations.

After preliminary negotiations that entailed my visit to Campbell's Camden, New Jersey, headquarters, housing museum-style the world's largest collection of soup tureens, I invited the Campbell's executives to a midday meeting in a private room of the Rockefeller Center Lunch Club. I had hoped to loosen up the Campbell delegation with cocktails in preparation for our sales pitch, but they followed the lead of their stony-faced boss and

257

declined alcohol in favor of Campbell's Beef Bouillon on the rocks (a concoction known as a "Bull-shot"). An executive from the sales department and I did the same. Our guests listened glumly to our presentation, went back to Camden, and that was the last we saw of them. No doubt they wondered, and with good reason, whether their customers, the great soup-slurping public, needed Lederman's magic wheel to tell them they could make puree mongole by mixing cans of tomato and green pea soup.

We had better success with the Mobil Corporation on a series of regional restaurant and lodging guides that Max had pitched to one of Mobil's directors, Grayson Kirk, Dwight Eisenhower's successor as president of Columbia University. The proposed Mobil guides were to be America's answer to the famous *Guides Michelin*. Michelin used forks as rating symbols (they had the sense not to choose tires or inflatable little men). Max wanted to use the Mobil emblem, a flying red horse, a great idea if you were rating filling stations. It took some doing on my part, not all of it tactful, to convince him that despite their promotional value, Mobil's horses shouldn't be on customers' minds as they cut into their Chateaubriands. Who would want to spend the night, I asked him, at a four-horse motel? For such mouthiness he came close to exiling me to Texas to do a dry run rating chili parlors.

Despite these ventures into tie-in and premium publishing, Max's sustaining passion was for the dissemination of knowledge, a goal symbolized by the publishing logo he and his partner Dick Simon had chosen decades earlier, a rendering of Jean François Millet's painting of a peasant sowing seeds in a field. The house motto, "Give the Reader a Break" (cast in bronze as a paperweight), conveyed a commitment to editorial civility and tact he and Simon considered vital to the publisher's job.

When I worked for him (and long before as well as long after), Max was in the grip of a scheme to put together and publish a great Summa, or Novum Organum, or Five (or fifty) Foot-Shelf to be called *The Inner Sanctum Library of Living Literature*. It already included spectacular publishing successes like Thomas Craven's *A Treasury of Art Masterpieces*, a special edition of *War and Peace*, and Ernest Sutherland Bates's *The Bible Designed to Be Read as Living Literature* (the title aroused a fair amount of indignation and amusement). Taking all knowledge for its province, *The Inner Sanctum Library of Living Literature* was to cover the full range of human culture—verbal, musical, practical, and pictorial—from Homer, Plato, and Montaigne to state-of-the-art advice on how to achieve peace of mind and remove cat vomit from upholstery. Max's own and cherished contribution was a well-received anthology, *A Treasury of the World's Great Letters*. With a passion for explicitness and elaboration, and in case you weren't yet sure what it was that you were holding in your hand, Max had subtitled his collection of letters *From Ancient Days to Our Own Time, Containing the Characteristic and Crucial Communications and Intimate Exchanges and Cycles of Correspondence of Many of the Outstanding Figures of World History, and Some Notable Contemporaries.*

M. Lincoln Schuster and Albert Einstein, 1946. *Used by permission of Pearl London.*

Max often expounded on the *Inner Sanctum Library* and on other publishing matters over lamb or chicken curry at the Rockefeller Center Lunch Club, a midday feeding place (at night the Rainbow Room) for heavy hitters in publishing, broadcasting, and communications. When one of Max's friends there, J. David Stern, a little roostery man who owned newspapers in Pennsylvania and New Jersey, announced as he left his table that he was going out to buy the *New York Post*, someone said, "Here, David, here's a nickel. Please buy a copy for me." Stern's ego, like that of another familiar figure there, the public relations mogul Benjamin Sonnenberg, was invulnerable to ridicule. The food at these table-hopping lunches was invariably preceded by Max's purely ceremonial order—a gesture of hospitality to his guest—"a little Scotch with a lot of soda." He never took more than a sip. When the main dish arrived he and I often tussled over the sauce boat of chutney—he assumed it was meant for him alone. He had a distressing habit of spraying food as he talked. You learned not to flinch but, between courses, to escape to the men's room to clean your eyeglasses. A good meal, in Max's idiom, earned "good reviews."

Lunch was his time for dispensing general wisdom, instruction, and merriment—he had an infallible sense of the comic and a Talmudic gift for cutting through nonsense, and he was as funny as he was shy. Behind thick glasses his eyes teared with laughter. "Even authors have rights," he told me, "although you don't have to invite them to dinner with you." When pressed for a decision that he wasn't yet willing to make, his trademark stall was, "Let's give him a definite maybe." He favored formula phrases like "hardening of the categories," "twenty-twenty hindsight," "faith, hope, and clarity." He had learned from experience that the manuscript delivery date in publishing contracts was only "a baseline for postponements." "Always read with a pencil in your hand," he told me many times—since then I've never been able to do otherwise. "Rule number one in publishing: Shoot the widow": he had learned this lesson in abrasive dealings with the estate of Rabbi Joshua Loth Liebman, author of one of the firm's most successful books ever, *Peace of Mind*.

The function of an editor, he often told me, was not to pass judgment on an author's work—anybody can do that—but to recognize whatever potential it had and either help the author dig it out or dig it out yourself. The supreme exemplar of such "creative editing," as almost every publishing novice knew, was the late and legendary Maxwell Perkins, credited with having nurtured Hemingway and Fitzgerald and turning Thomas Wolfe's trunkloads of manuscript into something like novels. The trouble with the Perkins exemplar, Max argued, was that some authors expected magic from their editors, abdicated responsibility for their work, and acted like children.

He was addicted to quoting from a four-page dittoed collection of epigrams—*The Wisdom of the S(ages), or, Short Sentences Based on Long Experience* (in other words, *Max-ims*)—that he compiled, updated from time to time, and distributed to friends. Among his favorites were "God is subtle but not malicious" (Albert Einstein); "There is no cure for birth or death except to enjoy the interval" (George Santayana); "Always do right; you will gratify some people, and astonish the rest" (Mark Twain); and "Great thoughts come from the heart" (Vauvenargues). Another referred to the denizens of Boca Raton, Palm Beach, and Juan-les-Pins, places Max and his wife often visited in the winter: "Shady people in sunny places." My own favorite during these recitations of gnomic wisdom was: "This too shall pass."

Max had a stock of inescapable routines and fetishes, like sending a messenger for an advance copy of *Publishers Weekly*—he had to be first with the news. Every morning at eight-forty-five he phoned whoever was in charge of publicity and asked, "What's

261

new on the city desk?" Another routine: "This bulletin just in. Someone was seen attempting to buy a book at Brentano's [or Doubleday, or Scribner's]. The manager called the police, and the man is now at Bellevue being held for observation." I attended these daily performances with an aplomb verging on catatonia.

As part of my training I had to learn Max's system of abbreviations and verbal algorithms, great time-savers when bucking letters down the line. His scribbled PAAIMA UYOJ DTN MLS at the top of a letter he had received meant, when decoded, "Please answer as in my absence. Use your own judgment. Do the necessary. M. Lincoln Schuster." The tiresome but officially approved formula for my replies: "In Mr. Schuster's absence from the office, I am taking the liberty of responding to your letter of such-and-such a date." (It was amazing how often he was supposed to be absent from the office.) His alphabet code was as much a Schuster trademark as the straight pins, a menace to beginners, that he used instead of paper clips (he abhorred them) to fasten papers together. Another trademark: the pink, blue, and green three-by-five slips, each color with a particular significance, he kept in his left-hand coat pocket. He used them for recording instructions, ideas, and, of course, maxims and then moved them to his right-hand or "out" pocket from which they would go to his secretaries for action or filing.

Drafting Max's own letters in triple space for his revisions and eventual signature, I became, in effect, a ghostly presence in his publishing affairs. Over his name I carried on phantom correspondences with all sorts of people, including Henry Ford II, whose equivalent phantom, impressively named Forrest D. Murden Jr., I once had lunch with. Each of us knew but neither acknowledged the other's role in the exchanges between our masters. In time I achieved a modest command of Schuster boilerplate, hyperbole, and formulaic closings and learned from him not to raise more than one question per letter if you wanted results, and always to close with a request for action (the "what to do next" paragraph). On my own I also learned that if you wanted to confuse and exasperate a letter writer who made the mistake of raising several questions, you had only to answer just one.

Working for Max Schuster, I thought, was like playing for the New York Yankees. I was proud that I had been recruited in the first place, lasted as long as I did (about five years), and worked with authors I admired and brought into the house—the sociologist C. Wright Mills, the memoirist Niccolò Tucci, the poet Muriel Rukeyser. Tucci's *Before My Time*, an account of his early years in Mussolini's Italy, was a work of genuine literary distinction, comparable to Vladimir Nabokov's *Speak, Memory*. Tucci had seen the rise and demise of fascism only to find himself living in the America of do-nothing President Dwight Eisenhower and Eisenhower's secretary of state, John Foster Dulles, the first, "crazy and cancer-ridden," Tucci raged in one of his operatic appearances in my office (making significant moves toward the open window), and the second, equally "crazy," bent on plunging the world into another hot war.

Muriel Rukeyser's *One Life* combined poetry, biography, reportage, meditation, and history in a boldly original way that was bound to baffle and repel some readers. It told the story of Wendell Willkie, a lawyer and corporate leader (president of Commonwealth and Southern, a giant utility holding company), a Democrat turned liberal Republican, who had entered the political arena, his critics joked, as a "barefoot boy from Wall Street." He ran for president against F.D.R. in 1940; he toured wartime England, Russia, and China as F.D.R.'s personal emissary; and in 1943 he published *One World*, a book (written with Joe Barnes's help) that described his travels, preached globalism, and sold about four and a half million copies by the time he died in 1944. A

263

foe of Amerian isolationism, Willkie had been one of my heroes. I would have voted for him in 1940 if I had been of voting age. But by 1957, when Muriel's book came out, he was pretty well forgotten or, if remembered at all, counted among the freaks of recent political history. The first book I sponsored when I came to Simon and Schuster, *One Life*, described by its author as "a story and a song," earned me as its editor a plea from *Post* columnist Murray Kempton, in his review in the *New York Post*, to get down on my knees and pray for forgiveness.

CHAPTER 14

During the early and mid-1950s there seemed always to be a party, small or large, at Bernie Winebaum's walk-up apartment at 950 First Avenue: a mix of writers (William Gaddis, Jimmy Merrill, and David Jackson, Frank O'Hara, James Schuyler), museum and gallery curators (William S. Lieberman, Jacob Bean), and occasional society night creatures. Bernie's impromptu, ad hoc parties simply happened, like flurries of snow.

I had known Bernie only from a distance when we were students togther in a freshman German course at Harvard. The instructor, Heinrich Kruse, said to have been an officer in the

Kaiser's army in World War I, recognized a natural victim in me, and after three weeks of systematic humiliation I dropped his course. Bernie, as I was to learn, soldiered on, and seven years later, when we ran into each other at a wine cellar in Paris, he recalled my ordeal in detail. It was impossible not to love him for such concern. In the intervening years he had acquired the confident manners and style of the WASP upper class along with a certain stylish fastidiousness, but he managed to do this without selling out his loyalty to middle-class Portsmouth, New Hampshire, where his father, prominent in the Jewish community, ran the Hearst news agency for northern New England, acquired valuable real estate, and prospered. When we met in Paris Bernie was on leave from a liaison job in Germany with the Hebrew Immigrant Aid Society, one of several organizations trying to deal with the vast tide of displaced persons the war had left in the hands of the victors. "Guilt and officialdom, dirt and depravity," he wrote to me from Schweinfurt. "You can picture, if you care to, sniveling Germans, black marketing DP's, bribe-taking petty officials, the habitual smut of occupation army people, *und so weiter*." He managed to do his job with the little German he had learned in Herr Kruse's class supplemented by a smattering of Yiddish picked up from his grandparents.

A year later he made a binary shift, from inferno to paradiso, from Schweinfurt in the Allied Zone of occupied Germany to the island of Ischia in the Bay of Naples. He rented an apartment there that he said looked a little like the Museum of Modern Art, took his meals with Wystan Auden and Chester Kallman, and joined a "small but ferocious American colony" that had touched down like a flock of migrating birds: Truman Capote, the poet James Schuyler (then Auden's secretary), Tennessee Williams, and an assortment of "literary chasers" and remittance people from New York.

When his money ran out Bernie left Ischia for New York. Endowed with considerable charm and worldly experience, a fluent writer and an accomplished artist, over the next few years he worked at a succession of prize jobs: at *Time*; at *Flair*, Fleur Cowles's glossy magazine of fashion and the arts; at a top advertising agency, Ogilvy, Benson, and Mather. He was never able to stay put, after a brief euphoria sinking into a state of chronic disgruntlement, picking fights with his employers, unable to satisfy whatever it was that he expected of himself. I hadn't begun to realize how constantly he drank—our favorite was a medium-price blended whiskey called Bellows Partner's Reserve—until one weekend when we flew to Miami to stay with an aunt of his and he vomited on the tarmac.

He started commuting to Athens where, with money from his parents, he bought a nightclub that he decorated with his own murals. He self-published a volume of his poetry, illustrated the work of a Greek novelist, and filled leather-bound notebooks with nervous and witty ink drawings. Driving his little Karmann-Ghia he steered with his elbows as he looked for a cigarette and lighted it, and this was terrifying enough, but he was also nearsighted and only at the last moment did he recognize that it was a person or a dog, and not some wisps of hay, that happened to be moving across the road in front of him. At his best, Bernie was generous, supportive, and tolerant, playful as a kitten, and in Mark Twain's phrase, as "sociable as a house fly." That he was gay and I was not never came between us. He and Annie adored each other, but before then there had also been women friends of mine he disapproved of, in a protective way, as not being up to the level of intelligence, sensibility, and native good judgment (he used the Yiddish word *sachel*) he thought I deserved.

Bernie knew everybody, especially people with impressive family trees and colorful connections, and he insisted on telling Annie and me about them at exasperating length. He was always meeting someone for drinks, weekending at Fire Island, Sag Harbor, Sneeden's Landing, or Stonington. As much as I loved Bernie there were times when I went out of my way not to see him, especially when his moods swung with alarming speed and unpredictability from high spirits to a rage directed against "liberals," "Communists," "faggots," and at least one family member. He became a vociferous supporter of Greece's right-wing military government. "What's the latest about Bernie," some of his old party guests would ask me. "Has he gone mad again?" He began to vanish from my life.

After Annie and I married, parties in New York no longer had their old romantic and erotic glow, their promise of adventure. Now they were largely a kind of education, an extension of office life: being a full-time editor was also an evening job. One night, in the crowded Central Park West living room of Tom Bevans, head of production at Simon and Schuster, Annie and I met the humorist James Thurber. Then in his midsixties, he talked nonstop, somewhat drunkenly, about his daughter and her favorite stuffed animal. Several times he had to interrupt his monologues to be led, like blind Oedipus, down a long hallway to the bathroom. Helen Thurber, his second wife, nudged me with her elbow, complaining in a loud whisper, "He's talking about that goddam daughter of his again." Except for her, the roomful of guests listened in battered silence, even the celebrity of the day, the quiz show champion Charles Van Doren, a Columbia University literature instructor and son of the distinguished literary scholar Mark Van Doren. In front of the television cameras he appeared to know everything, from astronomy to zootomy, along with the batting records of Ty Cobb and Tris Speaker. For fourteen dazzling weeks, locked in a glass-walled isolation booth (a trademark feature of *Twenty-One*), sweating and biting his lip as he strained for answers to difficult questions, Van Doren established himself as something unique in American popular culture of the day: the intellectual—or at least, the know-it-all—as hero. In November 1959, responding to a subpoena and open to charges of perjury for lying to a grand jury, he finally confessed to a congressional subcommittee that his spectacular ride to glory and $129,000 in prize money had been a put-up job: the producers of *Twenty-One* primed him with the questions and fed him the answers. We felt sold out, doubly ashamed because we should never have bought into this cheap spectacle in the first place.

Van Doren was like an earlier public figure turned notoriety, Alger Hiss. Annie and I met him and his wife, Priscilla, in 1956, shortly after he had finished serving in a federal penitentiary a five-year term for perjury. He told us he was proud that he had proven himself able to survive life on the inside without injury, especially since, as a convicted spy for the Soviets, he must have been a pariah among felons. "I can take care of myself," he said. That evening, after dinner at the house of one of Hiss's (and Max Schuster's) lawyers, Ephraim London, we planned to watch the televised newsreels of Grace Kelly's wedding to Prince Rainier of Monaco. To satisfy an American public that (like us) hungered for celebrity doings hot off the griddle, an RAF fighter had flown the films from Nice to Gander, Newfoundland, where they were loaded onto an American plane that took them to New York. The wedding films, melding studio royalty and casino royalty, were harmless enough entertainment by anyone's standards. But for Priscilla Hiss it was a matter of principle not to watch—and thereby to condone—a show-business spectacle that would "corrupt," she said, "the shop girls of America." Up to then I hadn't known even that we had "shop girls" in our country nor had I suspected that Priscilla may have been the driving ideological force in the Hiss family. We left her sitting alone in righteous protest and rushed downstairs to the TV room in the basement.

Another evening, writer and photographer Peter H. Buckley, the author of *Bullfight*, a book I was editing at Simon and Schuster, gave a champagne, brandy, and tapas party in honor of the star matador Antonio Ordóñez. With Ordóñez was his beautiful wife, sister of his arch-rival, another numero uno of the bullring, Luis Miguel Dominguín. Ordóñez managed somehow to present himself always in profile as he shook hands or conversed through clouds of cigarette smoke with the *New Yorker* theater critic and bullfight enthusiast Kenneth Tynan.

Buckley's party reflected the vogue for La Fiesta Brava during the 1950s. My own interest in the sport, as it was called, had barely survived seeing bulls butchered in the ring at Nogales, Mexico, years earlier: after some colossally inept swordplay the torero finished off the animal by driving a sort of screwdriver into its brain. Many of my friends who had never been closer to a bullfight than a second-balcony seat at *Carmen* fancied themselves aficionados of a sort. They read books about bullfighting by Hemingway, Tom Lea, and Barnaby Conrad, sat through the 1957 film of *The Sun Also Rises*, owned copies of Picasso's corrida graphics, and in solemn moments, with a little harsh *vino tinto* in their bellies, recited Federico García Lorca's lines for a dead bullfighter—

> At five in the afternoon.
> Ah, that fatal five in the afternoon!

Idioms of the bullring—"working within the danger of the horns," "the moment of truth"—became part of the lit-crit vocabulary: for serious writers struggling to go one-on-one with language it was always five o'clock in the afternoon, with blood already staining the sand. The bullfight's ritualized, balletic assassinations were supposed to reveal something profound about the Spanish character and our own craving for expiation. Despite Buckley's attempts to instruct me in *afición*, despite this evening in proximity to the great Ordóñez, what that something was I never found out.

Among the partying people I knew at all well alcohol was the thing and drugs did not play much of a role, except conversationally: the words *psychedelic, hallucinogen, acid,* and *trip* had entered our lexicon. In 1958 the young journalist Dan Wakefield, a transplant from Indianapolis to New York (he still said "Golly!" when impressed), tried to recruit me for a weekend-long experiment in LSD, a laboratory product reported to be many times, weight for weight, more potent than peyote. The gain for me, according to Wakefield, was to be the adventure itself along with a dramatic expansion in consciousness that would enrich my store of experience and make me a better editor. The gain for him was to be my moment-by-moment reactions and behavior, raw material for an *Esquire* article. In controlled circumstances (a private house up the Hudson near Croton), with Wakefield and his *Esquire* editor as observers (along with a doctor in attendance, just in case things got out of hand), I was to travel to a new plane of being with only Wakefield's casual assurance I would return to sea level with my mind in one piece. Enthusiastically, even passionately, urged on me over two long lunches, the project had undeniable allure as my introduction to an emerging spirit of the decade. Wakefield was the apostle Paul, but I remained the reluctant unbeliever Agrippa—"Almost thou persuadest me." "Almost" was not enough.

In 1958, when Susanna, our first child, was old enough to sit up at her table and eat baby food, Annie and I diverted her with propeller noises and daredevil swerves and swoops as we piloted the spoon from a hot plate of mashed carrots and applesauce to her mouth. "It's from Fidel, in the Sierra Maestra," we said, bringing the spoon in for a landing, "and it's for you!"

Fidel Castro was our hero, a middle-class professional (lawyer) who was also a revolutionist, a man of daring and action like Judas Maccabeus and the Lone Ranger. From his outlaw's hideout in the mountains, Fidel, Raoul Castro, and Che Guevara led a guerrilla 271

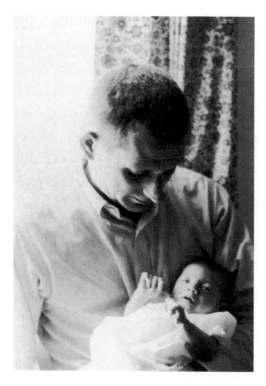
J.K. and infant Susanna, 1957.

band sworn to topple dictator Fulgencio Batista, banish the corruptive Yankee dollars, and, so we understood, bring democracy to
Cuba together with literacy. What a David and Goliath conflict,
what a good war Fidel was fighting! What a contrast to President
Dwight D. Eisenhower's indifference to civil injustices and to the
policies of his maniacal secretary of state, John Foster Dulles, who
preached massive retaliation and practiced brinkmanship! Before
Castro became our official enemy, a Communist dictator in our
own backyard, there were even elements of comedy to entertain
us: Fidel on the pitcher's mound; Fidel's numbing public speeches
that went on for hours; Fidel's cigars, signature beard, drab uniform; Fidel's survival, even diplomatic triumph in the face of
American attempts to humiliate him. A day after he arrived in
New York to attend a meeting of world leaders at the United
Nations, the Waldorf-Astoria management booted him from the

hotel, allegedly because his aides had been plucking chickens for *arroz con pollo* in the corridors. Fidel and his entourage moved to Harlem, to the Hotel Theresa on 125th Street. There Soviet Premier Nikita Khrushchev paid him a fraternal visit, a diplomatic and public relations disaster for the United States.

Through a wrench in perception, an exercise in cognitive assonance, we managed to live with the prospect of nuclear warfare while enjoying a time of economic growth and rampant consumerism. We had become "Utopia Limited in the Fat 1950s." *The Affluent Society*, the economist John Kenneth Galbraith called it in his classic 1958 book. In line with its growing control over our behavior and its demonic power to create desire, advertising— "Madison Avenue," familiarly—was the hot profession of the decade: glamorous, well paid, extravagantly self-marketed, and intrinsically fascinating. The daily capitalist soap opera had its distinctive cast of characters, "account executives" and "creative" people who carried attaché cases and bowed before "clients." At the end of their working day, they drank martinis and played gin rummy in the New Haven Railroad club car on their way home to Westport, archetypal exurb for people in the "advertising game." One of my authors at Simon and Schuster referred to me as his "account executive"—I set him straight with a few coarse words.

In the 1950s Annie and I were reading best-sellers like Frederic Wakeman's *The Hucksters* (its hero chooses "a sincere tie" to wear at a crucial interview), Vance Packard's *The Hidden Persuaders*, Martin Mayer's *Madison Avenue*, and Sloan Wilson's *The Man in the Gray Flannel Suit*, one of Dick Simon's most notable successes (Simon's protegé, Richard L. Grossman, posed for the jacket picture of the iconic Man). Writers we knew worked in advertising: William Gaddis, Anatole Broyard, James Dickey, L. E. Sissman, Joseph Heller, Richard Yates. Like movie mogul Samuel Goldwyn's malapropisms, advertising maxims, genuine or apoc-

273

ryphal, became part of our jokey language. "Run it up the flagpole and see if anybody salutes," "Smear it on the cat and see if she licks it off," "Put it on the 6:28 and see if it gets off at Westport," "Throw it in the pool and see if it comes up for air": the "it" being whatever slogan, headline, or campaign idea that might go over with agency bosses, clients, and eventually, us, the target public.

Advertising entertained us, but at the same time we knew we were surrendering some degree of control over our lives to enticing headlines and talking animals, to beer, razor blade, and laundry detergent jingles we couldn't get out of our heads. We were becoming part of a great homogenized American public with no will of its own, only a set of conditioned reflexes profitably studied by motivational researchers. (One expert, possibly fictional, is supposed to have predicted the quick demise of the Ford Edsel because of the vaginal shape of its front grille—"You can't sell a thing like that without hair around it.") There was plenty of informed support for this feeling of helplessness. According to the reasoned conclusions of David Riesman's *The Lonely Crowd* we had become "outer-directed" rather than "inner-directed," consumers rather than producers, on the edge of alienation. William H. Whyte Jr.'s *The Organization Man*, an important book acquired and skillfully published for Simon and Schuster by Joe Barnes, narrowed the focus to corporate culture. As a way of subverting conformity, a thumb in the eye for personnel managers, Whyte provided a valuable appendix titled "How to Cheat on Personality Tests."

What spoke to me even more directly, because they combined disciplined analysis, polemic, and a sort of Old Testament indignation, were two books by the maverick Columbia sociologist C. Wright Mills: *White Collar* and *The Power Elite*. Walt Whitman heard "America singing . . . strong melodious songs" of democratic joy and well-being. Wright Mills heard an upper-class oligarchy reveling in its ascendant strength, "money talking in its husky, silky voice of cash, power, celebrity." "American capitalism is now in considerable part a military capitalism," Mills wrote in 1956, five years before even Eisenhower, in a farewell address to the American people, warned of the "misplaced power" of "the military-industrial complex."

Like Fidel Castro (for a while), like F. O. Matthiessen (who killed himself in 1950), Wright Mills was an intellectual hero of the time and bearer of our best hopes, destined for failure though they were. He called himself objective but not detached, "a spiritual Wobbly," "a North American aboriginal." When I learned through his literary agent, James Oliver Brown, that Mills wanted to leave Oxford University Press, his publisher until then, I reported this to the Simon and Schuster editorial board. They allowed me to offer Mills an advance of $5,000 for a new book, to be called *The Causes of World War Three*. It turned out to be a typical Wright Mills effusion—bold, passionate, indignant, unsparing, totally engaged, a little grandiose and windy, a pamphleteering attack on what he called the "crackpot realism" that shaped the disaster-bound military and diplomatic policies of the United States and the Soviets. "For the first time in world history," Mills wrote, "men find themselves preparing for a war which, they admit among themselves, none of the combatants could win. . . . Yet men of power, even as they talk about peace, practice for war." The work of a Jeremiah, no longer an academic sociologist, Mills's book was perhaps overwrought, but it was important, and I worked harder than I had ever before done in publishing to promote it to a general readership and to a core audience of "opinion makers," in the jargon of the trade. Early one morning I dragged Mills off to appear on the *Today* show, a grotesque forum, given its commercial auspices and usual content, for doomsday convictions voiced by a combination of John the Baptist and Chicken Little.

The Causes of World War Three was only a moderate success, as 275 might be expected of a book that told people what they didn't want to hear, but Mills became my friend. He was big, voracious, and impulsive, a person of apparently ungovernable energies and often rudely indifferent to eastern and academic etiquette. He was "a figure of power," the critic Irving Howe said, "a fiercely grinding power that came down like a fist." Mills turned conventional sociology on its head: what he cared about was the flow of history, not "statistical stuff," "block surveys" that reported what people were thinking or how much they spent on whiskey. He had dozens of as-yet unwritten books and articles in mind, including *Listen Yankee: The Revolution in Cuba*. Wanting to rescue lower-case "marxism" from upper-case "Communism," he remained a Fidelista after Fidel became the State Department's chief local villain. Castro's betrayal of Cuban democracy left Mills behind the curl of history, even though he believed he was riding it into shore.

Given Mills's appetites, ambitions, and restless intellect, there could never be enough time for him to do all he wanted to do. He started the morning by brewing a quart of espresso on his kitchen machine—this was a potion that might have felled other people but only got him revved up to cruising speeds at his typewriter. He dressed like the foreman of a cattle ranch (he was born in Waco) in jeans, work shirts, and biker boots and drove around town, and to the house he was building in West Nyack, on a big supercharged BMW hog. Mills had earned a mechanic's certificate from the BMW motorcycle works in Germany, and as Annie and I realized at dinner one night, when we tried to steer the conversation away from motorcycles, he was prouder of his grease-monkey's diploma than of any of his academic degrees and honors. Drinking bourbon, eating cheese and walnuts all the while, although his doctor had warned him he was at risk of heart disease, he kept on talking about motorcycles at Castro-like length and to the exclusion of any other subject.

Another night he summoned us to his apartment near Columbia to see a newly arrived piece of teakwood furniture made to his specifications in Denmark. He took each of us by the arm and led us into the presence. We saw an altarlike hybrid of sideboard and bureau with drawers for Wright's shirts and pajamas and, above, about a dozen large pigeonholes that he had just finished labeling. SOCKS and HANDKERCHIEFS filled two of them. The others, also labeled, held notes and drafts of lectures, articles, and books. "Isn't that something!" he said, running his hands over the oiled teakwood. For a brief moment at least he had put the world in order.

Max Schuster entrusted me with editing of perhaps the most considerable literary book he was to publish, the poet Kimon Friar's translation (from the Greek) of *The Odyssey: A Modern Sequel*, a 33,333-line epic by Nikos Kazantzakis, perennial candidate for the Nobel Prize. "Blind Homer sings again!" Max announced to the trade—"A masterpiece of contemporary literature." I went through the enormous manuscript word by word and line by line, looking out for anachronisms and vagaries of meter and idiom. Meanwhile I had to deal with Kimon Friar's oily, insinuating, and spiderish personality. (The poet James Merrill called it "appalling." Merrill's father, founder of Merrill Lynch, had once threatened to have Kimon "rubbed out" for seducing his son.) Equally trying were Kimon's absences: when most urgently needed to answer editing queries, he was found to be visiting an uncle in practically unreachable Antofagasta, Chile. He even managed to be unreachable when a proofreader discovered at the last minute that two of the 33,333 lines were missing. From time to time Kimon complained to Max that Harvard had covered me with too "many thin layers of reticence" for me to be properly ecstatic about his work. He tried to get me fired, but face-to-face, over long lunches on my expense account, he was accommodating enough. And he did one thing that to my mind almost redeemed him. He had invited me to a twenty-fourth-birthday party he was giving for a young Greek poet, Stratis Haviaras, and I went reluctantly, as a professional duty. I had told Annie that the party wasn't worth getting a baby-sitter for and that she was lucky to be able to stay home. At one in the morning in Friar's dingy apartment off upper Columbus Avenue, I found myself dancing with Marilyn Monroe and gently kneading the little tire of baby fat around her waist. Her husband, Arthur Miller, looked on glumly as the party wore on. Friar, as I learned, was tutoring him in prosody.

At Simon and Schuster it was hard not to be infected by an extraordinarily high level of publishing energy operating in a largely improvisational, psycho-dramatic sort of way. Mysterious newcomers of indeterminate function came and went like Captain Ahab's "subordinate phantoms" living belowdecks. One of these phantoms, roundly named Rudo S. Globus, shut himself in his office one day and told me, "I'm going to smoke myself to death." In this freewheeling atmosphere an editor seized publishing opportunities the way the Bolsheviks, a minority faction, had seized political power—in a vacuum, or as it lay in the streets. You had to be ready and on the spot. When Jack Goodman, de facto editor in chief (Max held on to the title), died suddenly of a heart attack, I was on my way to La Guardia airport and two weeks on Cape Cod with Annie and our two baby daughters. I missed the meeting a day later at which the staff divided up Goodman's authors, projects, and agent contacts. That missed meeting marked my downward turning point.

Practically everyone at Simon and Schuster was an editor-publisher of sorts. We were derisive when we heard about houses like Prentice-Hall, where every publishing function was strictly compartmentalized. After passing down an assembly line, Prentice-Hall books emerged as "product," in much the same way packing-house porkers were turned into little breakfast sausages. Resisting tables of organization and lines of authority we kept the "business people" as far away from us as we could. We treated the firm's chief financial officer as if he were simply an office manager whose job it was to make sure we covered our typewriters and turned off the lights and air conditioners before leaving for the day.

It was *fun* to work at Simon and Schuster, not surprising to see editors staying long after hours to talk about books, trade industry gossip, and joke over office bottles of Scotch and gin. In the days before it was absorbed into a conglomerate the house was like a summer camp for intellectually hyperactive children.

Aside from Max Schuster, my most important tutor in the ways of book publishing was Joseph Barnes, former Moscow correspondent and foreign editor of the *New York Herald Tribune*. Barnes knew Russian and had traveled widely and often in Soviet Russia. At the opening of the McCarthy era this was enough to qualify him as a target. In 1951 the Senate Internal Security Committee put him through the wringer in a two-hour closed-door inquisition. Five witnesses, including Whittaker Chambers, said that over the years they had "heard" Barnes identified as a Soviet agent. The committee denied him the opportunity to clear his name in an open hearing. Max Schuster never wavered in his support of Joe in the face of pressures from inside and outside the house to have him dismissed as a liability. So far from being a liability he was a major asset, having known practically everyone in the upper levels of government, politics, journalism, and the academy. He had gone to China during the war with Wendell Willkie, worked with Dwight Eisenhower on *Crusade in Europe*, and 279 cofounded a boldly innovative liberal tabloid, *PM*. He and his partners on the paper hoped to make a go of it without having to sell advertising. The firm's intellectual eminence and social model, Joe was its major claim to class in the publishing industry. But the McCarthy ordeal had taken the fight out of him: he did his job, stayed out of office politics and power struggles, and was respected, even revered. After nursing it along for years, Barnes had been responsible for one of S&S's historic successes, William L. Shirer's *The Rise and Fall of the Third Reich*. But there was a sadness about him—I thought he was cut out for bigger things and suspected he thought so, too. In time my closest friend at S&S (I having survived a gentle probation), he introduced me to daunting carafes of martinis at the Century Association and the roast beef hash and lightly seared calves liver at P.J. Moriarty's on Sixth Avenue. For me, every outing with Joe was an education in the way the world worked when interpreted by a cultivated, tolerant, and seasoned intelligence.

A marathon lunch with him and Walt Kelly, creator of Pogo, went through cocktails and wine and ended with brandy in the late afternoon. Joe's strategy for maintaining relative sobriety was to drink beer before cocktails so that he wouldn't be drinking cocktails out of thirst. Strong drink, the obligatory lubricant of publishing lunches, sales conferences, and trade events, was an occupational hazard for editors and agents. I knew a young editor at Pocket Books who came back from a business lunch practically non compos. His boss sent him out to be sobered up by means of a fire hose played on his naked body at Reilly's Gymnasium, a place patronized by heavy-drinking actors needing to ready themselves for a performance.

An inevitable restlessness accompanied the ferment and excitement of working for Max's publishing house. Daily life there had something of the operatic atmosphere of the imperial Russian court in Mussorgsky's *Boris Godunov*. Nobles and peasants were in constant turmoil. True and false claimants to the throne walked on and then off the stage. Heads rolled. Richard Simon and Max Schuster seemed to be echoing Boris's dying words: "I am still czar." Neither had an heir apparent. "Loyalty," even in this fiercely liberal, anti-McCarthy political arena, became as important a criterion as editorial initiative. Simon and Schuster rarely spoke to each other. (The third partner, Leon Shimkin, had a separate fiefdom on the floor below.) Max (although not Mrs. Max) was restrained when commenting about Dick; Dick once took me aside to tell me that Max was lazy and had been getting a free ride for years. The two might as well have been headquartered in different boroughs instead of in offices a few yards away from each other, and in effect they were running separate publishing houses that just happened to be using the same production and sales departments. The one time I saw them laughing together was when I showed them a visionary manuscript submission of a business book titled *Dow-Jones 1000?* (The Dow-Jones average then stood at a little over 500.) They agreed the author was a bit mental.

Lower-level cabals formed and dissolved after secret conferences to plan breakaway publishing houses, always with an estimated start-up capital of two or three million dollars to come from no one knew where. I collected a drawerful of prospectuses and fiscal projections. George Joel of Dial Press, whom I had once asked for a job, took me to lunch at the Players Club and, on the basis of mischievous misinformation from Herbert Alexander of Pocket Books, offered to sell me 49 percent of his faltering company. Even if I had conceivably been able to raise the money, common sense would have figured 49 percent to be the same as zero percent: the controlling interest would still be held by Joel, who had to be, if not a madman or a bunco artist, at least a fool looking

The partners: Richard L. Simon and M. Lincoln Schuster. *Used by permission of Pearl London.*

for the legendary greater fool. His contract inventory, which he showed me with innocent pride, included, I noticed, several authors who had already taken money from Simon and Schuster for the same unwritten book.

A young editor had to learn to be something of a courtier and accommodate attractive overtures and tendentious histories from one faction or another. I heard seriously conflicting accounts of how the house acquired its spectacularly successful self-help book, Dale Carnegie's *How to Win Friends and Influence People*. In Max's version, he discovered Dale Carnegie all on his own, nosed out a potential gold mine, and assigned the firm's "little bookkeeper" to take Carnegie's self-improvement course and sign him up. The little bookkeeper, Leon Shimkin, the third *S* of S&S, remembered this differently: Dale Carnegie had been his idea from the start. During my time Simon, Schuster, and Shimkin were either selling their company to mercantile heir and newspaper owner Marshall

Field II, a champion of liberal causes, or buying it back from him, or spinning off their children's book division, Little Golden Books, or engaging in buyout intrigues against one another or planning a shoot-out at the corral. Squads of dark-suited, attaché-cased lawyers and accountants trooped through the corridors. With all his immense fortune and the power that came with it, Marshall Field seemed bewildered when occasionally he sat in on editorial meetings and got some inkling of how the business was run. Properly attired in dark suit and polished black shoes, he once made me uncomfortable by staring pointedly, and I thought reproachfully, at my chinos and canoe moccasins.

A lot of money changed hands in these transactions and the partners became even richer. (Dick Simon, who had a phobia about banks, was rumored to have kept Marshall Field's million-dollar certified check in his pocket for several weeks before depositing it.) The psychology of the house and of the partners had changed from shoestring to big bucks, but Max kept his grip on the real and tangible: in his clothes closet at home he kept a milk bottle full of pennies. When Max and Ray left their duplex apartment in the former Pulitzer mansion on East Seventy-third Street for winter vacations in Florida or Europe, she worried about the Braque still life that hung in the drawing room. Max made sure his penny collection was safe.

I let him down in many ways. Believing there was a book in the editor's regular essays, he had taken out a subscription in my name to a one-horse weekly newspaper called *The Carolina Israelite*. I examined one backwoodsy-looking issue, threw it in my closet, and did the same with the issues that followed, not even removing the wrapper. Frequent queries arrived from Max: "What are you doing about the *Carolina Israelite* idea?" I assured him I was either "looking into it" or "still very interested" or "still trying to find a handle." The reminders stopped coming, and sometime later I began to notice, at the top of the nonfiction best-seller lists month after month, a Doubleday book called *Only in America* by Harry Golden, a collection of his *Carolina Israelite* columns.

For this delinquency alone, attributable to snobbery and stupidity on my part, I should have been fired. I wanted independence from Max, to be primarily an editor instead of his assistant, and this, together with my undisguised reluctance to baby-sit some of the house's older authors like Will Durant (who continued to lay golden eggs), suggested disloyalty as well as negligence. Instead of being fired I found myself being moved farther and farther from Max's office until finally I saw him only at editorial meetings. The lunches stopped altogether, except when required by business. I was also in trouble with Max's wife for thoughtlessly balking when she asked me to write to his authors and friends and gather a bouquet of tributes as a surprise on his sixtieth birthday. She was angry with me again when she learned I was lobbying the editorial board to acquire Nabokov's *Lolita*, then a pariah book published in Paris by the Olympia Press on the same list with titles like *White Thighs* and *The Sexual Life of Robinson Crusoe*. She telephoned me to say, "I won't allow you to turn my husband's company into a publisher of dirty books." *Lolita* went to Putnam. Years later I heard that Nabokov circulated a story that a young editor at Simon and Schuster had made him an offer for the book contingent on his turning Lolita into a boy.

Max had assigned me to deal with Joseph E. Davies, F.D.R.'s wartime ambassador to the Soviet Union and author of the bestselling *Mission to Moscow*, a vivid but also notably gullible account of the Stalin regime during the show trials. (Davies's footnote about Joe Barnes playing tennis in Moscow with an NKVD officer was a major source of Joe's troubles.) Davies was embarked on a memoir, titled *The Days of Their Power and Glory*. Out of gratitude for the success of *Mission to Moscow* Max said we should make every effort to please Davies. His manuscript consisted largely of tributes to his favorite dictators, among them Generalissimo Franco and Portugal's António Salazar, in addition to Stalin. Insisting on being addressed as Mr. Ambassador, the eighty-one-year-old Davies, in black homburg, fur-collared black overcoat, and carrying a silver-headed ebony walking stick, showed up on whim and without warning to be announced in diplomatic style and escorted to my tiny office, where we would discuss his book.

I labored over the Davies manuscript, hoping to beat it into some sort of readiness so that we could at least publish it quietly— "privish it" as Max would say—and without too much embarrassment, like leaving a newborn on the orphan asylum doorstep. The book was already in type when Davies died in 1958, which was when I learned that several years earlier his daughters had declared him incompetent but allowed him to go through the farce of signing a contract and taking an advance: they had been using us since as occupational therapy, a diversion to keep him out of trouble and stroke his ego. His theatrical visits as Mr. Ambassador, real though they were to him, turned out to have been part of an extended make-believe. For a while there was some talk of handing over the Davies material to the family in exchange for the advance money, but this fell through. One day I took the boxes containing Davies's manuscript, galleys, photographs, and correspondence and stuck them in an electric utility closet, and that was the end of *The Days of Their Power and Glory*.

It was this sort of thing that had begun to erode my exhilaration at Max's "creative adventure" in book publishing. Even without the Davies farce my dealings with Kimon Friar, and by mail with Nikos Kazantzakis, always slyly politicking for the Nobel literature prize, and then his even more exigent widow, would have been enough to wear anyone down. I had also made the terrible mistake of signing up a supposed Civil War expert to write a book about the attack on Fort Sumter. The expert had been recommended by an editor at another house. What was operative here, I learned, was the principle of the bad penny passing from one editorial hand to another—I would have done better to sign up a monkey. This author, either drunk or in tears whenever we talked about his book, wasn't even able to get the distance right from the Battery at Charleston to Fort Sumter or keep track of who was going back and forth between the two places to negotiate a surrender—sometimes, inexplicably, five Secessionist negotiators left Sumter in a rowboat that arrived in Charleston an hour later with seven aboard. One evening, exasperated by an ongoing phone conversation with him over similar examples of incompetence, I drove a pencil through a pad of paper. The book was duly published, to my shame, despite heroic freelance rewriting by Annie, whom I had recruited to bail me out.

For about a year my mood at work, and at home, subsided into melancholy touched with ennui and a sense of failure and dread: my phone rarely rang, the mail room boys had little to deliver to me. My gloom was somewhat dissipated by the hope that "perhaps some day," in Vergil's line, "it will be pleasant to remember even this": an experience that, although not altogether happy, was indelible and too bizarre to have been missed.

PART V

CHAPTER 15

I had quit my job at Houghton Mifflin, using pregnancy as my excuse. I had done a writing job for Joe, trying to make an incomprehensible book by one of his authors about the firing on Fort Sumter minimally comprehensible. In the final stages of my pregnancy, we had moved to 175 Riverside Drive. As soon as Susanna was born I began to write short stories.

Awash in motherhood, I decided I needed help, someone to come in once a week and liberate me for half a day. It never occurred to me to ask my parents to baby-sit for Susanna, nor did they ask, except for one bright day when my father took two-year-old Susanna to Riverside Park for an hour or two. I happened to be looking out of the window just as they crossed Riverside Drive from the park, noticing, with a catch in my throat—probably because I couldn't pull up a single memory of his doing that for me—how gently he seemed to be holding her hand and how slowly he walked so that she could keep up with him.

I had never interviewed anyone for a job, and whatever questions—"Where have you worked before?" "Where do you live?"—I asked the mostly middle-aged women who came around to apply for the job didn't tell me what I wanted to know, namely did they really like small children? Enough to risk their life for them? How was their eyesight, their short-term memory? Did they drink on the job? I had to go with my instincts (even I knew that references invariably mess around with the truth) but had no more reason to

A.B. and Susanna, Riverside Park, 1959.

trust my instincts than I would have Susanna's. I hired May, who seemed both warm and smart. It turned out that I was right about her but had failed to notice (or deliberately hid from myself) that she wasn't too quick on her feet, and so I couldn't blame her when, on one of May's afternoons, the corner of a steel swing caught Susanna just above her left eye, leaving a gash that needed five stitches to close. Trembling and in a fierce panic, we took her to a surgeon who had reconfigured the faces of some of the women and girls living in Hiroshima when we dropped the first of two atom bombs.

Whenever May took the children to Riverside Park I treated myself to the movies. It didn't matter what was playing—*The Bridge on the River Kwai, Separate Tables, The Three Faces of Eve*. I went to be alone, silent, passive, and, above all, unavailable. Swallowed by the dark, I was nearly always surrounded by empty seats; almost no one but perverts went to the movies on a weekday afternoon. One day, at the Trans-Lux Theater on Madison and Eighty-fifth Street, I had to go to the bathroom. I walked down a wide staircase that looked as if it belonged in a museum, through a stygian underground area used for God knows what, and into a badly lit, deserted bathroom at its far end. I was peeing when I noticed a man's head close to my right foot, his eyes looking up at me. Terrified, I stupidly screamed, "What do you want?" I must have scared him, for he withdrew his head and barged out of the bathroom. The question now was should I try to cross the large room, where he might be waiting to pounce, or should I wait until someone came in to save me? This might be hours. So I took the chance that he had fled and made it safely back to my seat where I watched the rest of the movie, trembling with leftover terror. When I was old enough to go to the movies by myself, my mother had instructed me to take a sharpened pencil with me, so that if a man got "fresh" I could stab him in the balls with it.

Once a week I found myself drawn wholly into the lives of the characters on the screen and cut off from a reality I both loved and feared, for I was sure that I had been given more trust—in the form of an adorable child—than I deserved.

I never had enough time to see both movies of a double feature, but one was enough; I came back to our apartment as restored as if I'd spent a week being massaged and mud-bathed at Main Chance, Elizabeth Arden's luxury spa.

The camel's back gave way one hot afternoon when, probably for the hundredth time, it took ten separate maneuvers to jack-ass Hester's baby carriage into the elevator at 175 Riverside Drive. It was like trying to parallel park a car almost too large to fit into its space. This petty annoyance characterized what was no longer working for us in New York City: it represented the ultimate in trivial obstacles to living a well-oiled and productive life. Stuck in an apartment house elevator for five minutes—multiply this by a hundred or more and it's obvious that no one but an idiot would choose to spend their time this way. Having a choice made it a lot easier to chafe at life's minor frustrations than if, like so many New Yorkers, I'd been stuck in a fourth-floor walk-up.

Although outwardly quite different in temperament, Joe and I took the same view of decisions: make them quickly, with a minimum of fretting, hope for the best, and get on with other business. Although this is a risky way to maneuver past the traps in a life, it worked out for us more often than not. Eyes closed, we would head in a direction that could, had the circumstances been even a little different, have landed us in a foul swamp. The day I balked in the elevator of 175 Riverside Drive was not long after Joe quit his well-perked, well-paying editor's job at Simon and Schuster in order to start a biography of Mark Twain. By this time I had decided to leave the short story; it was too confining, both in terms of plot and emotional range. A short story is a drop of oil, self-contained. Every word in it has to count. A novel is a large splash of paint, and in it you can do almost anything—except be boring—and get away with it. It can be messy, loose ends need not always be secured in a tight knot, and it can stretch over one day or many years. For a writer who fought the control imposed by the short story, a novel was a better—and paradoxically, less demanding—form. I began to write *Short Pleasures*, a novel based on a one-inch story I had read in the *New York Times* about a young woman who ran away from a conventional marriage. The *Times* called her an heiress—thus the attention paid her story—but they were wrong—she was merely the daughter of an upper-level business executive. I thought I knew this woman, she was my Brearley and Wellesley classmates. I could hear her talk and read her mind, her appetites, and her taste for pretty clothes. She spoke to me in a somewhat querulous voice, wishing she had the nerve to step out of a role carved out for her even before she was born. The real-life woman changed her mind and went ahead and married the guy; the girl in my novel escaped.

For a week or two we considered our options. Since Joe needed a research library, the choice of where to move narrowed us down to three cities besides New York: Berkeley, Washington, D.C., and Cambridge. Berkeley sounded seductive, but neither of us knew anyone there and we were afraid of being swallowed or lost. We never seriously considered Washington, a company town of no particular appeal. Joe had spent seven years in Cambridge, first as a Harvard undergraduate and then as a graduate student in English, pulling everything he read into his spooky memory and storing it there.

If we chose Cambridge, it would be a step backward in the creative chain, as Cambridge was the place where ideas are born and nourished; when they reach maturity, they're off, most often in a flash, to New York, Washington, Los Angeles. You need quiet to think; excitement to persuade others to believe in you.

Moving is reputed to be among the most stressful of life changes, just below death of a loved one and getting fired. Our move from New York City to Cambridge was remarkably free of the horrors. Having lived for almost thirty years in a city with the world's fastest pulse, I was ready for a change, for a place whose dazzle resided in its slow heart rate. Streets and neighborhoods its residents regarded as urban seemed to me positively rural. There was a tree with great splashes of green leaf outside the bedroom window. There were weeds in the backyard! Instead of garbage trucks banging and crashing at dawn, little birdies sweetly sang in the maples and lindens. You could walk along the banks of the Charles with no fence between you and the water. A fifteen-minute drive out Route 2 took you deep into the country. If I wanted the children to get some fresh air I stuck them in the backyard. We acquired a beagle. Mr. Patchiavos came around in a beat-up truck once a week, parked outside our front door, and invited us to climb inside the truck where he took our order for fresh fruits and vegetables he had bought at Haymarket that morning before dawn. A woman we called Mrs. Chicken-lady delivered farm-raised chickens to us every week. We ate a lot of chicken.

I found all this almost intolerably exciting, not realizing that novelty can be mistaken for improvement. William Dean Howells liked living in Cambridge, he said, because he was so little distracted there; the most sensational thing he saw all during one winter was a cat crossing the street. Edmund Wilson, when he lived there, was excited by the weekly garbage pickup. And that's how it was. Cambridge was a hard nut to crack. It took seven years before any of our neighbors invited us for dinner.

If we hadn't had children we probably would have stayed in New York, the city of cities, the home of all you love and all you despise, the place of temptation and its opposite, namely the imposition of self-discipline—because if that isn't operating, forget about working toward anything concrete. A twenty-four-hour-a-day festival of shimmering light and frenzied dusk. Were we too cautious to raise our children where we ourselves were raised?

I was an experienced jaywalker by the age of ten. I could negotiate the underground transit system with my eyes half-closed. I knew how to get away from a predatory male with a single glance or a single word. What came to be called "street smarts" are built into a New York City child as soon as she's let off the parental leash. I knew where the best jazz was being played, how to stand on line—never in line—at the Paramount theater for three hours or more, waiting to hear Gene Krupa (bring along a friend, something to read, something to eat, and plenty of patience). I knew what to wear where, to bring along an extra pair of white gloves when I rode the bus or subway, knew how to waltz and do the fox-trot and the lindy hop. I knew what to order at Longchamps and Schrafft's—a mixed grill and a Napoleon at the former, a butterscotch sundae at the latter; knew to avoid pigeons and outdoor water fountains, the specter of infantile paralysis a shadow that stayed with you constantly. I knew how much to tip a waiter, a cabdriver, a hairdresser.

I was wise to the well-separated layers of New York "society," starting at the top with descendants of Dutch settlers who bought Manhattan for a pittance (these were the people Edith Wharton dissected and devoured). Then down a notch to the white-shoe crowd, mostly professionals, graduates of the Ivy League, then down once more to that postwar phenomenon known as "café society," men and women, often entertainers but also the newly rich, whose lives depended on being spotted and photographed at the Stork Club and similar watering holes. After that, well, it didn't matter much, a vast middle class, then the Irish, then the Jews, followed by people who looked different from you and me in one way or another. I could tell, after being with a person for just a few minutes, which rung of the ladder they had been born on. New York society before 1960 was richer than a wedding cake—and just as fragile.

I soon discovered that Cambridge—one of two ends of a mustache, according to Elizabeth Hardwick, the other end being Boston—was so much simpler, it was going back to the second grade at school. There were the Brahmins and then there was the rest of us. A couple of parallel stories I heard soon after we moved made this leafy New England area sound more like Antarctica than Eden. Someone asks an old-time Brahmin why she never leaves Boston. "Why should I go anywhere?" she says, "I'm already there." This same woman wears only one hat, day after day. When asked why she doesn't buy herself a new one, she says, "What for? I already have a hat." Bostonians, it seemed, didn't like to spend money on anything less trivial than investments.

George and Nancy Homans lived across the street from us on Francis Avenue. George was a direct descendant of two Adams presidents; his family was the closest thing there is to genuine aristocracy in America. When George's aged mother, née Abigail Adams, visited her son, she drove herself over to Cambridge from Beacon Hill in her black two-door Ford Pinto. That says it all. Except this: George Homans told us that, before he went to Harvard, his father had sent him to St. Paul's instead of Groton "because he didn't want me to become a snob." If ostentation was about as much in evidence in 1959 Cambridge as four-star restaurants were—that is, nowhere to be found—originality, invention, and grinding hard work were satisfactory substitutes; they prevailed.

CHAPTER 16

One of Herbert Alexander's several fixed ideas about me was

that I knew something about classical philosophy. He was sure of

this even though I had told him that my education there consisted

of irregular attendance at a one-semester college survey course.

Nevertheless in 1950, as editor in chief of Pocket Books, he had

hired me to put together an edition of the dialogues of Plato. For

a fee of $150, and within a month, I was to edit Plato's *Republic*

down to about a third of its length, select four other major dia-

logues, and write a general introduction and separate introduc-

tions for each of the five major components. Alexander instructed me to keep in mind that I was writing for the general reader (exactly what I myself was) and deliver a complete manuscript, including pasteups of the Plato texts. Terrified, I still managed to do the editing, squeeze out a couple of thousand words, and meet Herb's short deadline. He liked what I had done, asked me to double the length of my introductions, and added, apparently by way of contrast and compliment, that some of the high-income authors in his stable "didn't know shit from Shinola" and couldn't write "for free seeds." (He paused long enough to explain that "free seeds," corn and wheat, were what the U.S. Department of Agriculture used to send to farmers just literate enough to write a postcard asking for them.)

Soon after the Plato went into production, with my name on the title page ("Edited and with Introductory Notes by . . ."), he asked me to put together a similar edition of Aristotle, about whom I knew even less that I did about Plato. My survey course, given by a renowned Harvard Platonist, Professor Raphael Demos, had got up to Aristotle only in a slightly halfhearted way, this being based on Demos's conviction that all of us are born either Platonists or Aristotelians, not both. According to Aristotle's description of motion and change, Herb was the "efficient" cause of my entrance as a published author of sorts, serving members of Pocket Books' vast audience who, after scanning drugstore display racks, paid thirty-five or fifty cents to learn about Greek philosophy. Slightly intoxicated by approval I began to ask myself—this would have been Aristotle's "final" cause—whether my own stirrings in the direction of nonfiction made any sense, and if I did attempt to write a real book, what that book would be. This questioning, later making me uneasy in my day job for Max Schuster, had brought on a serious change of psychic weather. For good or bad this was the surprise lurking around the corner that one expected in New York.

Despite Herb's respect for "acts of culture," as opposed to "acts of commerce," the editors and executives at Simon and Schuster, Pocket Books' sister company, regarded him as an agent of marketplace greed and vulgarity: for them he wasn't a real publisher at all but an interloper who bought reprint rights in wholesale lots the way other sorts of businessmen bought rags and feathers. This was all the more disturbing for those who looked down on Herb because he was educated and informed, had imagination, wit, and a literary sensibility, and could have been respectable, on the right side, if he hadn't overvalued his Pocket Books salary, profit-sharing, expense account, and other rewards. His range of knowledge was amazing, from French culture, the fine arts, and modern medicine to aircraft maintenance and boxing history (thick-necked and barrel-chested, he was as bulky as the heavyweight champion Rocky Marciano). He had been a professional writer and put money in his empty pocket under the pseudonym "Herbert Videpoche." He had also, I suspected, done well for himself by trading on the black market during his time as a G.I. in Morocco and elsewhere in North Africa. Aside from Plato, Aristotle, Shakespeare, and other such prestige and public service items on the Pocket Books list (including Dr. Benjamin Spock's *Baby and Child Care*, as if from Sinai dispensing comfort and reassurance to anxious new parents), he was responsible for keeping happy Irving Wallace, Irving Stone, Harold Robbins, Mickey Spillane, and other layers of golden eggs. Max Schuster must have seen my discipleship under Herb as disloyal and corruptive, perhaps tantamount to consorting with known criminals. To descend the stairs that connected trade publisher Simon and Schuster on the twenty-eighth floor of 630 Fifth Avenue with mass-market Pocket Books on the twenty-seventh was like crossing Checkpoint Charlie into the Soviet sector of Berlin.

Every month or so, whenever he summoned me on short

notice, Herb and I met for marathon lunches, mainly at Louis XIV, one of several theatrically decorated theme restaurants in Rockefeller Center. "Louis Quatorze," as its maître d' called it, was tricked out as if for the Sun King's levee. Once in a while we met instead at Holland House Tavern half a block away, commemorating the glory days of Dutch colonialism; the Mayan Room in the International Building, Chichén Itzá minus human sacrifice; the Forum of the Twelve Caesars, furnished with faux-marble arches, toga-draped waiters, and wine coolers shaped like Praetorian helmets—it had an air of Neronic decadence and served up slabs of meat suitable for gladiators training for the main event ("Wild Boar Marinated and Served on the Flaming Short Sword").

Herb had a regular table at Louis XIV. His first drink of the day, a double Scotch, arrived unbidden as soon as he sat down. This and the others that followed fired up a practically nonstop free-associational monologue of worldly wisdom, critical opinions, obscenities, slander, and lurid anecdotes, mainly concerning people I hadn't heard of and who may well have been imaginary. Driven by mammoth verbal energies, he could out-talk and out-ridicule anyone I had ever known. He was affectionate, sensitive, and even autocratically possessive and challenging, always ordering more martinis for me than I wanted and insisting I drink them. At one of these lunches he gave me a brass-trimmed folding knife with a four-inch blade, a commando weapon suitable for cutting the throats of enemy sentries. He said that since I was probably too shortsighted and stingy to take a cab home at night, I was always to carry this knife and be ready to unlimber it when accosted by the muggers, drunks, and addicts waiting in alleys and basement areaways. Another time he insisted I accept and put on then and there the luxuriant brass-buttoned Italian knitted sweater-blazer he was wearing (I had made the mistake of admiring it). For an hour or two at these lunches he darted from topic to topic with no recognizable link among them. He left me on mental overload, jittery, punch-drunk, and drained, with only a tiny residue of this hypomanic performance to sort out when I tried to reconstruct what he had been talking about all that time.

What I came away with was the impression of having absorbed something at least atmospheric about the low state of book publishing; the villainy, ignorance, and nepotism of the editorial and corporate people he had to work with, in particular his boss—"smarter than a shit-house rat"—Leon Shimkin, the "third *S*" of S&S. I also heard about the barber chair in Herb's bedroom over on Riverside Drive (the man who had shaved his father arrived every morning to shave Herb as he read the papers); a friend of his named Marvin Small, an investor in odd and invariably profitable ventures; Herb's boxing instructor at Gallagher's gym; his racing bicycle (he rode it through Central Park, and when he got tired his chauffeur, trailing in low gear, picked him up and drove him home). He told me about one of his authors, a novelist whose standardized superheated product sold in the millions all over the world, who was so sure of his importance to future generations of writers and literary scholars, that he corresponded with Herb only by carbon copies; the signed originals went directly to the Harry Ransom Humanities Research Center at the University of Texas, Austin. Herb talked repeatedly about his doctor at Columbia-Presbyterian Hospital, a pioneer in the use of lithium as a mood stabilizer. Herb was apparently bipolar, although I only saw him when he was *up*, that is, north polar, a hardy specimen of *animal ridens*, the laughing creature. He said his father had died laughing and that he himself expected to go out the same way—"runs in the family."

There was no point attempting to dislodge Herb's idées fixes—they were, as lawyers say, stipulated. Early in 1959 he hatched a new idea: that I hated my job at Simon and Schuster but was unwilling to face the truth. The truth, I tried to tell him, was not that I hated my job. I hated myself for not loving it more and doing it better and for spending too much time looking out of the window at the crowds outside St. Patrick's and Saks. Instead of doing business with agents and authors I often ate lunch by myself: shad roe and bacon at the American Bar and Grill; pastina in brodo and sausages and peppers at La Scala, near Carnegie Hall, where I read the *Times Literary Supplement* and eavesdropped on one of the restaurant's steady customers, Dimitri Mitropoulos, the New York Philharmonic conductor, and his young male companions. In good weather I had a grilled cheese sandwich and milk shake at a drugstore counter and spent the rest of an extended lunch hour taking pictures along the Hudson waterfront. Quite recently, as I came back from one of these solitary outings and passed the Simon and Schuster reception desk, whose occupant was busy as usual buffing her nails and talking to her mother on the phone, I had an illumination, of sorts: I didn't care if I never became a long-term fixture at this or any other publishing house. I was happy to cede the future to brilliant and truly dedicated editors like Robert Gottlieb, Richard L. Grossman, and Michael Korda. I had had my fill of meetings, alcoholic agents, and infantilized authors who assumed editors were writing teachers.

Given these admissions, which, Herb reminded me, suggested that I was practically asking to be fired, he went to work on me like a thoracic surgeon: he spread my ribs, probed lungs, lights, and liver and concluded that the cause of my low morale and idleness—my "fucking the dog," as he put it—was that I was working on other people's books when all the while I wanted to be writing my own. This was probably true, I admitted: what I needed was a subject or an event that could be brought to a dramatic focus in individual lives: the Western explorations (and subsequent court-martial) of John Charles Frémont, for example, or the transformations of Ulysses Grant from reluctant soldier, bankrupt and drunk, to Civil War hero and U.S. president. That's as far as I had ever got with defining the sort of book I wanted to write if I should ever leave publishing, but I knew I was hopelessly in love with the American nineteenth century—it was just far enough and near enough in time to be both strange and familiar, historical and contemporary. Nineteenth-century photography—daguerreotypes, Mathew Brady's portraits—brought the dead out of their graves and gave them an eerie, compelling, staring presence, as if they had just brushed past me out of the dark and were about to whisper in my ear. What was it like to have lived their lives, to have seen the great pulsating nineteenth century through their eyes?

"A man's life of any worth is a continual allegory," Keats said, "and very few eyes can see the Mystery of his life—a life like the scriptures, figurative." Among such richly dimensioned lives that I had thought about, Thoreau was too pleased with himself for my taste, too sanctimonious about his self-sufficiency and long preserved virginity. Keats would have recognized the allegory and mystery of Walt Whitman's life, but the Whitman biographies I had read when I worked for Louis Untermeyer seemed to be trapped into telling the story of a disappearing act, a great poet evanescing into a cult object—"I depart as air" and this was not my idea of the kind of book I wanted to write or read. Maybe Whitman's story had to be told in reverse, in his words "a backward glance o'er travel'd roads."

In the spring of 1959 Hal Holbrook's one-man show, *Mark Twain Tonight!*, had just opened on Broadway at the Forty-first Street Theatre: three hours of makeup transformed a thirty-five-year-old actor into a seventy-year-old spellbinding monologist whose ghost story, "The Golden Arm," was so terrifying in the telling that it nearly sent Annie into labor, just as it had sent Mark Twain's daughter Susy into hysterics. "Think about Mark Twain,"

Herb said. This was an entirely new idea—Mark Twain had always been part of the literary landscape for me but not its commanding feature. In some ways I was as benighted as many of his contemporaries who thought of him as mere entertainer. "Yes, I like that a lot, more than anything," I said. "I'll look into it." Deliberate casualness aside, I was thunderstruck: in love with the idea.

Right after lunch I bought whatever I could find of Mark Twain at the Doubleday bookshop on Fifth Avenue. I spent the afternoon in my office reading *Roughing It*; the evening at the Harvard Club Library reading Albert Bigelow Paine's authorized biography of Mark Twain; and the next several weeks, on company time, doing the most single-minded and happiest thinking of my life. More awake than ever, more concentrated, at the same time I had the sort of warm, suffusing sensation (Keats's "drowsy numbness") you have when you suddenly find something valuable and necessary you've been a long time looking for and never altogether expected to find, in this case it was a vocation as well as a book idea. By the end of that time I had written a ten-page proposal for "A Narrative Biography of Mark Twain in the Gilded Age." "In telling the story of Mark Twain's triumphs and frustrations, his ambitions and conflicts," I announced rather grandly, "this biography will also reveal something about the terms of existence for the good life and for the creative life in nineteenth-century America."

Even in my ignorance I had learned enough about Mark Twain to recognize that he lived not only in the solitude of his work, as writers do, but also, to an extent almost unique among American writers, that he lived out in the world, fully engaged—wealth seeker, businessman, paterfamilias, world traveler, social creature, activist, dissident, professional celebrity. He was equally at home in the eras of the Pony Express and the motorcar, the river raft and the steam yachts of the plutocracy, the open frontier and the closed frontier, villages on the banks of the Mississippi and the great cities of six continents. He invited the biographer to exercise what Wright Mills called "the sociological imagination" and explore the intersection of history, society, and individual experience.

"Everyone is a moon and has a dark side which he never shows to anybody," Mark Twain said. Freudian analysis had left its permanent imprint, opening my eyes to the irrational, conflictive, and subliminal forces that make people think and behave as they do. It was Mark Twain's "dark side"—his mystery and riven identities—I wanted to explore: for all his rootedness in the quotidian he was also a nocturnal creature in the line of Poe and Hawthorne—guilt ridden and dream haunted, his middle life a daydream of glory, his later life a nightmare, his laughter breaking into tears. I proposed to begin my book not with an infant born in a cabin in Florida, Missouri, but with an adult in his early thirties, a classic turning point in the life cycle, Dante's "middle of the journey": one either made a decisive change then or resigned oneself to continuing on the same path. Starting Mark Twain's story in early midlife made sense: why enter into hopeless competition with him in writing about his boyhood in Hannibal, Missouri, and along the Mississippi? Just the words "When I was a boy" were a mantra for Mark Twain, an Open Sesame! for his memory and imagination. My book would begin, I explained in my proposal, with Mark Twain's arrival in New York in 1867, then as ever the scrambling center of American life, temple of trade and commerce, pattern of fashion and manners for the nation. "Make your mark in New York," he reports with a prophetic pun, "and you are a made man." My book would end in New York in 1910, with Mark Twain in his famous white suit lying in a casket at the Brick Presbyterian Church at Fifth Avenue and Thirty-seventh Street.

I couldn't wait to get started. Max Schuster was vacationing in Vienna when my proposal reached him. "Mark Twain project absolutely magnificent both in form and substance," he cabled. "Will discuss full implications on return." That was generous of him, since I was upsetting his sense of order and some publishing plans that involved me. But when he returned he called me into his office and showed a different face. Even twitchier than usual, clicking and sucking on his ballpoint pen, he told me that a great deal of valuable training was now going to waste, especially, he added, since after nearly five years I was just beginning to carry my own weight. Numbed and dry-mouthed by the Miltown I had taken in preparation for this encounter, I could hardly respond or blame him for this flick of the whip. He refused to have a final lunch with me: an ingrate who had scratched at his door for a long time and was now bolting. But he offered me a $5,000 advance, payable in three cautious installments, and I accepted eagerly. The contract, with Max as my editor and sponsor, was to be my exit visa from Simon and Schuster. I went about settling my affairs at the house as if preparing to depart for the next world.

As for Herbert Alexander, the ultimate author of these changes: he suddenly turned unreachable when I asked him to read the proposal. Either he was in one of his depressive phases or simply slunk away. Like Mary Shelley's Dr. Frankenstein, who had learned the secret of imparting life to inanimate matter, he had gone too far and was now reluctant to be held accountable for the actions of his creature. Several years earlier he had sent me off to the vocational testers at Stevens Institute of Technology to flush from my system the idea that I ought to be a social worker; he had once warned me away from a marital entanglement he compared to climbing into a Bendix washing machine; later on he had told Annie and me, separately, that it was okay for us to marry. Now, as a direct consequence of a suggestion Herb made over one of his hypomanic lunches, I was quitting my job and, never before having written a full-length book, much less a biography of someone

306

as flamboyant, enigmatic, and conspicuous as Mark Twain, committing myself to years of work on a venture that was all the more questionable in its wisdom because library shelves already had a running foot or two of Mark Twain biographies.

"This is a big league subject," Joe Barnes cautioned me. "Are you sure you know what you're doing?" As I realized after only a week or two of reading Mark Twain manuscript letters at the New York Public Library, what I was "doing" was to enter another mode of being: total focus on the life of a stranger, in this instance a resistant stranger fiercely jealous of his privacy. Everything I knew would have to come into play but without my having to use the pronoun *I*. It was clear to me right away there was no useful distinction between research and writing: even the first notes one took were acts of narrative and interpretation. This was the life of biography: solitary; messy, in many ways, because existence was messy; and chastening, because the "truth" of a life would always remain elusive and shadowy, a mystery that had to be respected because it could never be penetrated. Even apparently ineluctable "facts" of time, place, and relationship were not bricks of information to be laid course upon course—facts were magma flowing from a hot core of accident and personality. The life of biography was risky, because it involved speculation, imagination, and taking chances. It was demanding, because lives as lived don't have the shape of art, but lives as written ought at least to acknowledge efforts in that direction. And it was inexorably full-time, even in sleep, for I hoped to train myself to dream the New York of a century ago, a forest of steeples palisaded by the masts of shipping. In the New York Public Library's Berg Collection of English and American Literature I worked under the minatory gaze of its codonor's portrait: Dr. Albert A. Berg, Mount Sinai Hospital's longtime chief surgeon. During the mid- and late 1930s, before the introduction of sulfa drugs and other antibiotics, Berg performed annual and sometimes semiannual operations on my brother. At the age of eighteen, Howard had fallen seriously ill with osteomyelitis, a bone and bone marrow infection for which surgery was then the only available treatment. Howard suffered horribly but survived without a trace of self-pity, at least as far as I could ever see. In his portrait, as invariably on his rounds and in his visits to Howard's room at Mount Sinai, Berg wore a bloodred necktie and a bloodred carnation in his lapel. I assumed these were emblems of the surgeon's guild.

There was a sort of symmetry in my choosing to write about Mark Twain. When I began his story he and I were both at the watershed age of our early thirties. Just as he arrived in New York to make a new start I was planning to leave my city for the same reason. Cambridge drew me back: the open stacks of Harvard's Widener Library, an invitation to productive browsing and unexpected discoveries, the unfenced banks of the Charles River, the nearby countryside. The "style," such as it was, of Cambridge (and Boston) was regressive: decaying buildings; greasy spoon eateries serving grilled cheese sandwiches and coffee in cracked mugs; the sort of after-dark street life you'd find in Transylvania; a general air of neglect, of better days long since past. (According to the popular wisdom, if you wanted a good meal you went to Logan Airport and took Eastern or Northeast to New York.) But what had made life in New York so exhilarating—its surprises and accidents, marketplace chatter and competitive gossip, adrenaline-intoxicated style, its sense of itself as being the center of the universe—was not what I needed for my work, although I would miss the social traffic and easy companionship of the corridors, the trading of jokes and ideas. New York would always be the Promised City, but I needed a slower pulse rate, open space, perspective, a more deliberative life. Even Walt Whitman, the supreme poet of New York, I reminded myself, had said that for all its fierce and leavening energies the city was a great place to sell your crops, but not to grow them.

One morning in November 1959, soon after the movers left, we cleared out the last belongings from our Riverside Drive apartment, packed Susanna and Hester into a little blue Rambler station wagon, tied the baby carriage on the roof, and headed north. We drove past my old neighborhood at Ninety-sixth Street; Columbia (where Howard had gone to law school); Barnard, Annie's college, her mother's, and her aunt's; Harlem's Hamilton Terrace, where Georgia lived with her husband, Willie; Columbia-Presbyterian Hospital, where our daughters were born; the George Washington Bridge—my father and I had walked it in the 1930s; Riverdale, where I had gone to school at Horace Mann. Once on the Saw Mill Parkway in Westchester we were bound for the calmer precincts of New England.